D1399524

HOW TO INVEST IN THE MARKET

HG
4910
.S73
1990

HOW TO INVEST IN THE MARKET

The '90s Guide to Wall Street

Dan G. Stone

MADISON PUBLISHING ASSOCIATES

New York   New York

Copyright © 1990 by Dan G. Stone

All rights reserved. No part of this book may be used or reproduced in any manner whatsoever without written permission except in the case of brief quotations embodied in critical articles and reviews. For information, address Madison Publishing Associates, 20 Exchange Place, New York, NY 10005.

ISBN 0-933813-03-1

Printed in the United States of America

For permission to reprint copyrighted material, grateful acknowledgment is made to the following sources:

Cartoonists & Writers Syndicate for KAL Cartoon: Wall Street/Buy! Sell! © 1989 Cartoonists and Writers Syndicate.

Leo Cullum for Cat/Mice Maze cartoon © 1987 Leo Cullum

The New Yorker for Chas. Addams drawing © 1979 Chas. Addams

Random House, Inc., for quote from THE MONEY GAME by Adam Smith, copyright © 1967, 1968 by 'Adam Smith'. Copyright © 1966, 1967 by World Journal Tribune, Inc.

Fraser Publishing Company for quotations from REMINISCENCES OF A STOCK OPERATOR by Edwin Lefevre, and WHERE ARE THE CUSTOMERS' YACHTS by Fred Schwed.

To my mother and father
The best in the business

041442

041148

Acknowledgments

My sincere appreciation to Ann Finlayson and Sara Blackburn, my editors, and to Gloria Mosesson, my literary agent.

Also, many thanks to Sherry Segal, Laura Ripin, Chris Ryder, Judith Appelbaum, Stephen Braverman, Stephen Kiscadden, John Rock, Bill Stack, Paul Brauer, Seth Shalov, Helen Hotchkiss, Larry Lytton, David Halfpap, Doug Schmid, and Craig Stone.

Contents

PART II—THE FUN (Relatively Speaking)

PART III—LOOKING BACK, LOOKING FORWARD

PART IV—DEEPER INTO THE MARKET

PART V—THE BOTTOM LINE

Introduction

Get some good stock and hold it till it's worth more, and then sell. But don't gamble.

—*Will Rogers*

Wall Street, according to author Fred Schwed, is a street with a river at one end, a graveyard at the other, and a kindergarten in between. It's where some of the best minds in the country spend a tremendous amount of money to learn humility. As Adam Smith pointed out in *The Money Game,* "If you don't know who you are, this is an expensive place to find out." And yet, it's not all that difficult to be a successful investor, if you're really willing to *be* an investor.

Investing isn't a horse race or a crap shoot or a Ouija game; it is a way to make your hard-earned money grow. The stock market may seem like a maze, with the vast majority of investors groping their way down seductive dead ends, or relying on guided tours to nowhere. But the investment maze, like any other, is a great deal easier to negotiate once you know the lay of the land.

To most people, however, Wall Street is a strange and foreign country, where the natives are not only restless, they are often downright hostile. For those who don't understand the stock market—and are honest enough to admit it to themselves—investing can be a terrifying experience. It's as if you found that special New York cab driver who only relies upon the rear view mirror; he'll tell you ad nauseum what's just happened, but he's not too helpful about what's ahead. And even to the experts, whose business it is to be helpful or, at least, to be articulate about the future, the market can be unnerving. A good part of the reason is that the movements of stocks often seem inexplicable or inconsistent or irrational.

                        *   *   *

There will always be excesses in the market, because prices are determined by people. And besides, who would really want human nature to be totally rational anyway? Fear and greed, temporary irrationality and excess—these are the stuff that dreams are made of.

So, what can this book offer you? First, it will show you how to understand and analyze the market and its individual stocks. It explains why the market does what it does, and why it usually doesn't do what you think it should. More important, this book will show you how to invest successfully. Don't underestimate the gap that separates a good investor from a poor one—over your lifetime, the difference could amount to hundreds of thousands of dollars.

As an institutional equity salesman at a major brokerage firm, I had a firsthand look at how professional investors tackled the stock market. During eight years on Wall Street, I had the opportunity to observe the factors that were influencing the market, to determine those that really mattered and those that didn't. And with all these advantages, I still made a hell of a lot of mistakes (this isn't false humility; this is well-deserved humility).

Oddly enough, the best advice I picked up along the way came from books—most of them decades old. (The top choices are described in the Appendix.) Investing is a skill that lends itself to reading; since human nature doesn't change over time, the lessons of the past are the lessons of the future. The trick is to know which lessons are worth learning. That's probably why you bought this book.

I am not trying to promote a revolutionary new angle on the market, or to hype a clever concept that is exciting and marketable and useless. My goal is to give you a clear view of the investment world, to keep you from wasting your money and your time, and to show you what works and why.

The strategies that are recommended are not the type that make sense only in a bull market, or only in a bear market. The principles explained here are equally valid in a market 50 percent higher or 50 percent lower.

The focus is on *value investing*. Nothing is more logical than buying something for substantially less than it is worth. To a lesser extent, the book concentrates on *contrarian investing*, which recognizes the often illogical influence of human nature If you can buy what's undervalued and underloved regardless of the fears of the crowd, and avoid what's expensive, regardless of its greed, you will do very well.

The first chapter, "Understanding the Stock Market," describes the factors that form the foundation of our stock market and some observations on how it operates in the real world. "Rules of the Game," the second chapter, offers some simple dos and don'ts to remember when investing.

Most successful investors have earned their fortunes through expertise in stock picking, rather than in market timing. "Analyzing Stocks" shows you how to determine the prospects for individual companies and the attractiveness of their stocks. "Reading a Financial Statement" focuses on developing an understanding of a company's income statement, balance sheet, and flow of funds. Chapter 5, "A Case Study," applies the conclusions of the previous two chapters to an analysis of the Washington Post Company.

"Strategies" offers several possible investment approaches, depending both on your effort and on your discipline. The first highlights the basic strategy of perhaps the finest stock market investor of our time: that a company with a strong market position and a management capable of maintaining that advantage can be a terrific long-term investment *at the right price.* It is an approach—remarkable for its simplicity and its success—that allows an active investor to make a great deal of money without enduring a great deal of worry. Also, commissions to brokers are minimal with this type of long-term investing. It's rare enough to have motivation, discipline, and common sense; you shouldn't feel obligated to put someone else's kids through college, as well.

The second major strategy that is recommended concentrates on the sensible, low-risk approach of buying closed-end funds at a significant discount to the value of their holdings. The third focuses on mutual funds: Several of the best money managers currently in the market are identified, and their investment approaches are described. In a business where so many of the players are impressive and articulate, you shouldn't underestimate the value of knowing a few who are truly extraordinary. The fourth strategy involves stocks that are selling at a low multiple of their earnings, which may or may not make sense to you now, but it will by then

The following section on timing the market includes a simple rule of thumb for judging the stock market's attractiveness. In addition, several asset allocation strategies are presented to help you determine what percentage of your assets you want in stocks, bonds, cash, real estate, and gold. After all, you are certainly not going to put every dollar you own into the stock market.

"Wall Street in the 1980s" offers a straightforward appraisal of the Street and describes the practical realities of a fascinating, if confusing, decade. Among the topics are leveraged buy-outs, merchant banking, bridge financing, portfolio insurance, program trading, the dominance of the institutional investor, an extraordinary bull market, and an unprecedented crash. For the financial community, it has certainly been the best and the worst of times.

"The Outlook for the 1990s" presents projections for the future in personal interviews with five highly regarded professional investors: John Templeton, Julian Robertson, Phil Fisher, Stan Salvigsen, and Mike Aronstein. How will this decade compare to those that preceded it? Where are the greatest opportunities, and what are the most significant risks? Their thoughts on these questions, and others, make for valuable reading.

There is a saying that when all is said and done, there's a lot more said than done—an observation that certainly applies to investing. But if you develop an understanding of how the market should work and how it actually does, of why sentiment is important and value is crucial, and of how to analyze the market and its stocks, then a good deal will have been accomplished. This book may not make you a great investor, but it will certainly help to make you a better one and maybe a much better one. Perhaps even a great one, why not?

PART I

The Fundamentals

CHAPTER 1

Understanding the Stock Market

> Being a sound investor really just requires a certain control of your temperament and the ability to know what you know and what you don't know and occasionally act.
>
> It's just not necessary to do extraordinary things to produce extraordinary results.
>
> —*Warren Buffett*
> Chairman, Berkshire Hathaway*

Stock Ownership

When you are a shareholder, you own a piece of a company. You have a claim on a portion of its assets and its output. You probably won't own enough stock to have much say in how the company is run, but it's still nice to know. The management, from the mail clerk to the chairman of the board, actually works for you and the other shareholders. They are hired by the consent of the stockholders, they manage the company for the benefit of the stockholders, and they can be replaced by the decision of the stockholders—at least, in theory.

Dividends and Capital Gains

As a stockholder, you are entitled to your share of a company's earnings.† One way that you get these profits is by receiving dividends. Dividends are a direct payment by the company to its owners, usually made each quarter, a current return on their investment.

---

*On *Adam Smith's Money World.*
†As a bondholder, you are a lender to the company, and receive a fixed amount each year—no more, no less.

Since many investors rely upon dividend income and view it as a strong statement on the long-term prospects of a company, managements are extremely reluctant to reduce these payments. Therefore, a company's dividends are more stable than its profits.

That portion of the profit that is not paid out in dividends is reinvested in the company. The stockholder benefits from this reinvestment, since these retained earnings contribute to the company's growth. As profits grow, dividends grow with them. Also, the value of the company will grow along with the profits; over time, this increased value will benefit investors through increases in the price of the stock—*capital gains.*

A key factor in determining the price of a stock is the multiple: how much investors are willing to pay for each dollar of a company's profits. If all stocks sold at the same multiple, then the best company would also be the best stock. For example, let's say that companies A and B are both earning $1 per share this year, with both of their stocks selling at $10 (multiple of 10). However, Company A's profits are not growing, while Company B's profits are growing at 10 percent per year. Obviously, we would buy Company B's stock. In twenty years, A would still be earning $1/share, while B would be earning almost $7/share. If the multiple remains at 10, A's stock would still be at $10, while B's would have risen to over $65! This multiple, also called the *price-earnings ratio,* or P/E, is what separates the attractiveness of a company from the attractiveness of its stock.

All stocks don't sell at the same multiple precisely because all companies are not equally attractive. Some will grow their earnings more rapidly than others, and people will pay more for each dollar of these current profits because of the superior growth prospects. In our example, clearly we would rather own B's stock if it is selling at the same multiple as A's. But what if B's stock is selling at $20 (P/E of 20), while A's P/E is still 10? What if B's stock is selling at a multiple of 50, while A's multiple is only 5? Now it's not so easy anymore. Obviously, B is a better company, but A's stock at five times earnings may be more attractive than B's at fifty times earnings. This is what makes investing in the market challenging.

To confuse matters further, what if A and B are in two different industries? What if A has a new management? What if B has more debt? What if we really don't have much idea what A or B can grow at for two years, let alone twenty? This can get confusing.

As noted earlier, the portion of profits that is not immediately paid out as dividends is reinvested for future growth. If profits grow faster than expected, investors may be willing to pay even more for each dollar of profit—the multiple will expand—giving them a double-barreled benefit. For example, let's say that a company's earnings per share (EPS) double from $1 to $2. Investors are so impressed that their expectations for future growth increase, as well. Now they are willing to put a multiple of 15 on the stock, given its apparently improved outlook, whereas before the P/E was 10. In response to the doubling in earnings, the stock triples to $30 (15 × $2) from its previous price of $10 (10 × $1). But recognize that this cuts both ways: The stock may fall sharply in response to disappointing earnings and to a reduction in the multiple accorded these lower earnings.

In the real world, expectations are exceeded or disappointed on a daily basis for companies, their industries, and the economy as a whole. And prices will change accordingly to reflect the changing perceptions of people driven by fear and greed, while operating with imperfect knowledge. You certainly can't say it's boring.

Value Investing

One general approach to evaluating stocks is *fundamental analysis*. The focus here is on what companies do for a living and on how well they do it. After all, when you buy a stock, you are buying a company's future income in exchange for your money. An analysis of the company's income statement, balance sheet, management, industry, and economy should offer a reasonable estimate of that income. This is the basis for *value investing*, which focuses on determining the "intrinsic" value of a company through fundamental analysis, and then buying its stock at a price considerably below that value.

Benjamin Graham, author of the 1934 classic, *Security Analysis* (see Appendix), and the most famous value investor, used a simple and effective analogy to explain the market: Think of your investment as the partial ownership of a private company. Your partner,

Mr. Market, is a manic/depressive. On some days, or months, Mr. Market is in a great mood, exceptionally optimistic about the present and the future. He is willing to buy your share of the business for more than it's worth. On others, he is pessimistic and is eager to sell you his share for less than it's worth. Either way, you win. And that's the way that the market operates, swinging between its fear and greed.

Unfortunately, most investors mimic Mr. Market and his emotions. They are willing to sell undervalued holdings because of their fears and to buy overvalued positions because of their greed. But the world is such that our worst fears or fondest hopes are rarely, if ever, realized.

A big problem for average investors is that they really don't know what their "share in the business" is worth. And most have neither the skills nor the interest to determine the intrinsic value of their investments. Instead of taking advantage of the market's occasional extremes and ignoring the daily fluctuations in between, they allow Mr. Market to become their irrational role model rather than their benefactor. They would be far better off learning how to analyze and select stocks, which is the goal of Chapters 3–6.

Contrarian Investing

A second general approach to investing is *technical analysis,* which involves two different disciplines: *contrarian investing* and *chart reading.* Let's deal with chart reading first, and briefly. This method simply predicts future stock price movements solely on the basis of past movements. Chart reading has many followers, a catchy slogan—"the trend is your friend"—and few successful practitioners. Arguably, more money has been made by those who give advice in this field than by those who follow it—another variation on the theme: "Those who can, do; those who can't, teach."

The other type of technical analysis, contrarian investing, focuses on the sentiment, positive or negative, of the millions of investors whose decisions determine stock prices. This approach is based on the belief that a good way to predict how the stock market will act is to understand how its participants think. Emotions have an important effect on the movements of the market; they can cause stock prices to move toward fair value or—as success breeds excess—away from it. As an investor, you should recognize the influence of fear and greed, particularly during times of uncertainty and stress, such as when the stock market is open.

Stock prices discount the future or, more specifically, they reflect investors' perceptions of the future. As expectations change, prices will rise or fall.

What matters is not whether what happens is "good" or "bad" in an objective sense, but whether it is "better" or "worse" than investors expect. For example, consider this excerpt: "Golden Valley Microwave Foods, off 4⅛ to 26⅜, said sales and profits for the quarter just ended were up about 25 percent. That was well below the 40 percent it had led analysts to forecast." In this case, the 25 percent gain in earnings, however impressive in and of itself, was a disappointment to investors, and the stock declined sharply as a result.

Prices are based on expectations, and expectations are based on reality. At any given time, however, these perceptions of reality are heavily influenced by emotions. And the emotions of investors, especially when acting as a group, tend to oversimplify a complex world. Great companies often are easily confused with great stocks, as investors, in their enthusiasm, ignore price. Meanwhile, poor companies are often shunned, even though their stocks may be inexpensive.

The point is that inflated expectations are likely to be disappointed, and modest expectations are likely to create positive surprises. In effect, to use an old Wall Street adage, "if it's obvious, it's obviously wrong." By being brave when the crowd is afraid and timid when the crowd is greedy, you will probably find yourself buying undervalued stocks and taking profits when they become overvalued.

The Low P/E Approach

It is interesting that, over time, the lowest multiple stocks have produced the best performance. That is, the companies whose stocks have sold at the lowest price-earnings ratios have outperformed their high P/E peers. These low P/E companies are usually the least impressive, which indicates that the lousier companies have on average been the better stocks.

That the market has consistently created excessive expectations for the better companies was demonstrated in a study by Provident Capital Management. From 1959 to 1988, the top fifth of companies ranked by P/E provided an average annual return of 7.2 percent, while the dogs of the bottom quintile averaged 15.2 percent. To put this in perspective, $1,000 invested in the highest P/E companies would have grown to $8,000, while $1000 in the lowest P/E companies would have grown to $70,000—a difference of almost 800 percent!

The underperformance of high P/E stocks is really not difficult to understand. Companies that appear to have superior managements, great products, and attractive markets should have exceptional prospects—or so it seems. They become our heroes. They are written about by Wall Street analysts and business magazines. They are boasted about by those who were astute—or lucky—enough to get in early and profit by their early success. They are talked about by the late converts to the happy world of believers, who usually become their most fervent supporters. Investors as a group increasingly find themselves eager to believe the most optimistic expectations, naively assuming that the company's excellent—and well-recognized—growth in the past will continue into the future.

But there are many things that can go wrong with a great company. First of all, it may not be so great to begin with. Its management's chief strength may have been luck rather than insight, and its products and markets may fall victim to competition or to shifts in demand. One case in point is the Banana Republic division of Gap Stores, which saw its $20 million profit for 1986 disappear in 1987, as its safari-style clothing became unfashionable outside the Serengeti.

Less dramatically, a company's results may simply be affected by temporary setbacks. Even the best will occasionally stumble. The market may then extrapolate these problems unrealistically far into the future, just as it did the previous successes.

Or the company may do just fine, but not fine enough for its investors.

As you can see, the Low P/E Approach is a form of contrarian investing. What is less obvious is that it is also a roundabout way of value investing. Granted, this approach doesn't rely on the tried-and-true formula for value investors: Determine a stock's underlying value and then buy it substantially lower. Still, the track record of low P/E investing shows that it finds undervalued stocks, which highlights a noteworthy point: Value investing and contrarian investing are usually two sides of the same coin.

When a Concept Makes Sense

The ability to reduce the many investment variables to a simple concept or theme can certainly help your investing decisions, if you understand the importance of value.

With 20/20 hindsight, consider the state of our country in the late 1940s. It was a time of economic opportunity, low inflation, and flourishing technology. Meanwhile, the United States was one of the few industrial countries that had not been destroyed by six years of world war. According to economist Al Summers, no nation in history was in as strong a financial position as was the United States in the postwar period. Who could have asked for a better scenario for American corporations?

In this environment of extraordinary potential economic growth, stocks should have been selling for thirty times earnings, or more. And yet, the average P/E was only 7. Viewed from another angle, the stock market was offering an earnings yield—earnings divided by stock price*—of approximately 15 percent, five times greater than the competitive yield from bonds. (In contrast, the current earnings yield on stocks is *less* than the yield on bonds.) In 1949, even as people feared the onset of another Great Depression, an unprecedented economic boom began, to the benefit of the country and its stockholders.

Attractive concepts are certainly not limited to the stock market. For example, let's say that in 1981, you decided to ignore the details that might have dominated other investors' thinking, such as this quarter's dividends or next quarter's earnings, or next year's economic growth. Instead, you merely concluded that a 10 percent inflation rate was unacceptable to the most successful economic power in history. The new President, elected by a landslide, seemed to feel

---

*Earnings yield is simply the inverse of the price-earnings ratio; it is an indication of the return on your investment in a company.

very much the same way and was inclined to do what he'd said, when he could remember what he'd said.

You also might have decided that 13 percent, 14 percent, or 15 percent a year in risk-free government bonds was a pretty rare deal. After all, investors had earned less than that from the stock market during its five-decade bull market.

Even if inflation stayed at an extraordinary 10 percent a year, you were doing just fine. But the public sure as hell didn't want 10 percent—historically, inflation had averaged only 3 percent a year. Accordingly, you had reason to hope that inflation would decline and the value of your investment in bonds would increase.

There are examples of successful concepts in individual industries and companies, as well. Those who patiently waited for the media stocks to be recognized for the value of their unique products were greatly rewarded. Similarly, enormous profits went to investors who realized that the depressed oil stocks of the early 1980s were vulnerable to takeovers, since it became cheaper to prospect on Wall Street than in the oil patch.

Unfortunately, concepts are often driven by hope alone, without consideration of price, and such concepts are of no use to a value investor. Examples from the past include the gambling craze of the 1970s, which was triggered by the opening of the first casino in Atlantic City, and the home-shopping hype of the 1980s, which was driven by the market's dream of immense profits to be had by those who could satisfy the demand for costume jewelry.

In these cases, the subsequent bust was as cruel to the stockholders as the previous boom had been kind. Consider the saga of Home Shopping Network: Its shares rose from 7 to 47 within one year, and then fell to 4½ a year later.

What should be evident is that a concept can be powerful at the right price. But understanding the value that underlines a theme is crucial. Value tells the investor when it makes sense to bet on a concept, and when the market in its greed has overpaid for the story. A sense of theme, of what might eventually interest and excite investors, is important. But without the knowledge of underlying value, you might again find yourself at the mercy of the market rather than at its advantage.

What Drives the Market?

The players in the market love clever expressions. One that received great currency through the 1982–1987 bull market is that "markets climb a wall of worry." It is another way of saying that markets rise on positive surprises. When expectations are low, results are likely to unfold better than the market had foreseen.

When markets are dominated by excessive optimism, on the other hand, the future is likely to be disappointing. Even if the news is good, it may still fall short of the expectations already reflected in current stock prices. And the stock market tumbles down this "slope of hope."

It is no surprise, then, that markets tend to peak out when the news is excellent and the expectations high, while bottoms are created in an environment of despair. At the top, investors adopt an attitude that stocks should be held, since, even if they decline, they will always go back to new highs eventually. When the market dips, this decline is initially viewed as a buying opportunity—after all, the news is so good. Unfortunately, the rise in prices that created the peak has already taken the good news into account. Better news— much better news—that's what the market needs.

Positive surprises may drive a stock market boom in the beginning, but it is usually hope that drives it at the end. Gurus are adopted who tell the crowd what it wants to hear: "It's not too late to invest, not by a long shot!" Explanations that are temptingly plausible are given to show why, this time, it's different, why the booming market is *still* inexpensive. In 1929, for example, the argument that unending economic prosperity would make stocks cheap at any price was universally accepted.

Occasionally, the market may become more attractive to many, not because of valuation, but in spite of it. The overvalued market is expected to continue rising simply because it *has* risen. The Greater Fool Theory takes hold: someone, somewhere will be willing to buy your shares for more than you paid for them. Popular rationalizations are devised to explain away excessive valuation. In 1987, prior to the Crash, the rationalization was that the inflows of foreign money would keep the market climbing to new peaks.

The same emotional factors are at work with market bottoms. Stocks—the recipients of so much displaced faith—have disappointed once too often. Investors discard them, often in a brutal sell-off at the end. There is just no long-term case for holding common stocks, argue the poorer but not necessarily wiser. The business outlook is terrible, they say, and the experts are expecting more of the same. In time, investors accept the fact that stocks are cheap, but believe that they will get cheaper still. And so it goes.

The Purpose of the Stock Market

It certainly seems like a casino at times, but gambling is not the reason that we have a stock market. The purpose of this intricate, intense, and often irrational institution *is to raise money for corporations.* Companies need money to make money. Growth can be costly, because companies need to finance production facilities, distribution networks, and inventories of product, among other things. Without outside funding, many companies could not grow at the rate their opportunities offer them. Their product may be in great demand and their competitors in short supply, but if they can't produce, they can't provide.

Private companies—those not trading in the stock market—can finance their growth through reinvestment of profits, loans from banks and insurance companies, and investments by venture-capital firms. Eventually, they may grow to substantial size—and substantial needs—with a track record that inspires confidence in a bright future (or, at least, *a* future). At this point, they may "go public" by selling a portion of their equity in the stock market. This is called an initial public offering, or IPO. Over time, they can return to the market to raise further funding when needed or appropriate—a new plant may be necessary or an acquisition may require financing or the price of the stock may simply be high enough to justify selling shares to investors like you and me.

The abuses of the greedy and the corrupt may obscure the purpose of the stock market, but they should not diminish its importance. The opportunity for companies to raise capital from the public has been an important factor in the economic success of this country. It is no wonder, then, that both China and the Soviet Union are increasingly willing to twist the ideology of the workers' paradise to allow for stock markets of their own.

CHAPTER 2

Rules of the Game

Never play poker with a man called Doc.
Never eat in a restaurant called Mom's.
Never sleep with a woman who's got more troubles than you.

—Nelson Algren

A few simple rules can be invaluable in dealing with a complex world. The stock market is really no different. It certainly can be complex; if anything, it has become more so over the decades. And, even though the players have changed, human nature has not. Accordingly, certain rules can be relied upon to give you an advantage over the average investor. Here, then, are a few dos and don'ts to bear in mind:

Rely on Common Sense

Don't allow yourself to get caught up in the common wisdom unless that wisdom holds up to reality. Keep a sense of perspective. The arguments in favor of or against a particular stock may sound compelling. But ask yourself: Are they logical? Are they based on valuation, or do they depend on the emotions of the crowd?

Consider the case of Japan's favorite son, Nippon Telephone and Telegraph. At its peak, the shares were worth more than the *entire* West German stock market, selling at a P/E in excess of 200. Valuation was considered irrelevant—that is, until valuation became considerably less irrelevant and the shares fell by 40 percent in less than two years.

Another example of perception being removed from reality was the situation in the tobacco industry in April and May of 1988. The industry, which had never lost a tobacco product liability trial, was on the threshold of a possible defeat in the Cippalone case. Investors, fearful that a loss would open the litigation floodgates, drove down the prices of tobacco shares by several billion dollars in those two months.

Ironically, the shares bottomed out on the day that the industry did, in fact, lose its first case (and then doubled in value). But the important issue is that the legal battles, lost or won, are not a significant investment concern. Even if the industry loses one trial a week and even if the damages are a dramatic $1 million per case, the tobacco companies generate enough free cash flow to pay all their legal costs for the entire year by the third day of January.

Know More Than Your Competition

Your decision to buy or sell a stock usually reflects a belief that the shares are mispriced. But ask yourself: Do I know more about this company and its value than the collective wisdom of the market, as reflected in its current price? For the majority of investors, the answer will be no.

Moreover, most investors don't have a worthwhile strategy with which to compete against the market. The problem isn't a lack of available information, but often an excess of it. There is such an overload of public information that you're more likely to go brain dead than absorb it all, let alone analyze it correctly.

Here are two basic approaches to handling the onslaught of available knowledge:

Generalize. Rely on a few rules to reduce the investment cast of thousands to a few potential stars. For example, you might narrow the list by looking for businesses that are difficult to duplicate, those with a rare and valuable product, which engenders strong customer loyalty. Perhaps you would require that these companies are run by superior managers, as well. Or you may prefer to screen for stocks that are selling at low multiples of their earnings and cash flow.

If you stick to your rules, some sense of order should emerge from the chaos. These parameters will give you a starting point in ignoring the irrelevant and focusing on potential opportunities.

Specialize. Once you have found a few attractive stocks, become an expert in them. While the crowd races from one popular invest-ment patch to the other like a pack of piglets, you will be one of the few waiting patiently for your price. If you prefer to spare yourself the effort involved here, however, then the next rule is for you.

Diversify

In any investment, you must compare the expected return—the profit if you're right and the likelihood of being right—against the expected cost if you're wrong. The fewer your investments, the greater the penalty if one or more of your ideas goes awry.

Most investors are risk averse: They demand a higher expected return from those investments that are less predictable, more volatile. When you diversify by owning a number of stocks, your overall re-sults will show less volatility, as the occasional negative surprises are offset by the positive surprises.

Consider the toss of a coin: The chance of "heads" or "tails" is 50 percent. If you make a prediction for the next toss, you would expect to be right half the time. Flip it once, and you will be either completely right or completely wrong; flip it one thousand times, and you can be sure that overall you will be correct on almost exactly 50 percent of the tosses. As you can see, the more attempts you make, the more predictable the overall results.

For this reason, diversification makes sense for cautious investors in an uncertain market. By owning many stocks, they reduce the overall risk in their portfolios.

This approach is not without criticism, however, and some of it comes from several legendary investors. Their argument is that truly great investments are very rare indeed, and that a well-diversified portfolio of such ideas is unattainable. Therefore, they reason, in-vestors should take advantage of these occasional opportunities, as a professional baseball player should take a full swing at the occasional hanging curveball.

Their argument is a very compelling one. If you can find these ideas at the right price, you should invest heavily, with confidence and patience. The problem is that there are not many investors who are astute enough to find great companies, skilled enough to know the right price, and disciplined enough to wait for it. By the end of Chapter 6, perhaps you will be one of the few.

Admit Your Mistakes

Sooner or later, you are going to make a bad investment. If you are like many investors, you may have to fight your own grim determination to ignore reality. Nobody likes to lose, not even those who tell themselves hollowly, "It's only money."

But investment decisions are based on certain assumptions, and occasionally, those assumptions will be wrong. By the time you've begun to recognize that yours were wrong, more likely than not, your investment will already be in the red. But the important issue is not whether you're ahead or behind. The only question that matters is this: *Knowing what you now know, would you buy the stock at the current price if you didn't own it?* If not, sell it.

If you are honest enough to admit that you really don't know when or whether to buy or sell, find someone who does. If you prefer to make your own decisions, regardless, give yourself a lot of credit for self-awareness, but don't expect too much from your investments.

Don't Be a Trader

Trading generates commissions for brokers and income for specialists, which, frankly, reduces the potential profits from your investments. More important, considering the market's speed in reacting to events and the siren call of the consensus viewpoint, it is an achievement to be right even half the time.

One of the more interesting comments you may hear is that volatility provides good trading opportunities. A TV commercial offered this argument in describing the advantages of a multifaceted mutual fund aimed at small investors. The speaker earnestly praised the fund for enabling him to swap between stocks and bonds as quickly as the markets change.

But what makes someone think that he can react as quickly as a market that can drop 500 points in one day? And what makes someone think that he won't always be on the wrong side of the trades— buying when he should be selling, and vice versa?

Sure, volatility creates profits, but it also creates losses. Remember, for every smart buyer, there is a not-so-smart seller.

The dream of the quick buck is an expensive hobby to support. It appeals to several of the wrong instincts. Investing seems boring and unnecessary in comparison to easy potential profits from speculating. Our selective memories exacerbate the problem by reliving the triumphs and downplaying the disasters. It is the "coulda, woulda, shoulda" melodrama of fortunes waiting to be scooped up, if only we had bought some, or bought more, or sold when we knew we should have, or whatever.

Don't Buy on Margin

You are allowed to buy stocks on margin—borrowing up to 50 percent of the purchase cost from your broker—but generally, it's a bad idea. You should invest in the market without borrowed money, using funds that you don't expect to need anytime soon. This approach gives you room to ride out either adverse developments or adverse psychology in the short run.

If a sound business encounters some turbulence, margin debt can turn your investment into a short trip to disaster. The founding family of the exceptional Government Employees' Insurance Co. (Geico) learned this the hard way. It was forced to sell its margined shares when the stock plummeted due to *temporarily* unsound pricing. The problem was eventually corrected, and the shares have since risen seventy-fold from their lows.

A related problem with buying stock on borrowed money will occur when an unforeseen development triggers an excessive sell-off. In 1963, American Express was shaken by a scandal which drove the stock down by over 40 percent in three months. The company was a partial guarantor for Tino de Angelis, a fraudulent—and, subsequently, bankrupt—salad oil company. American Express decided to settle many of the claims rather than risk its greatest asset: its reputation. The financial consequences were less severe than investors had initially feared and, in the following five years, the shares quintupled. To date, the stock has risen some 4,000 percent.

Like most general rules, however, the one against investing on margin has an exception. If the expected return from an investment is significantly higher than the cost of borrowing, margin will increase your expected profit. For example, let's take a $10,000 investment: You've bought 500 shares of a $20 stock. If the stock rises to $25 in a year, you will net a profit of $2,500, or 25 percent.

However, let's say that instead you bought 1,000 shares for $20,000, borrowing $10,000—50 percent margin—at an interest rate of 10 percent. The profit would now be $4,000—the $5,000 increase in stock value minus your $1,000 margin cost—or a 40 percent return on your money.

If the stock instead drops 50 percent to $10, however, you will lose your entire $10,000 investment. And, to add injury to injury, you will have to pay an additional $1,000 in interest costs on the debt.

Even if the stock subsequently rises, good ole Mr. Market will have wiped you out before your analysis was vindicated. Remember that it is difficult enough to identify attractive investments, let alone to guess *when* their underlying values will be recognized. After all, there is no law that says that an irrational market cannot get worse before it gets better.

Investing without leverage is hardly a sure thing, but it does increase your margin of error—your chance of avoiding significant or total losses if you are early or just plain wrong. Besides, in the last ten years, the interest rate on margin debt—the *cost* to investors—has tripled. Meanwhile, the earnings yield on stocks—the *return* to investors—has declined by more than half. As a result, it now is rare for the expected return on an investment to significantly exceed the cost of borrowing to buy that investment.

And, believe me, you can live a full life without experiencing a margin call from your broker asking for more money.

Don't Underestimate Supply and Demand

The difference between capitalism and communism is clear: In capitalism, man exploits man; in communism, it's exactly the opposite. There is also the issue of free markets. Capitalism allows the forces of supply and demand to set prices; in turn, prices influence that supply and demand. As a system, it's hardly flawless but, as

Churchill said of democracy, it's the worst approach except for all the others.

A run-up in prices will eventually stimulate an increase in supply and a decrease in demand. Both of these factors will then put downward pressure on prices. In the last decade, this process was the same whether the product was food, oil, silver, or stocks. And this self-correcting mechanism works with equal efficiency in the opposite direction,* as lower prices encourage more demand and less supply.

Don't Play Turnarounds

Improving the declining fortunes of a company is a frustrating and time-consuming process. More important, turnarounds are generally a poor investment.

Many factors can put a company behind the eight ball. The company may be uncompetitive with other producers, domestic or foreign. A new product or production process may be delayed in development. Technology may render the company's product obsolete. The industry itself may be too competitive, characterized by similar products, aggressive pricing, and poor profitability. All of these unfolding problems may take significantly longer to overcome than the inevitably hopeful estimates.

In these circumstances, even talented managers may be outmatched. The management, however, is usually anything but exceptional, a factor which may have contributed to the company's problems in the first place.

Still, the occasional success stories will entice the media and the public. Investors will kick themselves for missing what seemed so obvious in retrospect. They will look for the next Chrysler, ignoring that company's unique confluence of favorable events: government loan guarantees, a new management, a consumer-led economy driven by falling interest rates and oil prices, and a shift in car-buying tastes toward the company's existing product line.

Certainly, it is difficult for the average investor not to wonder,

---

*Well, usually. The failure of the price mechanism for labor threatened to prolong the Great Depression indefinitely. Keynes argued that the influence of unions kept wages too high and employment too low.

"If only I'd bought Chrysler at 1½ . . ." However, if you can recognize this as an exception that supports the rule, you can focus your attention on the bets where the odds are in your favor: companies in which underlying business conditions are already positive.

Don't Play with Options or Futures

> There's an old joke in the stock brokerage business: "Two out of three people who trade options make a profit! The broker makes a profit, the specialist makes a profit—and the client? Hey, somebody has to lose."
>
> —Lee Crawford

An option is the right to buy 100 shares of a given stock at a given price within a given period of time, usually one to six months. And to put it simply: Them commissions, they'll kill ya.

Another problem with options is the wide spread between the bid price (at which you sell) and the ask price (at which you buy). For example, a quote of "2 bid—2¼ asked" implies only a ¼ point spread, but that ¼ point is actually 12.5 percent of the value of the contract. Therefore, the option must rise by over 10 percent for you just to break even, *before* commission costs. In contrast, the difference between the buy and sell price of IBM averages about ⅒ of 1 percent.

There is also the problem of time: It's not on your side. If your option is going to expire in three months, you not only need to be correct, you need to be correct fairly soon. And let's face it, in any three-month period, you are at the mercy of the market. The reasons you bought that option may become as irrelevant as they were impressive. Of course, you may also realize a quick profit for reasons that have nothing to do with your own thinking. But that is just luck, which is not exactly the key to long-term success.

Certainly, there is considerable leverage in owning options: A small bet can result in a large win, if you are right. We occasionally read how, when one company offered to buy out another, the news sent the price of some about-to-expire option soaring. However, the press has spent a lot less ink writing about the thousands of about-to-expire options that did expire worthless.

Just as in the lottery, where people overpay for the chance of a big win, buyers of options tend to overpay for the leverage. Add in commission costs plus the spread, and you have got a fairly poor use of your money. If you like a stock for good reasons, buy it directly and wait until it makes good.

There are similar problems with futures, which are contracts to buy or sell a stated amount of a commodity—pork bellies, corn, gold, even stocks and bonds—at a stated price at a stated time in the future. Most commodity futures contracts come due within three or six months; the short contract life again puts you at the weird whims of the markets.

As for leverage, the owner of a futures contract can turn a small bet into a large win or *loss*. An option buyer faces, at worst, the loss of his original stake. A player in the futures market can lose considerably more than that.

A speculator can buy a futures contract by putting down only 5 to 10 percent of the total value of the contract. This is considerably smaller than the margin debt you are allowed to borrow to buy stocks—currently 50 percent—and even less than the much-criticized levels of the speculative 1920s. Frankly, there is just no way that a 5 percent or 10 percent margin of error will permit you to ride out temporary fluctuations. Look at the United States stock market, the most sophisticated market in the world. It managed to decline by 22 percent in one day!

Another factor to consider is that your orders for these contracts are executed in what is called the futures pit, a term that can seem depressingly appropriate to the small player. Which is to say, you may not be too happy with the execution of your trades. The price you pay may be consistently more—and the one you receive consistently less—than the price at the time you place your order.

The free-wheeling reputation of the futures market recalls the glorious days of laissez-faire Rome, when private individuals owned the fire brigade, and occasionally rates were negotiated in front of the potential customer's burning house; accusations would even surface that these entrepreneurs had taken it upon themselves to drum up business directly.

As for the modern world, it has been noted that the average financial life-expectancy of a retail commodity player is six months.

There is a bright side to all of this, however. A single futures contract can rise or fall in value by thousands of dollars each day. If you are worried about where your kids are spending their summer afternoons, just give them one contract as a gift, and a Quotron to monitor it—you'll know exactly where to find them, at least during trading hours.

Don't Use Retail Brokers

If you are going to make your own investment decisions, consider using a discount broker, such as Schwab, Siebert or Quick & Reilly. A discount broker, unlike a full-service retail broker such as Merrill Lynch, simply executes your trades and does not provide company research or investment suggestions. Accordingly, you will pay less in commissions and will also separate yourself from the likelihood of poor advice.

Retail brokers are a distribution system. And the highest priority of the system is to distribute what's on the shelf, starting with the most profitable merchandise—namely, new issues. There is a Mischa Richter cartoon which illustrates this point nicely: It shows a chef standing before a ten-foot fish and telling his waiters, "Push the Scotch salmon with dill sauce."

Retail brokers are also inclined to market the easiest ideas, and as you probably know by now, the easiest stories to believe in are rarely the best stocks to own. To make matters worse, those brokers who don't know better probably don't realize this, or perhaps they just don't care; after all, the reality of this business is that brokers make money from your transactions whether or not you make money from their advice.

Does this mean that discount brokers are better than all full-service retail brokers? Of course not. (This is a favorite marketing approach: Ask yourself a ludicrously one-sided question and then answer it. This gives the illusion of insight.) A retail broker who represents his clients with integrity and insight, who measures his success with theirs, can be a valuable asset for an investor. Such a broker can be a useful sounding board for stock selections and can occasionally provide research from his firm that is both proprietary and incremental. However, retail brokers with these qualities seem to represent a small minority.

One final point: *Never* deal with any broker who calls you up out of the blue. The livelier the sales pitch, the likelier the risk.

Don't Buy New Issues

The purpose of the market, as mentioned earlier, is to allow companies to raise money from the public. If investors refused to buy new issues, there wouldn't be much need for a stock market.

Money would still be raised by companies from private sources, such as venture capital funds, insurance companies, and other corporations. Banks would allocate scarce capital in their consistent if not inspired manner. Still, without an active stock market America's ability to finance its future would be significantly impaired.

But there's no need to panic—people will continue to buy new issues. However, *you* probably shouldn't be one of these buyers. After all, you have no obligation to the free market to purchase a poor investment.

The reason that public offerings are usually unattractive is that they are rarely underloved and undervalued. More often, they represent industries that are highly popular with investors at the current time. For example, in 1983, investors, after watching the prices of small technology companies rise sharply during the previous eight years, developed an overwhelming demand for similar companies. Sure enough, a host of small, high-tech new issues surfaced to meet that demand. And, as the saying goes, beware of what you want because you just may get it—those overloved and overvalued technology stocks were soon decimated.

As you can see, new issues are usually a bull market phenomenon—rising prices are necessary to create the appetite both for initial public offerings (IPOs) and for subsequent offerings. In bear markets, demand wanes as investors lick the wounds from their purchases in the preceding bull market. Once burned, twice shy, they avoid new issues at any price—at least, for a while.

In considering a new issue, the question you must ask yourself is: Why should I want to buy stock from this company or its management? The odds are that you know a great deal less about the prospects for the company than these people do, and they are *selling*.

You also should be concerned about potential conflict of interest. Brokerage firms are the underwriters of new issues, representing both the sellers, who likely want the highest price possible, and the potential buyers as well—investors like yourself. To confuse matters further, your retail broker is probably not unbiased: the commission on a new issue is approximately ten times that of a normal trade. This is the basis for the saying that deals are not bought, they're sold.

This is not to suggest that most new issues will decline immediately; in fact, most do just fine—at first. The brokerage firm that underwrites an IPO has a certain responsibility to support the stock, to keep it from falling below the offering price. However, this obligation rarely extends beyond a few days.

Some IPOs rise sharply in price on the first trade. The only problem is that these shares—and their easy profit—will rarely, if ever, come your way. Deals that are genuinely "hot" are desirable because the demand for stock at the offering price is well ahead of the supply. Accordingly, the shares have to be rationed out, and you probably won't get any. After all, you are certainly not a major institution, and you are probably not even a major retail client.

In a sense, hot deals are the loss leaders that whet the public's appetite for the considerably less attractive offerings that fill the pipeline. And since you generally can't get what you want and shouldn't want what you can get, why bother?

There will always be those new issues that are wildly successful; there will always be brokers who will argue their merits, and a few investors who will prosper. But the overall historical record is discouraging. *Forbes* magazine determined that, of 1,236 new issues sold in the 1982–1987 period, 71 percent did worse than the average stock.

For most investors, an understanding of the odds and a few sensible strategies for the playing will serve them well. Which is to say, don't be obsessed with pearls unless you're really fond of oysters.

The End of the Beginning

At this point, you should have a sense of how the stock market operates and a general understanding of how to approach it. Now let's consider the process of long-term value investing, including what to look for in a company and at what price to buy its stock.

The next three chapters focus on finding exceptional companies at bargain prices. This strategy—the top choice among those recommended—may seem at odds with the Low P/E Approach (p. 25), which highlighted unattractive, out-of-favor names. Investing in inexpensive, excellent companies, however, is not in contradiction with investing in inexpensive, mediocre companies. In both cases, you're buying what's cheap.

There is more than one way to beat the market and many more ways to be beaten by it. You need a strategy that is worth your time and a commitment to see it through.

Recognize that your success as an investor will depend on your discipline, in addition to your effort and natural ability. Even if you are accurate in forecasting the prospects for a company, you will still need patience; it may take five years or more for its shares to reach fair value. Inexpensive stocks can often get cheaper before they rise, and overvalued stocks can climb farther before they correct—or crash.

The earnings that you predict may indeed come through, but the market may be temporarily unwilling to pay much for these earnings. Interest rates may have risen, the economic outlook may be poor, war may be threatening, or people may just be afraid to own stocks.

Maintaining the courage of your convictions in the face of all this is easier said than done. If the market refuses to reward you for your insights, and the stock just sits there, you can't help but wonder what it is that "they" know that you don't. After all, the market should be so smart, being the consensus of so many smart people. If your stock declines instead of rising, then there is the added pressure of lost money. Maybe it's time to wake up and smell the coffee, you think . . . maybe you're wrong . . . maybe you should cut your losses. It's not easy.

However, if you learn to invest with knowledge and discipline, the market should treat you quite well over time. Perhaps a good deal better than you might think.

CHAPTER 3

Analyzing Stocks

The race may not always go to the swift or the victory to the
strong, but that's the way to bet.
—Damon Runyon

The vast majority of successful investors have achieved that success through superior stock selection, rather than by trying to time
the market's moves. Their skill in picking stocks, in turn, has been
based primarily on a thorough understanding of the factors influencing the underlying companies.

This chapter offers a simple and sensible approach to the analysis
of companies and their shares. The approach concentrates on industry
outlook, company position, management quality, investor attitudes,
and economic considerations, focusing on high-quality companies that
enjoy unique products and superior managements.

Industry/Company Outlook

Prosperity today is no guarantee of prosperity in the future.
In fact, present prosperity may sow the seeds of its own destruction. Success will attract competition; if the industry or company is
ill-equipped to fight off that competition, then its success will not
last.

The level of competition can vary greatly among industries. Agriculture is almost perfectly competitive, with thousands of suppliers
producing a homogeneous commodity and each accepting the free-
market price. Newspapers operate in a different competitive environment, with a few suppliers—sometimes only one—having a great
deal to say about what they will charge for a very distinctive product.

Corn may be corn, but the New York *Post* is not *The New York Times*. A new farmer can enter or leave the corn business at will, but few publishers can successfully launch a new daily newspaper. For this reason, a newspaper is considered a strong "franchise"—it is a company that you wouldn't want to compete against.

Walter Annenberg developed an appreciation of the value of a franchise during a vacation in Cuba prior to World War II. He watched as gamblers lined up to buy copies of *The Daily Racing Form* at an exorbitant premium to its cover price. His ownership of this property, as well as that of *T.V. Guide* and *Seventeen,* eventually made him one of the richest men in the world.

When Warren Buffett—widely considered the country's foremost investor—analyzes a company, he asks himself: Will it survive the test of time, continuing to produce and profit well into the next century? Most investors would find the question irrelevant, but bear in mind that equities are really one of the longest-term investments you can make. Even if you hold a stock for only a few years, the price you receive from the next buyer will be a reflection of how he views the company's future at that time.

Buffett asks the same question in another way: Would you be glad to own the stock of this company if the market closed down for ten years?

Other questions worth asking: Is the company's product better than its competition's? Is the demand for it stable, or does it fluctuate up and down with the economy or with consumer fads? Is the company the leader in its industry or its niche in terms of market share? Is that market share growing or declining? Do you want a generic play (an average company) in a favorable industry, such as Gannett, or would you prefer a company whose performance will be relatively unaffected by industry trends, such as Polaroid in its heyday?

How important is research and development, and how successful is the company in translating research into results?* Does the company produce a product that must be ordered in advance, and if so, are those orders increasing and at a faster rate than shipments?

What will the company look like in five years? In ten? In thirty?

---

*If you are considering an investment in a technology stock, make sure that you understand—really understand—the company's products. Many investors do their learning when the stock is declining.

And don't forget the $64,000 Question itself: What can go wrong?

The answers to these questions should leave you comfortable both with the prospects for the industry you are analyzing and with the merits of the particular company you are considering.

Management

"Experience shows that really good management is practically never overpaid." What may surprise many investors about this quote is its source: Benjamin Graham, the recognized father of value investing. Graham's approach has become identified over the years as one of buying underfollowed, underloved, and undermanaged companies. But cheap doesn't necessarily mean valuable, and Graham acknowledged that few assets were of greater potential value than a motivated, qualified, and honest management.

Good managers may not be able to overcome bad industry fundamentals, but poor managers can often neutralize positive ones. And then there are the great managers, those who can make a difference, no matter how large their companies are. Examples of such people include Tom Murphy of Capital Cities/ABC, Jack Welch of General Electric, and Michael Eisner of Disney.

In evaluating the managers of a potential long-term investment, try to be certain in your own mind of their integrity. For starters, read what's been written about them in magazines and newspapers (libraries nowadays have user-friendly computers which can locate what you need in minutes). If you are willing to make the extra effort, you should seek out the opinions of those who have dealt with these people: employees, competitors, suppliers, customers, and social contacts. A company's public relations person can provide you with some initial leads, who can then suggest other names.

Also, don't be afraid to listen to your instincts if you have the opportunity to meet management in person, such as at the annual meeting. You don't want to rely on your gut when choosing a stock since that's unfamiliar territory where the obvious is often misleading; in judging people, however, you've had decades of experience, and you're probably damn good at it.

Once you are comfortable with the integrity of the managers, ask yourself if they excel at what they do, and why. Do they have a vision of what they want their company to achieve? If so, how do they plan to get from here to there?

Are they capable of making the difficult decisions, such as cutting overhead, which usually means putting decent people out of work? Or are they too willing to cut back, demonstrating an insensitivity to their workers? (Even in the coldest economic light, unfairness is bad business.) Are they interested in hiring the qualified and aggressive and ambitious—namely, the people who will eventually try to replace them?

Develop a sense of how the management views its bosses, the stockholders. Don't just read the words in the annual reports, which may ring with the banality of a campaign speech. Look at their actions. Look for a management that is really interested in maximizing shareholder value, especially one with a track record to prove it and two good reasons to keep on proving it—personal pride and personal wealth.

Managers should own large stock positions themselves; their intention should be to prosper personally by making their shareholders rich. Those managers who prefer large salaries to large stock positions are sending their bosses a message about their confidence and their competence.

Ideally, managers should be paid in *shares of stock*. Instead, many prefer to pay themselves some of their compensation in *stock options*. This practice is less admirable since such managers afford themselves all the upside potential of the shares, while assuming little or no downside risk.

Consistent with the ideal, management should own a significant, but not a controlling interest in the company—say, 10 percent of the outstanding shares. If for reason of ineptitude or circumstance, management has been unable to serve its shareholders well, it would be unfortunate if it had the power to preclude a better offer.

As with just about anything else in the market, there are exceptions. In general, however, an entrenched management is not desirable. In fact, some controlling family managements own so much stock that their wealth is assured beyond any reasonable needs—a factor that can dampen motivation.

Obviously, in searching for the ideal, you are going to spend most of your time being disappointed. But the closer you get to managers who prefer to prosper with their shareholders, the more likely you are to find yourself in an excellent investment. Warren Buffett pays himself only $100,000 a year, even though he owns more than 40 percent of Berkshire Hathaway stock, a position worth in excess of $3 billion. His priorities have been clear, and his performance has been remarkable: The price of the stock has risen by over 50,000 percent during his twenty-four-year tenure.

A manager or a board of directors who acts on behalf of the shareholders as readily as they speak on their behalf may be more the exception than the rule, but the exceptions can be marvelous. An April 1988 article in *Barron's* described a situation in which Honeybee's Board of Directors mandated a *higher* takeover price for the public than for the controlling family. Good for them, and good for their stockholders.

The Curse of Popularity

Have you ever been told by a broker that "you've gotta be in this stock," that the story was too good to be missed? At the time, the argument was probably more than a little tempting. But you know by now that a terrific-sounding idea is usually an invitation to trouble.

As an investor, you should beware of several caution flags. One particular danger sign is when a brokerage firm raises money to invest in a certain industry. This is done through an initial public offering of a *closed-end fund:* an investment company in which you are a shareholder. While other companies may produce widgets or corn flakes, closed-end funds are created to make investments—stocks, bonds, or real estate.

When those investments are targeted at the stocks of a specific industry, it is a reliable indication that this industry is already popular. Remember, brokers are generally interested in selling what people want to buy, since popularity is where the money is. If the fund is oversubscribed—with investor demand greater than the number of shares initially offered—you can be confident that the industry is too much in favor, and that the party in this sector is nearing its end.*

In addition to avoiding new closed-end offerings, you should be wary of *any* initial public offering. These IPO's, as noted earlier, are generally overloved, overpromoted, and overpriced.

Another caution sign is when a company already public announces a new stock offering, and nobody seems to mind in the least. This is particularly worrisome when, in addition to the sales by the company to raise money for its business, the company's managers are selling shares of their own. (The prospectus for the offering will state who is selling, and how much.) Again, ask yourself: Why should I buy when people who know more than I are selling?

Try to invest in companies that the managers think are cheap, and in which they are buying stock for themselves. Also, look to invest in companies which are generating more cash than they need, and don't have to raise money by selling shares, thereby diluting the ownership of existing stockholders.

The secondary offering of Texas Air shares in 1987 provided an especially grim example of the risk entailed by ignoring the danger signs. The stock, trading in the 40s at the time of the announcement, *rose* 5 percent on the news. One year later, the shares had declined by approximately 70 percent.

And be wary of favorable cover stories in the popular press, which have historically been reliable contrarian indicators. Since a general-interest magazine will try to focus on popular subjects, its positive articles on certain stocks, industries, and markets will be a reflection of current popularity. You might remember *Life* maga-

---

*Regardless of which investments a closed-end fund plans to make, there is no reason that you should buy it on the offering. The value of your investment will be immediately less than the price you were charged, since commissions are paid out of the proceeds, reducing the net asset value—the underlying value of the shares it owns. Also, since closed-end funds tend to trade at a 10–15 percent *discount* to net asset value, you can expect the fund's market price to decline by about 20 percent, even *if* the value of the assets doesn't drop!

To make matters worse, the assets probably *will* drop in value—after all, the fund is responding to an industry's popularity and that is usually a bad sign. Worse still, other players in the market will tend, in advance of the offering, to run up the prices of the stocks that the fund intends to buy, leaving it to pay top dollar. One example is the Duff & Phelps Selected Utility Fund, which was created to invest in the utility industry. It originally expected to raise $100 million; it actually raised $1.3 billion and went public the day before the utility index reached an all-time high.

zine's classic 1974 cover story questioning whether the stock market had a future, just a few months prior to a tremendous bull market.

As an investor, you should take advantage of people's natural tendency to want what everyone else wants. Be aware of the warning signals, avoid the investment fads, and look for the out-of-favor ideas. Since the market prices stocks at whatever investors are willing to pay—often regardless of value—the opportunities tend to lie with the unpopular.

Private Market Value

Up until this point, we have focused on what to look for and what to avoid in an industry, a company, and its management—factors that are primarily qualitative. Determining private market value is considerably more quantitative, and it is an essential step in analyzing a stock.

Private market value is the price that a company would sell for if it were auctioned off to the highest bidder. The acquirer, most likely another company in the same industry, could benefit from the synergies in production and marketing and, it is hoped, from improved management of the assets as well. Although few companies are ever put on the auction block, and antitrust concerns occasionally preclude the highest bidder, a sense of private market value is important in estimating a company's maximum potential price.

As an investor, you should try to buy shares in companies that sell in the stock market at a substantial discount to private market value—say 50 percent. In addition, you should want your money behind a management that will increase that private value over time. Eventually, you can profit both from the increase in the value of the company and from the narrowing of the discount between that value and its market price.

But, as Buffett warned at the 1988 Berkshire Hathaway annual meeting, be wary of private market values that seem to be removed from reality. Sometimes, in overly optimistic markets or in the heat of takeover battles, prices are paid that are unjustified by reasonable measures. In effect, you want to buy stocks considerably below the pro rata price that you would be willing to pay for the entire company, if you were an intelligent corporate buyer yourself.

Private market value is different from intrinsic value—what the company is worth on its own—although the two are related. Private market value is usually higher, since a buyer may have certain economies of scale that will improve the earnings potential for the acquired company. For example, if a company buys a competitor, it can consolidate research, production, distribution, marketing, and accounting.

If nothing else, private market value is easier to estimate than intrinsic value, because the purchase of one company, in whole or in part, offers a yardstick whereby you can appraise the potential value of similar companies. The takeovers of Carnation, Nabisco, and General Foods, for example, gave investors a clear idea of the value of the remaining food companies.

As a starting point in determining private market value, look at the multiples that are being paid in a takeover. Then make adjustments for differences between the acquired company and the remaining companies in the quality of products, distribution systems, and management. In addition, adjust for differences in the outlook for growth of revenues, earnings, and especially cash flow, which we'll consider in the next chapter.

Let's say that U.S. Widgets is bought out at two times current revenues, fifteen times earnings, and ten times cash flow. You have spent some time looking at its close competitor, W Industries, and you believe that it has superior management and products—in fact, a state of the art "midget widget" should be introduced in a few months. Accordingly, you project that it will easily outgrow U.S. Widgets. You therefore could reasonably estimate the private market value of W Industries at twenty times earnings, and you would be happy to buy shares for yourself at half that multiple.

If a company has extra cash on hand, net of debt, add this to the value of the ongoing operations in your estimate. For example, in the wake of the Crash, Dreyfus sold down to $16, not much above its net cash of $13 per share! Investors were paying only $3 for the company's mutual fund business, which was worth perhaps ten times that amount if sold to the highest bidder.

You should also keep an eye out for hidden assets which have considerable value even though they might not be generating much income at the current time. In the 1960s, Buffett bought shares in Disney because its film library alone was worth as much as the stock price; he reasoned that he was being given the company's businesses, management, and franchise for free. In general, the largest hidden asset that a company will own is land, which is carried on the books at cost and is usually worth considerably more.

Also, bear in mind that private market value is a concept that applies to ongoing businesses, as distinguished from a company's value in bankruptcy. As Graham warned long ago in *Security Analysis,* liquidation value is usually a disappointingly small amount.

A concept that is similar to private value is *replacement cost.* Ask yourself how difficult and expensive it would be to reproduce the company. How does that cost compare to the stock's current market value? A company that is selling for considerably less than its replacement cost is probably a good investment.*

The Big Picture

As an investor, you might want to give some thought to the economic outlook, both on a long-term secular basis and an intermediate-term cyclical basis.

The secular outlook is primarily influenced by the debt cycle, which is described in depth later. In general, a trend of credit expansion in the economy is positive for real assets—goods and services, such as land, commodities, housing, and labor—whereas credit contraction favors investments in financial assets—bonds, cash, and to a lesser extent, stocks.

The next macro issue involves the cyclical factors. Within a long-term secular advance or decline of credit, the economy will still fluctuate between cyclical expansions and recessions. The market tends to overreact to short-term economic upturns and downturns by over-

---

*Probably, but not necessarily. One argument frequently heard in the 1980s in favor of takeovers was that it is cheaper to expand by buying another company than by building new factories. However, in declining industries, companies may be better off neither building *nor* buying.

estimating their duration. Good times are expected to last, or even improve, and bad times to endure, or worsen.

Your attitude should be that this too shall pass. In recessions, look beyond the valley toward the factors that will create the next upcycle, and do the opposite for expansions. This attitude should put you in the nervous minority of those who are more often in the right.

If economic issues are unfamiliar to you, then ignore these factors when making investment decisions. Don't fall into the trap of: I call them as I see them and when I don't see them, I call them anyway. In fact, several of this country's finest investors argue that the economy cannot be accurately predicted. To them, economic forecasts are similar to horoscopes: interesting, but entirely unreliable.

CHAPTER 4

Reading a Financial Statement

I don't think we're in Kansas anymore, Toto.

—Dorothy at business school

Let me warn you up front: This isn't an easy chapter, especially if you're not very comfortable with numbers. If you find this stuff confusing, skip over it for now—you can do just fine without it, but you will do a lot better with it.

A clear understanding of a company's financials is worthwhile, even if the company is a high-quality name with a relatively predictable growth rate. You may not need to be an expert on the balance sheet or the income statement, but you should know its cash flow and free cash flow.

If you are interested in looking at a relatively unpredictable company, then a strong knowledge of financial statements is important. The balance sheet will give you a breakdown of the company's financial health, while the income statement will help you determine where revenues and earnings have come from and where they might be going.

For example, a cyclical company such as Bethlehem Steel or General Motors will see its earnings rise or fall dramatically with the economy's ups and downs. A look at past results can give you an idea of how sensitive the bottom line is to changes in sales. The statements will give you a sense of the firm's risk in bad times and its potential in good times.

At this stage of the game, however, it's best to focus on what the financial statements tell you about high-quality companies, those with the characteristics that were outlined in the previous chapter.

These financial statements are included in companies' annual reports, which are available at libraries, and from Bechtel Information Services (1-800-231-3282).

The Balance Sheet

The balance sheet is a portrait of a company's financial condition at a given time. Most public companies publish an interim balance sheet each quarter and a comprehensive one at the end of their fiscal year. (The vast majority of companies use the end of the calendar year as the end of their reporting year.)

Consider the example of Talking Buggy Whips Inc. (TBW), a hypothetical company whose balance sheet in 000's,* as of December 31, 1989, is as follows:

ASSETS			LIABILITIES AND STOCKHOLDERS' EQUITY		
Current Assets:			*Current Liabilities:*		
Cash	1,000		Accounts Payable		3,000
Short-Term Invest.	2,000		Notes Payable/Short-Term Debt		4,000
Accounts Receivable (less allowance for doubtful accounts)	8,000		Long-Term Debt Due within 1 year		3,000
Inventories	9,000				
Total	20,000		Total		10,000
Long-Term Assets:			*Long-Term Debt:*		30,000
Plant and Equipment (less accumulated depreciation)	70,000		Total		30,000
Goodwill	5,000				
Patents	5,000				

*This indicates that all of the figures presented below are in thousands of dollars. For example, cash is listed as 1,000; therefore, the actual figure is $1,000,000.

Stockholders' Equity:

Par Value ($1 par) (1.5 million authorized; 1 million issued and outstanding)	1,000
Paid-in Surplus	19,000
Retained Earnings	40,000
Treasury Stock	0
Preferred Stock	0

Total 80,000   Total 60,000

TOTAL ASSETS $100,000   TOTAL LIABILITIES/ STOCKHOLDERS' EQUITY $100,000

Our company's balance sheet is easy to understand if we look at it step by step. Current assets are those assets that are expected to be realized in cash within one year. Cash in the bank—$1 million in this example—is cash by definition, while short-term investments, such as stocks and bonds—carried on the balance sheet at current market value—can be sold for cash on short notice. Accounts receivable are the I.O.U.s that the company holds for products it has sold on credit and which are still outstanding at the end of the reporting year. The inventory account reflects the value of those Talking Buggy Whips that are in various stages of production, for sale in the next year.*

Long-term assets are primarily made up of plant and equipment, which are necessary to build our products. The next category, good-will, is the intangible value of an acquired company—in effect, it is the value of its reputation, its franchise. It is created when a company is bought for more than its *book value,* which is the amount by which its assets exceed its liabilities on the balance sheet. In our example,

---

*Keep an eye out for a large increase in accounts receivable or inventories from one year to the next. This would indicate, in the first case, that a growing proportion of sales are being done on credit, which may not be paid back. In the case of a jump in inventories, check with the company and its customers to see if its products are less in demand and, if so, why.

we have $5 million in goodwill left over from last year's questionable acquisition of Will-o'-the-Whips.

We have also recorded $5 million for the remaining value of our company's patents on the technology for talking; after all, buggy whips haven't historically sold too well when silent.

The total assets of Talking Buggy Whips Inc. were $100 million at the end of 1989, which is not bad, even for a fictitious company.

Current liabilities, those due within a year, are made up of accounts and notes payable (the company's I.O.U.s to suppliers and banks, respectively), short-term debt, and the portion of long-term debt that must be repaid in the upcoming year. The rest of long-term debt is carried on the balance sheet separately as a long-term liability.

Stockholders' equity looks more confusing than it is. Common stocks are assigned a par value, which is usually quite low and is essentially meaningless. The money that is raised from stockholders, in the initial public offering and in subsequent stock offerings, is allocated to the par and the paid-in surplus accounts, which have little importance. In this example, $20 million has been raised over the years for the outstanding 1 million shares. Since 1.5 million shares have been authorized by the stockholders, management could issue an additional 500,000 new shares if it thought that this would be in the best interests of the company.

Retained earnings are the company's accumulated profits over the years, after subtracting all the dividends paid out. The Treasury Stock account keeps track of the shares that have been repurchased by the company; these shares are considered issued, but not outstanding, and are not counted in determining per-share figures. And then there's preferred stock, which in this example is zero. We may be stupid enough to make buggy whips, but we're not about to finance them through preferred stock (see p. 226).

The total liabilities and shareholders' equity were $100 million, equal to the figure for total assets. This will always be the case, since a company's assets must be purchased either with money borrowed from creditors or with funds contributed by stockholders.

Now let's look at the income statement, and following that, we'll consider several valuable ratios that can be determined from the statements.

The Income Statement

The income statement is a picture in motion, recording the results of a company's operations for a given period of time—in this case, for a year. The recording of income and expenses is not really different from figuring your family budget, except that these figures might be a bit higher.

Income Statement

Revenues/Sales	$100 million
Cost of Goods Sold	60 million
Gross Profit	40 million
Selling, General & Administrative (SG&A)	15 million
Research and Development	5 million
Operating Profit	20 million
Depreciation/ Amortization	8 million
Interest Expense	3 million
Pretax Profit	9 million
Taxes (33%)	3 million
Net Income	6 million
Preferred Dividends	0
Net Income Available to Common Shareholders	6 million
Common Dividends	2 million
Retained Earnings	$4 million

Earnings Per Share (1 million shares outstanding) $6.00

Most of this is self-explanatory. The gross profit is the difference between the revenues from the products that were sold and the cost of producing them. The SG&A account involves marketing expenses and the general costs of running the business. Then there are the expenses for research and development.

The results are the operating profits, from which are subtracted the depreciation/amortization of the company's assets and the interest expense on its debt. Taxes are determined on the basis of the pretax profits. In this case, a 33 percent tax rate is assumed; a few years ago, the correct figure would have been 46 percent.

The net earnings are $6 million out of the initial $100 million in revenues. After subtracting dividends, the company will retain $4 million for future growth.

Financial Ratios for Fun and Profit

Operating profit margin: operating income as a percentage of sales; offers a picture of the on-going profitability of a company's goods or services. For TBW, this figure was 20 percent ($20 million out of $100 million) versus a U.S. corporate average of 15.4 percent in the latest available year.

Pretax profit margin: pretax income as a percentage of sales; indicates a company's profitability after deducting its interest costs, which are fixed charges that must be paid in full and on time. TBW's pretax margin of 9 percent was slightly better than the corporate average of 8.6 percent.

Net profit margin: net income as a percentage of sales; reflects the amount of each dollar of revenue that is left over for shareholders after all expenses. You may prefer to focus on pretax margin rather than net margin, since pretax figures are unaffected by temporary distortions in the tax rate caused by tax credits or net operating loss carryforwards.

Current Ratio: Moving to the balance sheet, we can determine the current ratio—current assets divided by current liabilities. This ratio offers an indication of a company's ability to meet its short-term obligations. In our example, the ratio is 2 ($20 million in current assets to $10 million in current liabilities), which is an adequate showing.

Quick ratio: Some conservative investors may be concerned that the accounts and notes payable will come due before the inventories are sold. For them, the quick ratio—cash and accounts receivable and short-term investments divided by current liabilities—is a useful measure of liquidity; at our company, the ratio is 1.1 ($11 million in cash, short-term investments and receivables divided by current liabilities of $10 million), a bit above a comfortable level of 1.

Debt/equity ratio: An important measure of financial leverage, this is simply the long-term debt divided by the stockholders' equity on the balance sheet. A reasonable D/E ratio is 1/2—$1 of debt for each $2 of equity. For Talking Buggy Whips Inc., the debt/equity ratio is, in fact, 1/2 ($30 million in long-term debt to $60 million in shareholders' equity). This highlights one of the advantages of a fictional company: It's easy to manage.

Some debt is usually desirable, since most businesses can earn a greater return from the money than the cost of borrowing it. However, excessive debt leaves a company ill-prepared for bad times.* The interest costs must be paid regardless of the revenues, and if an interest payment is missed, the company is liable to be thrown into bankruptcy. (That is, unless the debtor owes so much that its creditors are unwilling to let the loans default. Welcome to the exciting world of Third World lending.)

Interest coverage: Another measure of leverage is the interest coverage, which is operating profit minus depreciation divided by interest expense. In our company, the ratio is 4, indicating that mandatory interest charges are covered four times over. This figure is better than the ratio of 3 that was suggested by Benjamin Graham as

---

*One argument in favor of greater debt is that the "true" D/E ratio should be based on the market value, not the book value, of companies' stocks. The problem with this argument is that market values can reach unsustainably high levels, making further borrowing appear justified. The subsequent declines in the stock market will then raise the "market-adjusted" D/E ratios to uncomfortable levels, and leave companies especially vulnerable in the next economic downturn.

a minimum for industrial companies, and significantly exceeds the coverage ratio of 1.0 for RJR, the largest buyout in history.

Return on equity: This is one of the most important ratios to an investor. It is a measure of the company's rate of return on the money provided by its owners, and is determined by dividing the net income by the shareholders' equity. The ROE is most useful as an indicator of what the company can earn in the future on the net income that it chooses to retain. In our example, the ROE was 10 percent ($6 million in net income divided by $60 million in equity),* which is below the 12 percent average for public companies in the past several decades.

The ROE measure is not always a reliable guide, however, for it is only as accurate as its components. Look for distortions in the earnings figures—a large variation in the bottom line from one year to the next is a good indicator—and adjust for them. A misleading figure can arise from an unusually low tax rate which will overstate earnings. Or the net earnings number may not be a true reflection of operating results in any given year due to extraordinary or nonrecurring items. Focus on the earnings from the company's continuing operations, fully taxed, exclusive of one-time gains or losses.

Some "one-time" losses, Graham warned, are really just accumulated operating mistakes made over the prior few years. If you believe that the earnings from continuing operations are overstated because of these excessive special writeoffs, reduce the figures accordingly. For example, if our company took a one-time writeoff for the unsold buggy whips that have piled up over the years, this would be misleading. Since selling buggy whips is an integral part of our ongoing business, this loss should be included with operating results. To be accurate, the writeoff should be allocated to the relevant years when the whips were made.

On the other hand, if TBW took a one-time charge for a loss on the sale of a separate division, this would be considered a nonoperating expense and should not be included as part of continuing opera-

---

*If you want to be precise, the ROE was actually a bit higher, since you should use the *average* of last year's and this year's equity rather than just the year-end figure. This year's number was $60 million; last year's was $56 million (the $4 million difference was the amount of earnings retained by the company—net income minus dividends paid out). Therefore, average shareholders' equity was $58 million and the ROE was 10.4 percent

tions. Let's say that our company sold its buggy hubcap subsidiary for a $1 million loss. This would not affect our $6 million net earnings figure from ongoing operations.

Certainly, deciding which writeoffs are truly nonoperating is not cut and dried. Just use your best judgment and, if in doubt, be conservative.

The ROE measure may also be inaccurate because of factors that overstate or understate shareholders' equity. For example, a new issue of stock will boost equity more rapidly than earnings, and this will temporarily depress the ROE. Or a special writeoff may significantly reduce the shareholders' equity account on the balance sheet. This will cause the ROE to soar, even though the company is no better off than it was just before the writeoff.

Another factor to consider is that the return on equity measure does not adjust for the risks of leverage. A company with a great deal of debt on its books may be able to earn a terrific ROE during good years, since interest costs are both fixed and tax-deductible; however, this company may be unprepared for a bad year when revenues decline but interest costs do not.

Earnings Yield: This critical ratio is the return on investment (ROI) for public stockholders like you. Your expected return on investment is not the same as the company's ROE, unless the stock price is at the book value per share. If the market price is above the book price—as it usually is—your return will tend to be less.

As we noted earlier, the earnings yield is merely the inverse of the P/E. Let's say that the shares of Talking Buggy Whips were selling at 72, which, given earnings per share of $6, is a P/E of 12. Therefore, for each $1 of earnings, investors are willing to pay $12, and their initial return on investment is 8 1/2 percent.

Earnings Yield on Total Capital: If a company has a debt/equity ratio above 1, you should compute the return on the total capitalization, as well. This will tell you what the earnings yield would be if the company had not taken on significant debt; it is the *unleveraged* return on investment to investors.

To do this, first recompute the net earnings, assuming no interest expense—add back the after-tax cost of interest to the net income figure. Then divide this number into the total market capitalization, which is the sum of debt plus the market value of the stock (current price multiplied by the number of shares outstanding). For TBW Inc., the yield on total capital was approximately 8 percent ($8 million in adjusted net income divided by total capitalization of $102 million).*

Bear in mind that no matter how many ratios you compute and no matter how complex and thorough they seem, they are only as good as the numbers that go into them. And even when the figures are completely accurate, remember that these rates of return are based on past history—they may not always be reliable indicators of what the company can do in the future.

These ratios, however, do help to separate the potential winners from the living dead. They will give you a "feel" for the financial strengths and weaknesses of a company, which is particularly useful if you want to analyze names that don't meet the standards of the previous chapter. Putting together the financial ratios doesn't take much effort, and you should find some interesting facts in these boring figures. But none more worthwhile than you'll find in the following section on cash flows.

The Flow of Funds Statement

The purpose of the Flow of Funds statement, officially known as the Statement of Change in Financial Position, is to track where a company's money is coming from and where it is going. The example on the next page of TBW's flow of funds for the year ending 12/31/89 may look difficult at first glance, but a brief review will show it to be fairly straightforward.

---

*The $8 million in adjusted earnings is arrived at by adding $2 million in *after-tax* interest ($3 million in interest expense minus $1 million in taxes saved at a 33 percent tax rate) to the $6 million in unadjusted net income. The $102 million in total market capitalization is the sum of $30 million in long-term debt plus $72 million in market value—1 million shares times a stock market price of $72 per share. Review this example a few times—it's not as difficult as it might seem at first.

Sources of Funds—Operating (important):

Net Income	$6 million
Depreciation of Plant/Equipment	$7 million
Amortization of Goodwill/Patents	$1 million
Total	$14 million

Uses of Funds—Operating (important):

Capital Expenditures	−$8 million
Total	−$8 million

Other Sources and Uses (not too important):

Change in Working Capital:

Increase in Accts. Receivable	−$1 million
Increase in Inventories	−$1 million
Decrease in Short Term Investments	$2 million
Decrease in Notes Payable/S-T Debt	−$4 million
Dividends	−$2 million
Change in Long-Term Debt	0
Sale of Stock	0
Acquisitions/Divestitures	0
Total	−$6 million

Net Change in Cash Position	0

$ 14,000,000
− 8,000,000
− 6,000,000

Cash at beginning of the period	$1 million
Cash at the end of the period	$1 million

The flow of funds is directly related to the change in the balance-sheet accounts from one year to the next. The figures for the latest two years at our imaginary company, again in 000's, are included to show you exactly how each source and use of funds was generated. If the balance-sheet figures that follow are helpful, great; if they're just confusing, forget them—the important information comes after the numbers.

	December 31, 1989	*December 31, 1988*
ASSETS		
Current Assets:		
Cash	1,000	1,000
Short-Term Invest.	2,000	4,000
Net Accounts Receivable	8,000	7,000
Inventories	9,000	8,000
Total	20,000	20,000
Long-Term Assets:		
Net Plant and Equipment*	70,000	69,000
Goodwill	5,000	5,200
Patents	5,000	5,800
Total	80,000	80,000
TOTAL ASSETS	$100,000	$100,000

LIABILITIES AND STOCKHOLDERS' EQUITY

Current Liabilities:		
Accounts Payable	3,000	3,000
Notes Payable/S-T Debt	4,000	8,000
L-T Debt Due w/i 1 year	3,000	3,000
Total	10,000	14,000
Long-Term Liabilities:		
Long-Term Debt:	30,000	30,000
Total	30,000	30,000
Stockholders' Equity:		
Par Value	1,000	1,000
Paid-in Surplus	19,000	19,000
Retained Earnings	40,000	36,000
Treasury Stock	0	0
Preferred Stock	0	0
Total	60,000	56,000
TOTAL LIABILITIES/ STOCKHOLDERS' EQUITY	$100,000	$100,000

*The $1 million increase in net plant and equipment in 1989 was the difference between the $8 million of capital expenditures and the $7 million of depreciation during the year

The most important figure that you can derive from the Statement is the *free cash flow*. This is the excess money that is available to the company on an ongoing basis. It is the difference between the funds generated from its operations minus the expenditures on maintaining and replacing plant and equipment. These *capital expenditures* assure that the company will be able to continue producing competitive products and, therefore, to stay in business.

To compute the free cash flow from operations, simply subtract capital expenditures from *gross cash flow* (net income plus depreciation/amortization). These expenditures usually run a great deal higher than the company's depreciation, since inflation raises the cost of maintenance and replacement over time. In our example, the free cash flow was $6 million ($14 million minus $8 million).

If you want to be more precise, you should also take into account changes in *working capital*—current assets minus current liabilities. An increase in working capital should be deducted from gross cash flow, since funds are required to finance the increase. Working capital needs tend to increase over the years; as the business grows, more money is necessary to keep things running smoothly. The most important components are accounts receivable and inventory—the larger you are, the larger your credit sales and the larger your inventories of products to sell.

An increase in assets is a *use* of funds, since the company is exchanging cash for that asset—be it investments, inventory, or whatever. An increase in liabilities is a *source* of funds, since the company is receiving cash now in exchange for an obligation to pay cash in the future. Accordingly, a decrease in assets is a source of funds, while a decrease in liabilities is a use of funds. Eventually, the liabilities will be paid off, reducing cash, and the assets will be sold, raising cash.

In any given year, free cash flow can be boosted or reduced substantially by unusual nonoperating factors such as divestitures or sales of stocks/bonds. However, your focus as an investor should be on the free cash flow from operations, with particular attention to the trend of that free cash flow over time.

The simplest way to incorporate free cash flow into your analysis of a potential investment is to view it as a boost to the growth rate of a company. Extra cash means extra income, beyond what the firm can earn from its current operations. The free cash can be used to repurchase stock, to make acquisitions, or to repay debt, all of which should add to earnings per share.

The company may choose, instead, to spend its extra funds to increase the dividend payment. This would benefit shareholders by raising their dividend yield, whereas the previous three options would improve their prospects for capital gains. As an investor your hope is that management will deploy these excess funds in a manner that will maximize the long-term value of the company.

Don't underestimate the importance of this concept: A dollar of free cash flow is just as valuable as a dollar of reported earnings. In addition, since this point is widely misunderstood by investors, an understanding of free cash flow offers you an edge on your competition in finding a great investment.

A good deal of free cash flow is generally a good deal, but there are exceptions. As mentioned earlier, free cash flow is gross cash flow minus capital spending. What complicates this analysis is that all capital expenditures are not created equal. A company that must spend all its cash flow just to survive in a competitive business is unlikely to be an attractive long-term investment. Conversely, one which spends its funds to take advantage of an unusual opportunity is treating its shareholders right. For example, you should not penalize Disney for expanding its hugely popular studio tour, or Pepsi for buying one of its bottlers at a good price; these actions will reduce excess cash flow currently to the greater benefit of each company's future.

This is expanded upon in the section headed "A Closer Look" on page 204.

Rules of Accounting

- Revenues are usually accounted for under the accrual method, which means that sales are recorded when the transaction is made, whether it is for cash or credit. When the credit sales are paid, the only change is on the balance sheet. Accounts receivable are reduced by that amount, and cash is increased.

- The three primary methods of valuing the products that are produced and sold are "last in, first out" (LIFO), "first in, first out"

(FIFO), and "average cost." (There is also the notorious FISH— "first in, still here"—for those companies often destined to end belly up.)

The LIFO method assumes that the last product produced is the first product sold. In inflationary times, the costs of production will rise, and our cost of goods sold (CGS) will be higher than if the FIFO system was used. Accordingly, our costs will be higher for any level of sales under LIFO, and our pretax profit will be less. This will reduce our taxes.

Since LIFO will tend to understate both earnings and taxes, a dollar of LIFO earnings is of better quality than a dollar of FIFO or average cost earnings. As an investor, you should generally expect a higher P/E for a company using LIFO than for a comparable company using a different method. On the balance sheet, inventories under LIFO will tend to be understated, which is just the flip side of CGS being overstated. Bear in mind that inventories are just goods waiting to be sold; when they are, they will show up on the CGS line.

• *Depreciation* is an accounting convention allowing for the loss of value over time of the company's assets. If we need to replace our production plant and equipment every ten years, then theoretically these assets lose 10 percent of their value each year.* This approach is called straight-line depreciation, which most companies use for reporting to their shareholders.

The other approach is accelerated depreciation, which will increase the amount of depreciation in the early years and decrease it proportionally later on. This serves to understate profit—as with LIFO accounting for CGS—and reduce taxes in the early years. Since a tax dollar saved now is worth more than one saved later, companies like to use this approach for reporting to the IRS. Either way, the value of plant and equipment is reduced each year by the amount of depreciation, leaving us with the Net Plant and Equipment figure on the balance sheet.

*This assumes that the assets have no residual, or salvage, value at the end of their useful lives; if the salvage value was 20 percent, then the annual depreciation would be 8 percent for ten years.

- *Amortization* of patents is spread over forty years and is deductible against taxable income. Amortization of goodwill, on the other hand, is *not* deductible for tax purposes. However, it is supposed to be treated as an expense and deducted from net earnings, a fact which was ignored in our income statement.

  Frankly, goodwill amortization should not be treated as an expense. Like depreciation, goodwill amortization is a noncash accounting charge; unlike depreciation, it is not tax deductible. More important, depreciation reflects the fact that plant and equipment will wear out and will need to be replaced. In this sense, depreciation is a valid operating expense.

  Amortization, however, should not be subtracted from earnings in the first place. It is a noncash charge to reflect the cost of an acquisition in excess of book value. But that acquisition cost is already being reflected elsewhere on the income statement. To the extent that the purchase was financed with debt, it is reflected in a higher interest expense; to the extent that equity was used, the cost is reflected in an increased number of shares which will dilute per-share earnings. Therefore, goodwill amortization should be ignored and not subtracted from reported earnings.*

- If a company has a convertible bond outstanding, analyze the earnings projections on a *fully diluted* basis, which assumes that the bonds are converted into stock, thereby increasing the number of shares. On the positive side, the interest expense for these bonds is eliminated.

- *Unusual items* may be listed separately on the income statement as "extraordinary," "nonrecurring," or "special." The results of a discontinued operation are usually excluded from what the company considers its true operating performance. Most of the time, separating unusual items is justified in order to present an accurate picture of the ongoing business. Occasionally, however, a management or three might sneak a nonrecurring gain into operating profits or remove a normal operating-related loss from operating results.

*An excellent discussion of this widely misunderstood topic is presented in the 1983 Berkshire Hathaway Annual Report.

Red Flags

Always be on the lookout for any legerdemain in financial statements. One good place to find questionable accounting practices or potential bombshells is in the footnotes to the company's annual report. One misrepresentation to the shareholders will tell you more about the qualities of management than 100 pages of glossy pictures and promises.

Other suspicious items to watch out for include a "modified opinion" from the auditors. Turn to the page prior to the footnotes in which the auditors sign off on their work; their comments should state that the results *"present fairly"* the company's financial position without qualification. Any potential operating or legal problem mentioned on this page should encourage you to look elsewhere for a place to invest your money.

Another factor to be wary of is a change in the accounting approach for cost of goods sold, such as shifting from LIFO to FIFO, thereby raising reported earnings (and, consequently, the tax bill) without improving the quality of earnings. In addition, be concerned if a company has a large unfunded pension liability, whereby they have failed to set aside the required funds for their employees' expected retirement benefits.

Understanding the various rules of accounting is neither easy nor fun, but it is necessary. The Generally Accepted Accounting Principals (GAAP) are the language of business, as Buffett has noted, and a knowledge of the native dialects is important. Unfortunately, even the fluent have difficulty interpreting exactly how well a company is doing in the real world. There will always be a certain measure of confusion, not to mention an occasional display of creativity. The next financial statement you look at may bring to mind the accounting job applicant who, when asked what two plus two equaled, replied, "What do you want it to be?"

PART II

The Fun
(Relatively Speaking)

"YOU WILL NOTE THAT THEIR ABILITY TO COMPREHEND, ASSESS AND PROCESS INFORMATION INCREASES DRAMATICALLY WHEN PROFESSOR PODHERTZ THROWS IN THE CAT."

CHAPTER 5

A Case Study: The Washington Post Company

We believe the principles on which the company has long been managed—a commitment to quality, careful control of expenses and investment in the long term—will continue to serve us well.
—Katherine Graham, Chairman

Now that we've considered how to analyze stocks and read financial statements, let's apply what we know to a review of an exceptional company, the Washington Post. First, we'll see how this company measures up in terms of the categories that were described. Then, we'll make a reasonable forecast of what the company will look like in several years and what we, as value investors, should be willing to pay for it now.

Much of the information provided in this chapter is derived from a straightforward, one-page summary of the company in the Value Line Investment Survey, which is available at most libraries.

The Basics

The Washington Post Company (symbol: WPOB) publishes one of the finest newspapers in the country, as well as the *Everett Herald* (a Washington State daily) and *Newsweek*. It also owns four TV stations and fifty-three cable systems. WPOB has approximately 13 million outstanding shares. Stockholders' equity is on the books at less than $900 million, whereas the market value of the equity is some $3.6 billion. The company also has approximately $150 million in long-term debt; however, after taking its cash position into account, it has no net debt. Therefore, its debt/equity ratio, effectively, is zero.

The Big Picture

Let's start with a biased look at today's macroenvironment—the economic conditions in which the WPOB functions. The levels of debt—personal, corporate, and government—are at all-time highs, but what is considerably more relevant is that the amount of debt relative to the economy's size is at a ratio that is even higher than in the late 1920s.

Moreover, as money managers Stanley Salvigsen and Michael Aronstein have pointed out, the credit expansion process has already ended in agricultural, energy, and Third World borrowing. Perhaps the Crash of 1987 marked the beginning of the end of the financial lending boom, as well. In short, banks are running out of places to lend and are being forced to focus on the deflationary process of getting their money back—not a good secular environment, if correct.

On a cyclical basis, the economy at first seems to be experiencing neither boom nor bust. However, here at the beginning of the 1990s, it does appear to be getting late in the business cycle; there has not been a full-scale national recession since 1982. Meanwhile, the economy has begun showing some late-cycle signs of tightening labor markets and scarce raw materials, accompanied by rising inflation. At this point, the consensus among Wall Street forecasters is for an economic slowdown ("soft landing") in the near-term.

This forecast, however attractive to investors, ignores the long-range shift that seems to be occurring and that threatens to overwhelm the usual cyclical influences. If we look at the last six years in the context of a long-term secular shift from expansion to contraction, the outlook is different.

Our economy has arguably been in a dichotomy, with widening depressions in some business sectors because of recent credit contraction and aging booms in others as a result of decades of credit expansion. The economic statistics that average the booms and busts of our country's various industries and regions tell a story of slow, steady growth; however, the reality may be one of economic expansions and contractions occurring simultaneously, with the expansions becoming rarer and contractions more frequent

Regardless of the relative merits of the secular versus cyclical argument, it is fair to say that our economy is no spring chicken. As an investor, these considerations should encourage you to err on the side of caution when deciding at what price to buy the Post Company.

Industry/Company

At the industry and company level, the outlook is quite different. In most of its markets, the newspaper industry is a wonderful business, since it has a tendency toward natural monopoly, which is just great if you're the monopolist. Every city and town needs a daily newspaper to supply information and advertising. But they really don't need two, and the number-one player tends to attract a loyal readership—and, accordingly, the bulk of the local advertising dollar. To put this in perspective, of the more than 1,400 United States cities in which daily newspapers are published, approximately 90 percent have only one paper!

Once a daily newspaper develops a monopoly, it is extremely expensive for a new paper to compete, and rare indeed for it to succeed. Fortunately for all concerned, most of the players realize this and prefer to buy existing franchises, rather than try to develop new ones. Unfortunately, the increasing use of direct-mail advertising packets has cut into the cream of local newspaper retail advertising, while preprinted inserts have reduced profits. In addition, the growth of weekly local papers and shopping "throwaways" presents a competitive threat that is difficult to quantify but difficult to ignore.

The flagship of WPOB, the *Washington Post,* is a monopoly newspaper of national reputation, generally considered one of the top five papers in this country for excellence in reporting. It caters to a city whose primary industry is politics, one of the least cyclical businesses in any country. There is a great deal to say for an industry that never seems to decline, regardless of its popularity.

Management

The Post's publisher, the Graham family, has voting control of the company through its ownership of 100 percent of the super-voting 2 million A shares and 14 percent of the 11 million publicly traded B shares. An unfriendly takeover is, therefore, out of the question.

Normally, the use of dual classes of stock—A for the family, B for everybody else—is a caution flag for the prospective shareholder. You should tread carefully when considering a company in which a few managers are entrenched due to disproportionate voting power. However, let's not be too rigid. Without the dual stock, this company might never have gone public, since the family members may have been unwilling to risk loss of control. Besides, they are good managers, as the phenomenal performance of their stock demonstrates.

In fairness, it should be noted that they have benefited from the influence of the company's second largest shareholder, Warren Buffett. He bought 12 percent of the company in 1973 for less than $6/share and has been an active friend and adviser to the Graham family over the years. His attitudes toward superior management and shareholder orientation are very positive factors in considering whether to buy this stock. Although Buffett was required to resign his seat on the board of directors when he became a director at Capital Cities, his investment and probably his influence are intact. In general, you should always pay close attention to a stock that attracts a large investment by any of the few exceptional investors, particularly if that investor becomes an active adviser.

Popularity

The company is of exceptional quality and the stock has clearly been a winner, two characteristics that usually attract a Wall Street cheering section. According to Jay Morse, WPOB's chief financial officer (202-334-6662), the stock is followed by about five major brokerage firms, and is currently recommended for purchase by Drexel Burnham and First Boston. (Value Line assigns the shares a "timeliness rating" of 2, at the higher end of its 1 to 5 scale.)

My perception is that the "high" price of the stock—currently near $300 per share—has managed to discourage a more widespread following among analysts. For one thing, brokers are not eager to market high-priced stocks, especially to their retail clients. In addition, the current price highlights how much of the move in the stock has already been missed, an argument that is as seductive as it is irrelevant.*

The point is that a high price for a stock, *in and of itself,* does not mean that the stock is expensive. Can you imagine how thrilled you would be if you had sold your shares of Capital Cities at $300/share only because the price was "high" and watched it rise to its recent level above $500/share?

Let's now consider insider transactions at the Washington Post, the buying and selling of its shares by the people who know the company best—its managers. The figures on WPOB's insider transactions (included in Value Line) don't tell you much, with only two buyers and two sellers among its management in a nine-month period. Although the ratio is favorable (one buyer for every seller is considered a neutral reading), the volume of transactions seems insignificant. A tremendous number of shares are already owned by insiders at the Post—a few shares more or less don't make much difference.

Ideally, as a contrarian and a value player, you would want this company to be extremely unpopular with Wall Street analysts, who both create and reflect investor sentiment, and to be clearly popular with insiders, who have the best information. This is not the case here. However, even though WPOB doesn't rate highly by these two measures, neither does it show up poorly.

Growth Potential

On average, companies will grow in line with the economy; after all, economic growth is comprised of increases in the production of products plus increases in the prices of those products.

The newspaper industry is certainly affected by the economy, since the three main components of its sales are retail advertising, classified advertising, and circulation revenues. Meanwhile, costs are primarily composed of equipment, labor, and newsprint.

---

*A related issue concerns stock splits. The 1983 Berkshire Hathaway Annual Report included a compelling argument that stock splits serve no useful purpose—after all, 1 million shares at $100 each is no different from 10 million shares at $10 each. What is relevant is the total value of the company. An individual who would rather own a $10 stock than a $100 stock doesn't really understand what drives stock prices over the long term. (A friend of mine once ordered an entire pizza for himself; when asked whether he wanted it divided into four slices or eight, he replied, "Cut it into four—I don't think I can eat eight.")

The Washington Post has maintained growth well above the average; over the past ten years, earnings per share at the Post Company have quintupled, while those of the average company have doubled. On an annual basis, per-share earnings have grown by more than 15 percent a year over a ten-year span and by more than 20 percent a year over the past five years.

WPOB's exceptional growth has benefited from its substantial generation of free cash flow. In recent years, the company has produced about $.80 of free cash for every $1 of earnings, while the average company has produced less than $.30 of free cash for each $1 of profit.

The free cash flow of the Washington Post has historically been reinvested in acquisitions, which have improved the growth rate of revenues and earnings. Other options would have been to retire debt, which would have increased net income, or to buy back stock thereby boosting earnings for the remaining shares. Alternatively, the company could have paid out the free cash flow as dividends without jeopardizing its ability to grow at an average rate. Each of these four approaches is employed by various companies at various times, though few generate free cash flow as effectively as the Post Company.

Projections

Looking forward, let's make a reasonable assumption: Earnings will grow by 10–15 percent a year from 1990 to 1995. This forecast may seem too conservative in light of past growth rates but bear in mind, if economic growth continues to slow, particularly in the East, the growth of WPOB is likely to slow as well. In addition, 10–15 percent growth is considerably faster than that of the economy.

Using the midpoint of our 10–15 percent growth estimate, our EPS projection for 1995 is almost twice Value Line's 1990 estimate of $17/share. Specifically, our 1995 estimate is 80 percent above the 1990 figure, or $31.*

---

*To this we should add the amortization of goodwill, which, as discussed earlier, should not be subtracted from earnings in the first place. Unfortunately, Value Line doesn't provide the amortization figure. However, with a little help from an annual report or an analyst, you would learn that the figure is about $.65 per share. If you have trouble finding this number, then do your analysis without it—just recognize that your estimates will be a little on the conservative side.

For reasons of simplicity, we'll ignore amortization since it is not a meaningful amount in the case of WPOB. If, however, we were analyzing a company with a great deal of goodwill on the books, we would not ignore it. For example, the goodwill amortization of Coca-Cola Enterprises increases the earnings figure by some 70 percent.

Finding the Right Price

At this point, we can apply a reasonable multiple to our 1995 estimate of $31, an approach that was suggested by Benjamin Graham decades ago. Let's say that in 1995, you would be happy to receive a return of over 15 percent on your initial investment. Therefore, a fair multiple on 1995's estimate would be 6×, and your buy point on the stock would be around $185. At this price, the P/E on the 1990 estimate of $17 is 11.

A simpler approach would be to use the following rule of thumb for great companies (but only for great companies): *Buy aggressively when the earnings yield on the latest twelve months' results is greater than the Treasury-bond yield.** Over the past ten years, this rule of thumb would have recommended buying WPOB during 1979 and 1980 at prices ranging from 16 to 26. Since then, the total return for an investor has averaged over 30 percent per year.

For WPOB, the current buy point would be near $200, since the relevant earnings were above $15 and the T-bond is currently yielding below 8 percent.

If you really want to be demanding, wait until the earnings yield on the latest twelve months' profits is 10 percent or more. A multiple of 10× on $15 of earnings would give you a Sale of the Century Price of approximately $150. If Mr. Market forgot to take his lithium and offered to sell his shares at this price, you would be given that most elusive gift: the one-decision stock. You would then own an asset with an excellent current and an exceptional future return. (Your return would be made up of capital gains—through earnings growth—plus dividend yield.)

Digression

You might wonder why, if the stock is so far above our estimate of attractive value, hasn't Warren Buffett sold his shares? The answer is that he won't sell his shares at any price; he stated at the 1987 Berkshire Hathaway annual meeting that he views his position

---

*The stock pages will usually include the P/E for each company, based on the latest twelve months of reported earnings. The earnings yield is the inverse of this P/E ratio.

as he would a holding in a private company that is not publicly traded. This is not to imply that he feels that the stock or its industry is inexpensive; in fact, he pointed out in the 1986 annual report that the expression "attractively priced media company" has become a contradiction in terms, much like "military intelligence" or "more equal than others."

Private Market Value

In 1973, when Buffett purchased his shares of WPOB, the total market capitalization of the company was $80 million. He believed that any of several other companies would gladly have paid $200 million or more to own it. This didn't stop the stock from declining 25 percent in the next year. More importantly, however, the market's fears didn't stop the company from increasing its intrinsic value by going about its business, and doing it well.

Currently, the market capitalization of WPOB is $3.6 billion. As for the private market value (PMV), one Wall Street estimate exceeds $5.5 billion, some 50 percent above the current price. The assumptions are as follows:

Private Market Value, WPOB

DIVISIONS	OPERATING PROFIT	ACQUISITION MULTIPLES	TOTAL
Newspaper	$206 million	14	$2880
Newsweek	34	11	370
Broadcasting	87	12	1040
Cable	65	13	850
Other	14	9	130
Equity in affiliates			80

Total: $5.35 billion plus $180 million in cash net of debt divided by 12.7m shares = $435/share

(Source: Drexel Burnham Lambert)

This private market value figure is not available in Value Line, but a phone call to the company could get you an answer. Jay Morse indicated that various PMV estimates range from 425 to 500 per share. If you wanted to buy the Post at 50 percent of PMV, your buy point would be 210–250.

But, be warned, these private values are usually based on estimated multiples for each division, as in the example above, and these acquisition multiples will vary both with interest rates and with the level of the market. Therefore, the private market value will decline in a bear market along with the stock.

A similar approach is to determine the company's LBO (leveraged buy-out) value: What is the maximum price that a buyer could pay and still meet the interest payments, assuming that he borrowed the entire purchase cost? If the government must pay almost 8 percent to borrow currently, a leveraged buyer could expect to pay at least 10 percent. Accordingly, he could afford to pay $10 \times$ operating profit.

The Value Line estimate for operating profit in 1990 is approximately $400 million. A multiple of ten times this figure equals $4 billion, which, after adding cash and deducting debt, is approximately $330/share. This is well below the estimate of private market value. (Normally, private market value will exceed LBO value, since a strategic buyer—most likely another company in the same industry— may be able to reduce redundant costs or may be willing to accept losses on its investment for a while.)

Another issue to keep in mind is that LBO value will also vary with interest rates. That is why an estimate of private value or LBO value is a helpful input, not a sure thing.

A related question is: How much would it cost to replace this company? Many companies can be easily re-created, and some for less than their current market value, which is a clear signal to an investor to look elsewhere. But for the WPOB, the answer is easy: It can't be replaced at any realistic cost.

The Post Versus the Market

Let's address another interesting question: How does the stock of the Post Company compare to the market? WPOB should have an operating margin of 25 percent in 1989 (five-year average: 23.2 percent) versus 15.4 percent for the Standard & Poor's Industrial Index of the 400 largest companies in 1988 (latest year available). Net margin is estimated at 13.7 percent (10.7 percent average over 1985–1989) versus 5.4 percent for the market.

On the P/E comparisons, WPOB sells at a 20 percent premium to both the S&P 400* and the S&P 500. (The better comparison is probably with the S&P 400, since the 100 financial companies which distinguish the S&P 400 from the S&P 500 are really not comparable to a company like WPOB.)

The total market capitalization—debt plus market value of stock—of WPOB is more than double its revenues. In contrast, the market cap of the average stock in the S&P 400 is less than its 1989 revenues—a more favorable showing. (Ideally, an investor would like to find a superior company like WPOB when its market cap declines to near parity with its revenues.)

All things considered, WPOB is more attractive than the average stock given its superior franchise, free cash flow, management, and margins, while selling at a reasonable P/E premium to the general market. This is not encouraging. Here we have a stock that is fairly priced relative to the market, but which we wouldn't want to buy for ourselves until it declined significantly.

Summary

The Washington Post Company would be an attractive buy at about $200/share, some 30 percent below the current price, based on an analysis that would take you an hour or two to put together yourself. In time, that buy target will rise, as the company's growth continues. Also, the discouraging possibilities for the economy as a whole—and investors' penchant for overreaction—raise the odds that you will get an attractive buying opportunity for this and other great companies at some point.

The fact that the stock is overpriced at the current time does not

---

*The Post Company sells at 17.8× its earnings for the last four reported quarters; the S&P 400 sells at 14.8×. Earnings figures for the S&P can be found on the Market Laboratory page in *Barron's*; all other S&P information is available in the *S&P Outlook* in your library and from the Standard and Poor's Corporation (212-208-1351).

WPOB reports earnings on a calendar basis. However, if you are analyzing a company with a fiscal year that doesn't end in December, you must calendarize the earnings before you make comparisons with the S&P, which is based on a calendar year. For example, if Company XYZ had a June fiscal year and had reported $2.50/share for fiscal 1988 and $3.00 for fiscal 1989, the calendar 1988 number would be $2.75/share.

suggest that there is nothing to do in the meantime. A serious investor should stay active, developing an up-to-date expertise on the company, while waiting for excellent values to reappear.

Examine WPOB's annual reports; look at the results of the various divisions over a period of several years, in terms of relative size, profitability, and growth. Also, look at how the operational performance has been presented. However, you needn't be paranoid: Exceptional companies such as the Post are rarely in the business of misleading their investors with questionable one-time items and suspicious accounting footnotes.

Beyond this, you should also become familiar with similar companies, such as Dow Jones, the New York Times, the Tribune Company, and Times Mirror. Ask yourself: How do their revenue/cash flow growth rates compare, and what do the differences suggest? Are their margins higher, more stable, or more sustainable? What do the competitors say about the prospects for each other and for their industry? What about capital expenditures? (Jay Morse of WPOB indicated that a new printing factory may be needed, but that it would cost considerably less than the $300–400 million dollars that *The New York Times* is spending on its facility.)

What about the industry's future growth rate? In addition to the impact of more effective competition from local weeklies, new competitors may appear. AT&T recently requested approval to provide electronic publishing, which would offer the public an alternative means of receiving news and other information. Meanwhile, the Baby Bells—the seven regional spinoffs from AT&T—are lobbying Congress to let them enter this potentially lucrative field as well. Ask yourself how badly the newspaper publishers would be hurt if these formidable potential competitors became actual competitors.

What about other factors that will effect WPOB's revenue growth? Are there reasons to believe that circulation or advertising—retail, classified, and national—will grow at meaningfully different rates in the future than in the past? Will the industry become more aggressive in expanding overseas, as suggested in a *New York Times* article? The Post is already represented by its partial ownership of *The International Herald Tribune,* which is currently sold in 164 countries; will it seek to expand into European broadcasting to take advantage of the deregulation trend? If so, at what immediate cost, and for what eventual benefit?

And so on.

After reading this chapter, you might be wondering why you should bother with a thorough company analysis when you could rely instead on the simple rule of thumb suggested on page 81. The reasons that you should make the effort are twofold.

First, great companies do not grow at the same rate. Accordingly, they should not be bought at the same multiple of earnings, which is what the rule of thumb would have you do.

Second, things change. Companies, even great companies, will evolve over time or they will face an unusual development; rarely will they grow at steady, predictable, trend-line rates. The introduction of a new product, the groundbreaking of a new plant, the opening of a new market, or the onset of an economic recession can create abnormal results for one year or several. If you are willing to do your work, you may be able to anticipate some of these changes, to determine their long-term significance (if any), and to profit from them should the crowd overreact or fail to react. In other words, you'll be a first-rate value investor.

CHAPTER 6

Strategies

In case of doubt, decide in favor of what is correct.

—Karl Kraus

High Noon

Many people invest for the wrong reasons. They may need to prove that they are not stupid or irrational, or that they are. They may want bragging rights at their country club. Or perhaps they picture themselves as a modern gunslinger—long on pride, short on thought, quick on the draw.* People who invest for reasons of ego or insecurity are going to do their own market-timing and pick their own stocks, and they probably won't do a very good job of it.

Other investors will make their own decisions for the reason that they want their money to grow, conservatively and intelligently, and they are confident in their own judgment. If you consider yourself part of this group—and you should—here are a few suggestions.

The Buffett Approach: The Essence of Value Investing

Sensible, straightforward, and successful, this is the strategy for those who recognize the profit potential for a long-term value investor.

---

*It's an interesting historical footnote that the gunfights of the Old West—which have had such influence on our imaginations—never actually occurred. But the legend has outlived the reality, and for good reason. We like the concept of a score being settled, face to face, no discussion. The current version of "my lawyer will speak to your lawyer" just doesn't quite fire up the same glands. Let portfolio managers complain about the cult of short-term performance—that's nothing compared with the short-term pressures on two guys racing each other for their guns. It is an exciting and appealing image, particularly if we're not directly involved.

Concentrate on those few companies whose franchises cannot be duplicated, whose private market values are well above their market capitalizations, and whose managements are superior in integrity, effort, and competence. Learn these companies inside and out, since a little knowledge is probably worse than none. Determine attractive prices at which to buy them, based on conservative assumptions with a margin for error. Then wait.

Patience in an overvalued market works to your advantage in several ways. As you wait, you can earn a return on your money from bonds or cash, while stockholders will face losses if the market drops. Meanwhile, the buy points on your targeted stocks will rise in time as the intrinsic value of the underlying companies grows. This is especially true if interest rates decline as well; obviously, if they rise instead, the improvement in company results will be somewhat offset.

You might wonder how this approach relates to the popular view that greater reward entails greater risk. The concept seems so simple and logical that it's difficult to accept the fact that it's often wrong. Stocks will trade within a wide band of values, ranging from undervalued to overvalued. The more undervalued the stock, the greater the potential reward and the *less* the potential risk. If you knew exactly the lowest possible valuation, you would have maximum upside with no downside at all.

The fact that you'll never know the valuation limits means that there will always be some risk. However, for the true value investor, this risk is unimportant, since expensive stocks will eventually fall and cheap stocks will eventually rise.

Here is a short list that can take the serious investor a long way:

Ten from Your Show of Shows

The Washington Post Co.
Dow Jones
The New York Times Co.
Dun & Bradstreet
Capital Cities/ABC
Kellogg
Philip Morris

Interpublic Group
Disney
Coca Cola

You can probably find a few other names that belong on this list.

Buy these companies right, and you may never have to worry about when to sell them.

Closed-End Funds

The simple fact is that some people are better at this business than others, and a few are a great deal better. Fortunately for the small investor, several of these superstars manage money in closed-end funds and in mutual funds.* Unfortunately, in many cases, these portfolio managers are already handling huge sums. Accordingly, their future performance is made that much more difficult—after all, it's harder to find $5 billion worth of compelling new ideas than $50 million.

Closed-end funds associated with exceptional money managers offer an extraordinary opportunity for the ordinary investor. As noted earlier, you should avoid initial public offerings of closed-end funds; however, once they are trading publicly on the stock exchange, they are worth considering. The reason is that, occasionally, a well-managed fund will sell down to a substantial discount to the underlying value of the stocks that it holds. According to Mike Price, an excellent money manager in his own right: "There is no better bargain than buying Mario [Gabelli]'s closed-end fund or John [Neff]'s closed-end fund at 20 percent discounts—unless they go to 25 percent discounts."† (At which point, you should look to own more.)

As an investor, you can benefit over time from an increase in the value of the fund's stock positions and, perhaps, from a narrowing of the discount of the fund's price to its asset value.

The quickest way for that discount to narrow is if the fund converts itself to an open-end fund, either voluntarily or as a result of an unfriendly takeover. Accordingly, you should be wary of any closed-

---

*Mutual funds are also known as open-end funds, since investors may either buy or redeem their investment at net asset value—the current market value of the fund's holdings.
†Gabelli and Neff are two of Wall Street's most successful money managers.

end fund with antitakeover provisions. On the other hand, a fund that is authorized to buy back its own shares can help its investors by repurchasing its stock whenever the discount to net asset value becomes meaningful.

Buy any of the following funds at a discount to net asset value (NAV) of 15 percent, with the intention of selling once the fund trades up to a 10 percent premium to NAV:

1. *Comstock Partners Strategy Fund (Symbol: CPF; 212-943-9100)*

Stan Salvigsen and Mike Aronstein have been among the most successful investment strategists of the 1980s. After a long stint with Merrill Lynch, the two formed their own investment firm, Comstock Partners. Their fund, which went public in mid-1988, is permitted to invest in any area, and to position itself for a market decline. Accordingly, this fund is riskier than your plain vanilla common stock fund. (On the other hand, common stocks may be one of the riskiest prospective investments of all.)

2. *Gemini II (GMI; 1-800-662-7447)*

John Neff is brilliant, intense, and disciplined, qualities which are downright charming in someone managing your money. His preference is for low P/E, out-of-favor stocks which meet certain minimum quality standards and offer a generous yield. His approach is to project a company's earnings into the future, assign it a "fair" P/E to determine a reasonable target price, and buy it at a significant discount to that price. "We take stocks from undervalued to fairly valued, and if someone else wants to play greater fool, well, that's their business," Neff noted in a 1986 article in *Institutional Investor* magazine. "Our definition of an irrational market is when we don't do well."

3. *The Zweig Fund* (ZF; manager: Marty Zweig; 212-486-7110)
4. *Gabelli Equity Trust* (GAB; Mario Gabelli; 203-625-0028)
5. *Royce Value Trust* (RVT; Charles Royce; 212-355-7311)
6. *Growth Stock Outlook Trust* (GSO; C. Allman; 301-654-5205)
7. *Schafer Value Trust* (SAT; David Schafer; 212-644-1800)

* * *

Investing in international stocks is particularly difficult because of the different cultures, different financial disclosure requirements, and different market regulation involved. One sensible approach, however, is to purchase the Templeton Emerging Markets Fund at a 20 percent or greater discount to net asset value (NAV). In addition, various closed-end funds which specialize in a particular region or country occasionally sell well below asset value. For example, the scudder New Asia Fund—offered publicly at a premium to NAV—recently traded at a 25 percent discount and would probably be attractive at a one-third discount or more. In the case of the Korea Fund, however, the shares sell at a significant *premium* to NAV, reflecting the fact that the Korean stock market is closed to most outsiders until 1992.

Open-End Funds

Open-end funds (mutual funds) have a few disadvantages relative to their closed-end cousins, though they are considerably more prolific. One problem is that several mutual funds charge you an up-front sales fee, which will reduce your expected return. (Both closed-end and open-end funds charge an annual management fee, usually less than 1 percent.)

Perhaps the strongest argument against mutual funds is that a bear market might trigger a devastating round of redemptions. In a market decline, nervous investors will redeem their positions, forcing mutual-fund managers to raise cash by selling stocks, at whatever price the buyers demand. And you can bet that at that time these buyers will be far from eager. We've already had a taste of this at the time of the October Crash.

The mutual funds that are suggested in the following pages are less likely to be heavily invested in an overvalued market—that just isn't their style. Their particular portfolio managers will probably have more than enough cash on the sidelines in the event that mutual funds experience the equivalent of a run on the bank, to draw a cheerful 1930s analogy.

Here are five excellent funds (for additional choices, look in the annual Business Week review, published each February):

Sequoia Fund
($714 million; no sales charge; 212-245-4500; currently closed*)

When Warren Buffett terminated his partnership in 1970, he recommended this mutual fund to his limited partners. The Sequoia Fund has not been accepting new money since 1983 and is currently some 35 percent in cash. It is an unusual show of character when a portfolio manager is so unimpressed with investment options that he refuses to manage your money, even though he would earn a fee regardless of the fund's performance. But the day will come when the opportunities reappear and the doors reopen, perhaps when the average investor would prefer to see the Stock Exchange burned to the ground.

Fidelity Magellan Fund
($12.5 billion; 3 percent sales charge; 1-800-544-6666)

Peter Lynch manages the largest mutual fund in the country, and, fortunately, he is also one of the best money managers in the business. His manner is unpretentious, unbiased, and self-deprecating, but his intelligence and commitment are obviously superior. He does not try to be a market timer or an economist. He looks for good companies in simple businesses, especially those in which the insiders are buying stock. Over time, he believes, the performance of a well-chosen stock will track the company's earnings growth.

"Other people don't do as well because they're usually out of the market too early," he noted in *Fortune.* "If you make mistakes, sell them. But if the fundamentals of a stock get better, buy more. Most people cut the flowers and grow the weeds."

Lynch visits with more company managements in a year—about 500, on average—than most portfolio managers do in a career. "Of my really good stocks, I think if 100 people had seen them, 99 would have bought them," he observed in a September 1987 *Institutional Investor* article. "People make this business out to be incredibly more complex than it is."

Mutual Shares
($3.6 billion; no sales charge; 800-448-3863; currently closed)

---

*If a fund is currently closed to new investors, keep that portion of your money in the bank until the fund reopens. All of the funds will allow you to add to existing positions over the years as your savings increase.

Mike Price's approach is to focus on special situations, perhaps a bankruptcy workout or an overlooked convertible preferred. Unusual investments such as these historically have hidden in some of the most inefficient corners of the market—after all, few people are qualified or eager to analyze the bond indenture of a Chapter 11 company. Unfortunately, the fund is up to $3.6 billion in size, which makes the smallest—and usually most attractive—special situations irrelevant.

Baron Asset Management
($48 million; no sales charge if held more than three years; 212-759-1500)

Ron Baron is another value player, focusing on stocks selling at a substantial discount to their private market value. He is a fairly young investor, which is both an advantage and a disadvantage. On the positive side, it is great to find an excellent portfolio manager before the size of his fund begins to limit performance. (Baron's performance—up 83 percent since the fund's inception in June 1987 versus 23 percent for the market—supports this argument.) On the other hand, there is a lot to say for experience in this business.

In this case, the pluses easily outweigh the negatives.

Lindner Fund
($579 million; no sales charge; 314-727-5305)

This fund, currently headed by Robert Lange, has four things going for it:

- an excellent track record
- an operating history of more than ten years
- an extremely conservative, income-oriented philosophy
- a willingness to close its doors to new money

The Lindner Fund seems to define the philosophy that the first step to getting rich is not to get poor.

Investment Managers

A related strategy is to hire an investment manager to make the decisions for you. When choosing among the thousands who are willing and eager to manage your money, narrow your list to those whom you trust personally and whose investment approach is consistent with what you believe.

Also, make sure they have a (verifiable) track record that justifies your confidence, and a fee structure that you think is fair—management fees vary greatly, from less than 1 percent of assets to more than 20 percent of profits. (Remember, however, that a good manager may do better for you taking a chunk of your profits each year than a poor manager will do taking a small percentage of your assets.)

The Low P/E Approach (Again)

This method is for the investor who prefers to be active and diversified—certainly, your broker will prefer it. The Low P/E Approach acknowledges the fact that most individuals who manage their own money don't know their investments as well as the collective intelligence of the market. If you feel that you are one of these investors, you can rely on the market-timing suggestions described further on and invest in a well-balanced group of stocks that should outperform the market averages over time.

Look for low P/E situations—names that sell for less than a market multiple on latest twelve-months earnings—which historically have both lower risk and higher expected return. Specifically, focus on those names that are generating free cash flow and are reporting purchases by insiders.* One of the most useful clichés of Wall Street is that insiders may sell for a variety of reasons, but they will buy for only one reason: because they expect their company's stock to rise.

In addition, since most low P/E companies are in competitive industries, look for those that are the low-cost producers—if things turn ugly and competition becomes cutthroat, a low-cost company will be a survivor.

Review and update your portfolio annually.

---

*Portfolio manager John Sturges makes a compelling case for paying particular attention to "quality insiders"—namely, those managers who have been unusually successful at making money for their shareholders over the years, as reflected by historical price performance of their shares

Catch a Rising Star

An alternative strategy is to focus on small companies which have extraordinary growth rates and ordinary multiples. "You out-perform others," money manager Donna Diamond argues, "by buy-ing in early into companies with strong financial characteristics, strong balance sheets, little debt, and a high return on equity." (And, again, those with substantial insider purchases.)

The goal is to find companies such as these *at the right price,* before they find their way into institutional portfolios and onto Wall Street buy lists. Peter Lynch recommends that you purchase their stocks when the P/E is less than half the future growth rate.

A note of caution: as with the advice to do what everyone else is doing but do it first, this strategy is easier said than done. And, bear in mind, a small company's shares trade infrequently and in small amounts, so plan on buying when they're out of favor and selling when they're not. If events turn sour, the exit for these shares will be very narrow and very crowded.

The Best of the Rest

The following sources can be used to screen for new ideas:

- *The Insiders' Portfolio,* published by The Insiders (1-800-327-6720; $145/year). The performance of this model portfolio—based on in-sider purchases vs. sales—has been exceptional, according to the results provided in each bi-monthly newsletter. The average gain for the seventy-three stocks recommended over time has been 64 percent; the *annual* return has averaged 18 percent.

- *The Contrary Investor* and *Follow-up,* published by Fraser Manage-ment Associates (309 South Willard St.; Burlington, Vermont 05401). Since 1963, they have recommended the purchase and sale of 530 stocks with an average gain of 56.1 percent, over three times the average 16.4 percent increase in the DJIA. They are currently recommending fifty-three stocks. (In addition, Jim Fraser offers worthwhile written comments on the psychology of the market and on trends in our society.)

• *The Value Line Investment Survey* ($495/yr; 1-800-633-2252; also available in public libraries for $495 less). Value Line, created by Arnold Bernhard in the 1930s, rates stocks for timeliness on a 1 to 5 scale based on proprietary technical factors. Its track record over a twenty-three year period has been excellent.

Value Line also provides a number of quantitative screens, such as price-earnings ratios, returns on capital, yields, and free cash flows.

Placing an Order

When you buy or sell stocks, regardless of the investment approach you choose, consider using *limit orders*. If you are buying, place your limit at or just above the current asked price; the shares will be bought at this level or lower. If you are selling, put your limit at the current bid price or just below; the stock will be sold at this price or higher. Of course, you run the risk that the price will run away from your limit, and your trade won't be executed. Still, a limit order does help to protect you against poor execution of your trades.

When to Invest and Where

Market timing under the Buffett Approach is essentially irrelevant. After all, you are simply buying stocks when they are cheap and avoiding them when they are not. However, it might help to have a sense of whether the entire market is expensive or attractive.

For the low P/E and other approaches, you can rely on the following simple rule, which goes to the heart of stock valuation. It addresses the question of whether stocks are undervalued relative to bonds, which are an alternative investment of your money.

Simply compare the earnings yield on stocks to the interest rate yield on bonds. To compute the earnings yield for this indicator, take the average of the latest two years of earnings for the S&P 400 (available weekly in *Barron's* magazine on the Market Laboratory/Stocks page). This average figure should smooth out any large fluctuations due to a recession or a recovery year.

Divide the average earnings into the current price of the S&P 400 Index to determine the earnings yield. For the comparable bond yield, use the thirty-year Treasury bond interest rate. If the earnings yield is higher than the bond yield, you should be happy to own stocks. If not, you should wait.

Since the earnings yield is based on the *previous* two years of earnings, this indicator will favor bonds over stocks. However, as a potential investor in stocks, you should prefer a conservative measure such as this; when this indicator tells you that stocks are attractive relative to bonds, you can believe it.

Once you have bought shares using this approach, the next question is, when do you sell them? A suggested rule-of-thumb is to wait until stocks are *overvalued* relative to bonds by a comfortable margin, say 25–30 percent. This strategy will protect you against excessive buying and selling in your account.

A less complicated approach to market timing was suggested by Benjamin Graham in *The Intelligent Investor.* It was designed for "defensive investors" and incorporates both stocks and bonds. Divide your financial investments evenly between the two, making readjustments whenever either becomes too great a percentage of the total, say 60 percent. This simple formula will force you to sell into prolonged strength and buy into weakness. It will also keep you diversified between equity and fixed-income investments.

Given the debt situation in the United States, my suggestion is for you to put the bond portion in Treasury bonds. You shouldn't underestimate the comfort of lending money to people who can print it, if necessary. Also, the high quality corporate bonds of today may be the junk of tomorrow, for reasons ranging from competition to takeovers.

Another advantage of T-bonds is that they are subject only to federal income taxes, and rates at the federal level are considerably lower than they were at the beginning of the 1980s. In addition, unlike other bonds, they are *noncallable*—they cannot be repurchased from you at a preset price, sometimes below the fair market value. This feature allows greater upside if interest rates fall.

You can buy T-bonds directly from the Federal Reserve without paying a commission; just call (212)720-6619.

No set rule can determine what percentage of your financial assets should remain in cash. One approach is to hold a comfortable level of cash—at least 25 percent—when stocks are not attractive *and*

T-bonds are yielding less than 10 percent. This affords the flexibility to move easily once values reappear in the stock market.

Some investors will prefer to be fully invested at all times. There is a great deal to say for separating yourself from the pressures to screw up; many investors will do themselves more harm than good by market timing and stock picking. It is one thing to read about being a value investor and a contrarian; it is another actually to bet your money against the crowd and probably against your own instincts. You can always see the wisdom of buying when the market is cheap and selling when it is dear, in retrospect. At the time, however, the logic is never so clear, even for the minority of individuals who understand valuation.

The major potential problem with a fully invested position in stocks alone is that the next ten years may not be like the last forty. We are not the same economy we were in 1950, when we enjoyed the most favorable set of circumstances for any country at any time throughout modern history. And our attitude toward the stock market has changed even more dramatically, from national disdain to fascination. Throw in the wild card of a possible secular decline in debt, and you might prefer a fully noninvested position. As Will Rogers once noted, "I'm less concerned about the return on my principal than the return of my principal."

There are two strong arguments against such a pessimistic outlook. First and foremost, these concerns may not come to pass or may already be reflected in stock prices by the time you read this section. Second, common stocks historically have been a terrific investment. John Templeton, an exceptional money manager, asserted in a 1989 Shearson ad: "If you're truly an investor and not just a temporary trader, you can be sure in the long run that almost every bull market will carry you to new peaks of prosperity."

In fact, common stocks have outperformed almost every other investment over almost every time frame to the present. In the 1885–1985 period, stocks provided an average total return of about 9 percent per year; by comparison, high-quality bonds and short-term commercial paper averaged less than 5 percent annually.

Bear in mind, however, that although you may have averaged a 9 percent total annual return in the last century, you would have suffered greatly during certain periods. The most obvious example is the September 1929–July 1932 period, during which the market declined by 89 percent! The market did not return to its 1929 peak level for almost one quarter of a century. It would not have been easy to stick to your convictions then about a fully invested equity position, not only through that brutal decline, but also through the two decades of extreme volatility that followed.

You might have noticed that I've sidestepped the question of what percentage of your investments should go to financial assets and what to real assets, primarily real estate. If you own a home, you probably have already made a major investment in real estate. Even after deducting the unpaid portion of the mortgage, the equity in your house is probably your biggest investment.* Therefore, you can allocate the balance of your portfolio to financial assets—bonds, stocks, cash—and still have diversification. Also, since stocks are partly real assets, your exposure here will put you in both camps.

An unscientific approach to the issue is to ask thirty to fifty friends, family, and coworkers the following question: Which do you think will be a better investment in the next five years, a government bond or a house? You will want to bet the reverse of the consensus, if that consensus is overwhelming. Keep an eye out for the fellow who practically assaults you for asking such an "obvious" question. Although this approach sounds a bit silly, I suspect it will play better than it reads. Ask yourself what the answer to this question would have been in 1980. Since then, financial assets have significantly outperformed real assets, on average.

On a more rigorous level, consider whether the after-tax cost of owning a home or co-op is more or less than the cost of a long-term lease to rent a comparable place. (Assume that you are borrowing the entire purchase cost, with an adjustable-rate mortgage.) If the after-tax cost of owning, including maintenance expenses and taxes, is similar to or less than the rental cost, then ownership makes sense.

Another (simpler) approach is to follow Graham's suggestion and set fixed percentages for stocks, bonds, and real estate, such as one-third of your assets in each.

Last, and possibly least, is the issue of investing in gold, a favor-

---

* And your best place to borrow, if necessary. Home equity loans are fully tax deductible up to $100,000. On the other hand, the interest payments on credit card charges, auto loans, and installment purchases are almost entirely *non*deductible. One of the best investments you will ever make is to avoid these outrageously expensive debts.

ite subject of overzealous retail brokers. There is a strong case to be
made that gold should be left out of your portfolio.

Gold is considered a long-term hedge against inflation, but your
home should serve the same purpose. More important, gold has little
intrinsic value: it has few practical uses and generates no income for
the owner.

Any asset that is only worth what someone else will pay for it is
not worth buying in the first place.

To summarize: The Buffett Approach is the preferred strategy
among those recommended. But to make this approach work, you
must spend some time and use some discipline in analyzing your companies, choosing your buy points, and waiting for the right opportunities to arise.

Of course, you could just rely on the simple rule of thumb mentioned on page 81; like the other recommended strategies, it doesn't
require a great deal of judgment on your part. This reduces the
chances of making a really poor decision, but it also reduces your
chances of making a great one.

Regardless of which approach you use, your results should improve—perhaps in a big way. Nothing I say can make you as good an
investor as Warren Buffett, since nothing I say can make *me* that
good. Still, if you understand why these recommended strategies
work and how they work, you have a right to expect good things
from your investments. If nothing else, you will be nobody's fool.

The next section looks at the past and the future. Chapter 7
examines the ins and outs, ups and downs of the investment community and the stock market over the last ten years. Wall Street is an
intriguing and, for many, an intimidating place, well worth a closer
look. A better understanding of what makes the Street tick and what
drove the market in the 1980s will also give you a head start on this
decade.

The following chapter considers the outlook for the 1990s, as
forecast by five of the smartest investors out there. Their comments
touch on a wide range of issues, and will give you a good idea of what
they think and how they think.

PART III

Looking Back, Looking Forward

CHAPTER 7

Wall Street in the 1980s

We measure success one investor at a time.

—*Dean Witter*

I help people with their investments until there's nothing left.

—*Woody Allen*

This chapter focuses on the major issues in the financial community during the 1980s: the growing importance of institutional investors, investment bankers, and risk arbitrageurs; the controversy over program trading, portfolio insurance, and corporate takeovers; the mixed emotions of an exceptional bull market and an unprecedented crash. All have influenced the events of the last decade, and have set the stage for the 1990s.

The average investor has watched these events unfold with a mixture of awe and envy, fear and loathing, and confusion. This chapter should help to demystify Wall Street in your eyes. You may be surprised to realize that the machinations of the pros have, in fact, shifted the odds in your favor.

Institutional Investing: Wall Street Blues

The stock market is dominated by institutions, such as banks, mutual funds, insurance companies, investment advisers, and corporations. As an individual investor, you may be intimidated by this fact, but you really shouldn't be. From your perspective, the influence of these "buy-side" institutions is more of a positive than a negative.

The bad news for you is that you're not an institutional investor

You don't have the access to information that institutions have; you can't assimilate and analyze all the data you're barraged with as quickly and as thoroughly as they can.

Information is valuable, and timely information can be very valuable. Not surprisingly, when something new happens, large institutions that control millions of commission dollars are likely to get the first calls. In addition, they can rely not only on the analyses of the Wall Street brokerage firms, but also on their own in-house talent. In theory, large institutions have an advantage over smaller institutions, and smaller institutions over retail investors like yourself.

The good news is that you're not an institutional investor. You don't have to face the extraordinary pressures to be right—and right now. Institutions do. They are increasingly being judged on quarterly performance, a time frame that precludes investing in any real sense of the term—that is, for long-term success. The demands for short-term results, particularly from those who control the various pension funds, often force money managers to go against their better instincts. In this fast-paced environment, no one wants to own the out-of-favor groups, and no one feels comfortable watching the current favorites from the sidelines.

As if these pressures aren't enough, institutions have to worry about their fiduciary duties, their legal responsibility in managing other people's money. Under the unseen glare of the "prudent man" rule,* portfolio managers learn that it's better to be wrong than stupid. Which is to say, when you're wrong, make sure you've got a good reason. And there's no better reason than a stack of research recommendations and no better place to hide than in a crowd.

It is extraordinary to think that an industry comprised of such intelligent and rational people could increasingly find itself working under such irrational requirements. Perhaps the impressiveness of the participants is to some degree responsible. Portfolio managers, on the whole, are a formidable group—knowledgeable, articulate, and hardworking. They make the goal of short-term performance seem more attainable than it really is, and one can see how their clients expect superior performance.

---

*Fiduciaries are legally required to make decisions consistent with those of a fictional prudent person; this usually is interpreted as an endorsement of investments in conservative, superior companies, which all too often are conservative, inferior stocks.

And if that short-term performance is lacking from one particular money manager, there are hundreds of others who will have done better in the latest quarter and are eager to explain why they will keep doing better. Meanwhile, those who have underperformed find themselves under the gun to perform better, and soon. To hell with long-term investing, they think; Keynes said that in the long run we're all dead, and he was right—just look at him.

The counterparts to those who manage the institutional portfolios are those who offer advice. The "sell-side" is represented by the research, sales, and trading departments of the major brokerage houses. If the focus of the money managers is on quarterly performance, then that of the sell-side is increasingly on daily commissions. As the time horizon of the clients has narrowed and especially as commission rates have plummeted, the brokers have become more short-term-transaction oriented. What has changed since yesterday, or earlier today, they wonder, and what should portfolio managers buy or sell because of it?

Sell-side analysts, in general, are an impressive, accomplished group—conscientious, motivated, and personable. A first-rate analyst, however, needs to be a gifted workaholic, and few people in this world are either. They must keep up-to-date on what has just happened or will soon happen, and they must be attuned to the shifts in the underlying trends of a company, an industry, and an economy.

They must also write about all these things, so that the buy-side will have the hundreds of reports on which to base their prudent decisions—and barricades to hide behind if the market acts "imprudently." Meanwhile, sell-side analysts are trying to be visible, which in a people business means talking and meeting and getting along with people—particularly those people who vote for the "best" analysts in the annual Institutional Investor and Greenwich Research polls.

For the analysts who find the time to become experts on their companies—and most of them do—accurate stock-picking is still a formidable challenge. An in-depth knowledge of a company and a close relationship with management can often hurt the valuation decision. It is easy to lose the forest for the trees when your world is dominated by a few companies and a truckload of their statistics.

Expertise about facts does not necessarily confer insight about stocks. Especially if that expertise is based on using management as the source of information; that can be like relying on *Pravda* for an unbiased look at Soviet society.

Those few analysts whose research extends far beyond management have a great advantage over their counterparts. They will have access to information about current developments or shifting trends at the same time, or even before, the company's management. Their competitors, on the other hand, will find out only after the management or the market has alerted them. These competitors comprise the unfortunate majority whose forecasts *react* to movements in stock prices, rather than *anticipate* them.

Even those analysts who make the time for serious independent research, however, may not reach the correct conclusion as it relates to the long-term value of their stocks. They may not recognize a significant new development that's gotten lost in the chaos of the input. Perhaps a new trend seems too remote in the future to be of importance to a portfolio manager obsessed with the next three months. Perhaps these facts seem insignificant, since they are inconsistent with the general consensus. Perhaps all of this implies a new conclusion that is too controversial to be easily marketed.

The relationship between the buy-side and the sell-side is self-reinforcing in certain ways. People want to hear what they want to hear, or so I hear. More often than not, portfolio managers want their advisers to tell them to buy the successful, attractive company whose stock has been doing so well. And they give more of their business to these advisers. From the other perspective, sell-side analysts prefer to recommend successful, attractive companies whose shares have been doing well. And not just because of their clients. Good fundamentals, sharp management, price momentum—these make a good story and a strong sales pitch.

The buy-side and the sell-side are the ones who establish the consensus. By definition, what they like as a group is popular, and what they avoid is unpopular. The professional pressures to be part of this crowd should not be underestimated. The few analysts who choose to argue against the Street's malaise or enthusiasm, to recommend an unpopular course of action, learn the truth of the Anthony

Gaubis comment: "If you warn 100 men of possible forthcoming bad news, eighty will dislike you right away. If you are right, the other twenty will as well."

And then there's ego. We tell ourselves so often in so many subtle ways that, yes, we are smart. And more—we are smarter. And if the facts don't always fit our theory, then to hell with the facts. Because we are smart, and therefore we should be right. We trumpet our correct plays and allow our mistakes to slip into the fog. We often confuse motion with progress and we too easily dismiss bad judgment as bad luck.

All of which is good news for the individual investor. If you thought that the deck was stacked, recognize now that if it is, it's stacked in your favor. In a sense, it is the institutional investment community's short-term focus on performance and commissions that has helped to make long-term value investors rich.

We may pay tribute to these value players, and to contrarians as well, but we dance to the frenetic tune played out on the Quotrons in front of us. And that offers quite an advantage for you, if you're willing to use some discipline and common sense.

Block Trading: Profitless Prosperity

The research and sales operations at the brokerage firms are responsible for creating and disseminating investment advice. In return for this advice, retail and institutional clients buy and sell stocks through the trading operations of the firms, generating commissions for these brokers.

For half a century, Wall Street was content, even insistent, about limiting its exposure to losses. It focused its operations on *agency* business, executing orders for others and taking a commission. During the last few years, however, the trend has been toward *principal* trading, in which firms risk their own capital rather than simply put together buyer and seller. Meanwhile, those firms that have been reluctant to take on the additional risk have found themselves at a competitive disadvantage.

The growth of institutions as the major factor in the stock market was the catalyst for this change in the trading equation. The abolition of fixed commissions on May 1, 1975, allowed large institutions to use their influence to negotiate sharply reduced commission rates, often at discounts of 60–80 percent. Even smaller institutions now routinely trade at rates 40–50 percent below those that prevailed before May Day. (How many other goods or services can you think of that currently cost less than half their price of a dozen years ago?)

The reduction in rates has hurt the brokers significantly. This is a high fixed-cost business—the rent, heat, phone, and light bills have to be paid, regardless of sales. Somewhat offsetting the pain of reduced commissions per share has been the massive increase in the number of shares traded each day. Trading volume on the New York Stock Exchange averaged 160 million shares each day in 1989, up from 14 million in 1974.

As institutions became a larger and more powerful force in the stock market, they have also encouraged the growth of principal transactions, in which the brokers themselves act as buyer or seller of last resort. This occurs when the market won't accommodate large trades. For example, if an institution wants to sell 600,000 shares of IBM, and there are only buyers for 400,000 shares, the brokerage house might buy the other 200,000 for its own account. Now the broker is at risk; if the price falls ¼ before the shares are resold, the broker loses $50,000 on its 200,000 shares. This loss more than offsets the commission (on the full 600,000 shares) which might average $.06/share, or $36,000.

The majority of principal transactions lose money. In this example, once the 400,000 shares have been sold, there are few if any natural buyers left for the remaining 200,000. Supply will initially exceed demand, which is not encouraging for the one with the excess supply.

The bottom line is that the brokerage industry no longer enjoys the immense profits at low risk that once it did, as institutions demand lower commission rates and higher capital commitments. Meanwhile, individuals seek lower rates at discount brokers.

Well, you might ask, if it's such poor business, then why do it? Because success in the brokerage business is closely related to distribution. The brokers want to be on good terms with their customers, particularly the large institutions, in order to get the opportunity to underwrite lucrative new issues. A primary attraction of one broker over another to a company issuing stocks or bonds is the broker's ability to distribute the securities broadly to investors at a favorable price—for the company, that is.

Investment Banking: Nice Party; Nasty Hangover

Trading has increasingly become a loss leader for a brokerage firm's investment banking transactions, where brokers advise companies on restructuring, public offerings, mergers, and acquisitions. For several decades, investment banking fees were substantial, particularly in the boom years of the 1960s and 1980s, and the brokers focused on providing advisory and underwriting services. However, here too an ominous trend toward greater risk-taking has developed.

Envy and greed are hardly limited to investors. Investment bankers are similarly inclined to look at the past and project the same rosy picture into the future. For fifty-five years, while these investment bankers have primarily limited their involvement to giving advice, the value of their clients' companies has soared. And now these advisers increasingly want to invest their firms' own money in future deals. It's not all that different from the situation in which you and I watch the stock of a company we know well, and we see it rise and then rise further. Finally, greed replaces reason and we become convinced that it must keep going higher and higher, because that's all it has ever done. So we buy it, often to our regret.

Wall Street, in recent years, has resuscitated a term from the glory days of turn-of-the-century American finance: *merchant banking*. At that time, bankers such as J. P. Morgan created huge industrial corporations to provide for and profit from this country's extraordinary growth in the 1900s. These bankers were not only the principal lenders; they also became major shareholders.

The concept became less fashionable after the 1929–1932 bear market, when the equity values of highly leveraged companies were decimated. It is probably unnecessary to remind you that leverage cuts both ways. In good times, once the interest on the debt is paid, all that is left goes to the shareholders; in bad times, if the debt isn't paid, there's usually nothing left for the stockholders except lawsuits. Still, merchant banking has an impressive ring to it, with its British origins and its centuries-old tradition.

Another concept that reads better than it plays is *bridge financ-*

ing. This is when the investment banking department of brokerage firms lend huge sums of their own capital to allow a client to proceed immediately with a takeover. In time, the broker sells bonds for the company and uses the proceeds to retire its loan.

This approach has been forced on the industry by the overwhelming competitive edge that Drexel Burnham created in distributing high-yield bonds. Bridge financing has become a method of preempting Drexel's advantage in placing bonds quickly. The client acquirer gets its money immediately, and the investment banker gets its money back eventually (it is hoped) once new bonds are floated.

There's a certain Russian roulette aspect to it, with each "click" implying repaid bridge loans and huge fees. And so far those clicks are about all we've heard (the most notable exception being First Boston's $250 million loan to Campeau Corp.). It's somewhat similar to the story of the fellow who jumped off a roof and announced as he plummeted past the fifth floor, "So far so good."

Risk Arbitrage: Playing the Percentages

If investment bankers have become famous for their role in initiating, advising, and financing takeovers, risk arbitrageurs have become infamous for their bets on the outcomes of these takeovers. Which is a bit of a bum rap. Their generally poor reputation is based not only on the reality of government investigations and convictions, but also on what's in a name. *Arbitrageur* sounds mysterious and foreign; the shortened version, *arb,* sounds like something you don't want to brush up against. At the same time, managements portray them as selfish, shortsighted, and soulless traffickers in corporate ownership to the highest bidder.

And yet, my personal contacts with arbs have shown them to be decent, hardworking professionals. *Risk arbitrageurs* play the odds, buying positions in companies that have received takeover offers. If, for example, Company A announces an offer for Company B at $50, B might trade up immediately to $48. An arb must determine if it is worth buying the stock for the last 2 points. Let's say that there's a 95 percent chance of the deal being completed within three months, and a 5 percent chance that the deal falls through and the stock drops back to $40. The expected gain is $1.50/share (.95 × $2 profit minus

.05 × $8 loss). On a percentage basis, the expected annual return is 12½ percent ($1.50 × 4 quarters ÷ $48 cost).

The trick is to have enough such deals to invest in that the odds work themselves out. This is similar to owning a casino: Although you might lose to any given player, you will win a predictable percentage of the thousands of bets placed. As one casino owner put it, "What I love is the risk; some nights we make money, and other nights we make more money."

The challenge to an arb is much greater than this, however. Arbs don't have thousands of deals on which to spread the risk, and the odds of success are never clear. They must thoroughly research the valuation of the target company, the resources of the potential acquirer, the strategic fit of the two companies, the legal issues, the personalities of both managements, the possibility of a poison pill, a white knight, or greenmail*, and the chances of a higher bid.

In addition to the weak science of valuation, they also rely on the weaker art of "reading the tape," trying to detect the strategies of all sides through the patterns of stock purchases and sales. Theirs is a business of small wins and large losses, none larger than those of October 1989, when the arbitrage community lost hundreds of millions in a few weeks. But, over time, risk arbitrage has been a very profitable profession and will probably continue to be in the future.

Some players prefer to anticipate deals rather than react to them. Interestingly enough, the best at this game are the aggressively unflashy value investors. They buy companies selling at a fraction of their underlying value, and then wait—and wait—for that value to be recognized by the market. Occasionally, that value is recognized sooner than expected in the form of a takeover bid. Unfortunately, a few conspicuously nonvalue players have preferred to pay for illegal inside information and have contributed to the negative perception of risk arbitrageurs.

Another contributing factor to the poor reputation of arbs has been the criticism that greedy arbs replace concerned shareholders in determining the future of a target company. But think about it for a

---

*When a management repurchases the shares of one stockholder at an unfairly high price to eliminate the threat of a takeover.

minute: Who did the arbs buy the stock from in the first place, if not these shareholders?

The Takeover Boom: The Good, the Bad, and the (Occasionally) Ugly

Now that we have considered the major Wall Street players in the takeover game, let's look at the boom itself.

Stockholders are the owners of public corporations and, as such, have the legal right both to hire and to fire managements. The reality, however, has generally been one of entrenched managements. Like a government bureaucracy, the primary concern of many of these managements has become the maximization of their power base, rather than the maximization of their owners' wealth. When those two goals were compatible—when increasing the revenues was the best approach to increasing the stock price—as during the growth decades of the 1950s and 1960s, there was no conflict.

By the 1980s, this had changed. Low growth had reduced the number of attractive opportunities for expansion. At the same time, high real interest rates had made the cost of expansion that much more expensive. Meanwhile, the 1981 tax law improved the cash flow of corporations, and low equity prices often made stocks the most attractive investments for that cash.

In fairness, for some industries, restructuring—repurchasing stock, selling off less efficient divisions, streamlining the remaining operations—was not the best method to improve the stockholders' wealth. For them, prospects were still improving, and expansion made sense. Other industries, as strategist Burt Siegel pointed out, had benefited from rapidly rising prices in the 1970s and were suffering from stagnant, or declining, demand in the subsequent decade. For them, contraction was the correct course.

All of this made for tension between shareholders and their managers. A management that wants to expand its domain tends to define its influence by the size of the company. But in the 1980s, the maximization of shareholders' wealth was often best accomplished by buying back its stock rather than by trying to expand sales through acquisitions or expansions into other markets.

This was not easy on the ego of managers. After all, managers are only human: They want to stand on the ramparts and look as far as the eye can see and say, "Someday all of this will be mine." Let's face it, "Someday all of this will be sold" just doesn't have the same ring to it. This is particularly true of managers who don't own much stock and therefore won't benefit from the maximization of its value.

Management might prefer to increase its domain at the expense of its employers, the stockholders; however, the market will tend to reflect this misallocation of resources in a low stock price. This depressed price might be significantly less than the potential value of the company, if its assets were managed efficiently. In effect, the low price of the shares implies that the whole is worth less than the sum of its parts, reflecting the skepticism of investors: They doubt that management will realize the potential value of those assets.

These factors set the stage for the takeover boom. After all, if the stock price of a company is at a substantial discount to its asset value, an acquirer can afford to pay a premium for the stock and still make an attractive profit on the sale or restructuring of those assets.

Until the 1980s, most large corporations were immune from outside pressures to restructure their assets, since banks and insurance companies were hesitant to finance multibillion-dollar deals. This was especially true of the riskiest portion of these deals—the subordinated debentures (in the event of bankruptcy, such bonds have no claim on any specific assets and are repaid only after senior debt holders have been paid in full). Perhaps there was also a sense among banking executives that gentlemen shouldn't finance raiders.

The growth of the high-yield debt market provided the additional financing that made size a considerably less effective deterrent to takeovers. Investors in these bonds—commonly referred to as "junk bonds"—received higher yields in return for accepting the greater risk. Stockholders received a higher price for their shares. The acquirer made a relatively quick profit on his investment that, in the last decade, has ranged from impressive to obscene. The management all too often received a generous severance payment, known as a golden parachute. And the remaining company, as well as its sold-off divisions, was forced to operate with maximum efficiency, in order to meet the interest payments on the new debt.

Everybody wins, right? Hell no, say the critics. Buzzwords like "efficiency" and "rationalization" are often a fancy way of discussing layoffs, they argue. Meanwhile, highly leveraged companies are that much more likely to find themselves in eventual trouble or in bankruptcy, creating severe losses for the company's employees, lenders, and investors.

Managements who oppose unfriendly takeovers also criticize the short-term mentality of the stock market, as they see it. How can we operate for the long term, they ask, if a raider may step in to buy the company before the benefits of our planning are reflected in the stock price? Or, why should we feel forced to repurchase stock or restructure just to boost our stock price in the short term?

From the stockholders' point of view, the argument against takeovers is an interesting one. Even at a takeover premium to the current price, shareholders will not benefit from the additional profit that the raider receives. In time, the stock price may have risen to its "true" value. Why should a short-term profiteer receive the windfall that the astute and patient investor would eventually have realized?

And what of the counter-arguments to these criticisms?

- Yes, there will be defaults on these debt-laden takeovers. In fact, the sad outcomes of the lending booms for real estate, oil, agriculture, and the Third World would indicate that the defaults will be much worse than expected. But that is the risk that these high-yield bond investors, primarily institutions, are supposedly being paid for. (This argument should not be used to defend those institutions, mismanaged thrifts in particular, that carelessly speculated with federally insured money.) On the positive side, takeovers make it possible for many long-suffering stockholders in undermanaged companies to benefit from their investments.

- The issue of layoffs is more important. Takeovers do involve putting people out of work. But, in many cases, these layoffs were already inevitable, made so by competitive pressures. There were few takeovers in the steel or auto industries. What devastated employment here was international competition, and competition isn't about to get any easier.

- The argument that the stock market is too short-term oriented is seductive and is perhaps true at any given time in any given stock.

Still, a lot of money has been lost by underestimating the intelligence of the market over time.

• The concern that shareholders should not be forced to give up their potential profits to a raider or other buyers, in return for a quick but smaller gain, is a strong one. One sophisticated counterargument is that an immediate profit, often in excess of 50 percent, is nothing to sneeze at. Moreover, the gains from one undervalued stock can be invested in another with similar characteristics and, let's hope, with similar results. Rarely is there only one such situation; the market factors that created one opportunity will tend to create many.

• The increasing use of "stub equity" has offered stockholders an excellent method to benefit from an undervalued situation immediately without giving up their shares. In these situations, the company borrows heavily to pay shareholders a substantial dividend without repurchasing and retiring the stock. Therefore, current shareholders can participate in the company's future growth, rather than sacrifice this profit to a takeover artist or corporate acquirer.

• Probably the strongest argument in favor of the takeover boom in the 1980s is that the threat of being acquired has forced managements to be more accountable to their shareholders. Executives who must consider how their actions will affect the value of their companies will tend to spend their stockholders' money more wisely. It is a shame to see the managements of companies invulnerable to takeovers show more concern for themselves than for their shareholders. For example, three of the ten largest industrial companies in America made huge acquisitions in the 1980s that have arguably cost their stockholders tens of billions of dollars.

Let me finish this description of takeovers with an anecdote from *Grant's Interest Rate Observer* that captures the lost sense of purpose by many managements—or, at least, by this one. At an annual meeting, the management announced that they were selling their corporate jet. One shareholder got right to the point. "If it serves a valuable purpose," he asked, "why are you selling it? And, if not, why did you buy it in the first place?"

Management Buy-Outs: Looking Out for Number One

This form of takeover is particularly controversial and probably unfair. In this situation, the managers—the people who are responsible for maximizing the stock price—instead purchase the outstanding shares of their company for themselves. They pay a premium for the stock—often a substantial one—and usually finance most of the purchase price with debt, a transaction known as a leveraged buy-out (LBO). What distinguishes this from any other takeover is the fact that the managers know more about their company and its prospects that anyone, even their employers. (Frankly, they had better know more, since that's their job.)

Obviously, a management that proposes a buy-out believes that the stock is undervalued relative to its existing or potential assets. Otherwise, why else would they want to buy it? The point is, however, that it is their responsibility to realize the value of these assets for you, not them. If the company is being undermanaged due to insufficient expertise, or poor strategic fit, or excessive overhead, it is ludicrous to allow the ones who caused the problem to profit from it. And yet they have.

If stock prices had fallen and interest rates had risen during the 1980s, and management LBOs had collapsed instead of prospered, would this argument have been different? No, only less relevant. In the stock market, no one is given the right to profit from material information that is not available to the public, least of all the people who are paid—and paid well—to make money for their investors.

Program Trading: A Bumpy Ride

One of the most widely criticized aspects of Wall Street since the Crash of 1987 has been *program trading*. It has become the scapegoat that short-selling* was a half-century ago. The spirit of the moment was captured by a cartoon in which a veteran investor is asked by a disingenuous rookie, "Were there bear markets before program trading?" It's the same old story of hope and glory: People simply don't

---

*A short sale is the sale of a security that you don't own, which is borrowed from a brokerage firm. You hope to buy back the shares at a lower price.

wish to accept the basic fact that overvalued markets will eventually decline, and sometimes with a vengeance.

Program trading is another form of arbitrage, this time in the classic sense. It involves buying one asset and simultaneously selling an identical asset at a higher price. No risk, no problem.

In this case, the two identical assets are the 500 stocks that comprise the S&P 500 Index, and the Index itself. The stocks are traded on the New York Stock Exchange, while the S&P 500 Index is traded in the futures market, on the Chicago Mercantile Exchange.

An investor can buy or sell the Index at some time in the future although most of the volume will be in the nearest contract. If this is January, the next maturity will be March, followed by June, September, and December. If you buy the March S&P 500 Index Futures, you are betting that the value of the Index, comprised of those 500 stocks, will rise between now and then. Obviously, the seller expects the opposite.

The March contract should sell at a premium to the current value of the Index. If you buy the futures contract and put up the minimal margin of 5 percent, the balance of the amount due at the settlement of the contract (the 95 percent) can be earning interest in the meantime. For example, if the S&P 500 is selling at 250 and the contract is two months away, you can earn approximately 1 percent on your money in those months. Therefore, the futures contract should sell at a 1 percent premium to the current "cash" market, which in this case would be 2½ points.

Program trading becomes profitable when the spread between the current price and the futures price varies from this equilibrium. If the spread widens, it makes sense to buy the stocks and simultaneously sell the Index Futures. If the spread narrows or becomes negative, a trader should buy the futures and sell the stocks.

Either of these approaches will push the markets back to their correct spread. In the first case, an excessive spread will be narrowed by bidding up stock prices and driving down the prices of the futures contracts. In the second case, an insufficient spread is widened. Neither affects the amount of money in the market, and neither should cause the market to begin an upward or downward spiral, as we saw on October 19, 1987.

Unfortunately, the practice of program trading has been poorly represented by some of its practitioners. Brokerage houses which executed program trades for their own account ahead of their customers' orders were in the wrong. In addition, situations in which the volume from programs overloaded the system that handled small orders should not have been permitted.

Under the wave of blame that has made it a less significant factor in the market, the occasional abuses of program trading may become little more than an historical footnote. In fairness, though, an understanding of the subject reveals that program trading alone would not have caused or exacerbated the October Crash. Rather, it was program trading in combination with *portfolio insurance* that laid the foundation for 1987's homage to 1929.

Portfolio Insurance: Back to the Drawing Board

The basic idea behind this investment technique was to "insure" portfolios against major declines by selling the S&P Index Futures once the market had suffered a moderate decline. Prior to 1987's Crash, an estimated $60–80 billion of such insurance had been acquired; currently, the amounts are a fraction of that figure. The impact of portfolio insurance was felt in one inglorious week in October, and it is unlikely to be of much consequence in the future. The problem was that it worked, but worked badly. The concept made sense in theory but, in practice it was—in the words of Roy Campanella—not just wrong but loud wrong.

The assumption that the relatively tiny futures market would willingly absorb large sellers proved to be seriously flawed. Although the total value of stocks in August 1987 was well over $3 trillion, the value of outstanding contracts for the S&P 500 Index Future was only $50 billion. When the market declined sharply in the week of October 12, portfolio insurance was triggered and large-scale selling hit the futures market. Not surprisingly, many previously optimistic and eager futures buyers stepped away, hoping to wait until the selling exhausted itself. Futures prices were driven to severe discounts to current prices.

The program traders stepped up to buy the futures while simultaneously selling the stocks, thereby locking in an arbitrage profit. This, in turn, drove down the current prices on the stock market, at times violently, as specialists on the NYSE became unwilling or unable to maintain orderly markets. The decline in stock prices stimulated further selling by portfolio insurers.

This spiraling effect threatened to create a situation of panic. All major futures and options exchanges, except the Major Market Index, were temporarily closed on October 20. An extraordinary rally in the MMI around noon restored confidence and is credited with saving the day—a tired but, in this case, valid cliché.

So who's to blame? The market rose sharply throughout most of 1987 and then collapsed even more suddenly. It ended the year relatively even with its beginning level, an ironic conclusion to the most volatile year in more than half a century. All things considered, the main culprit was emotion, a factor which can hardly be legislated or regulated away.

One point that is rarely mentioned is that portfolio insurance may have contributed to the market's spectacular rise in 1987. Money managers may have felt that they could capture any further upside with limited downside risk. This would have encouraged them to remain fully invested, even against their better judgment. In the past, these managers may have sold stocks to raise cash as the market rose, thereby limiting its move.

Certainly, the low margin requirements for futures contracts exacerbated the situation in both directions. Another contributing factor to the debacle was the creation of yet another "sure thing," this insurance that would protect a portfolio manager's downside. But when the financial community's Mount Rushmore transformed itself into Mount St. Helens under the weight of the real world, the ones who were hurt the most were those who had relied upon it. The indiscriminate selling of severely depressed futures contracts was a costly exercise for those who had put their faith in this device, and who will be reluctant to do so in the future.

The failure of portfolio insurance will be the reason for its demise, which is as it should be. But there will be those who will miss it, since it was at times the least rational player in the market. And, since it is irrationality which creates opportunity, perhaps we should lament its faded influence.

The Great Bull Market: Was It Good for You?

Now that we've described both the major players and the most significant issues of Wall Street on the 1980s, let's consider the main event: the glorious bull market, during which stocks and bonds soared, fortunes were made by others, and investors still managed to suffer. . . .

Beginning in mid-1982, shareholders enjoyed a market climb of almost 2,000 points on the Dow Jones Industrial Average. And yet, many probably have mixed emotions about the ride. Unless you bought in August 1982 and took a seven-year vacation, you were continually under pressure to make the wrong decisions. Even when rising, the market tended to do whatever it took to make the maximum number of investors miserable.

By August 1982, stockholders were beaten, battered, and bruised. The double-digit inflation of 1979–1980 had been met by tight monetary policy from Volcker's Federal Reserve; beginning in late 1979, the Fed had targeted money supply growth rather than interest rates. As a consequence, three-month T-bills soared to an unprecedented peak of 16.3 percent in 1981 At the same time, investors suffering from inflation paranoia drove the long-term Treasury bond rate to an all-time high of 15.4 percent.

This rise in interest rates to double-digit levels was the major cause of the worst recession since WWII, with its consequent impact on corporate profits. Meanwhile, Mexico was at the brink of defaulting on its foreign debt, threatening an unraveling of the debt structure worldwide. Pessimism was at its highest level since 1974. The Dow Jones Industrial Average slid to 777, within 50 points of the level it had first reached in 1961, over twenty years earlier!

The result of this seemingly hopeless mess was the bull market of which we are all now so envious. The Fed, in response to the recession and the debt crisis, eased aggressively. Short-term rates fell an extraordinary three percentage points in as many months, while long-term rates continued to decline from their 1981 peak. The stock market bottomed on August 12 and rose 35 percent by the end of the year.

By mid-1983, the Dow was over 1200, and the economy was eight months into recovery. Enthusiasm for stocks was particularly strong in the smaller names, which had been outperformers since 1974. IPO's were prevalent, trying to satisfy what seemed an insatiable demand for these small capitalization stocks.

The aftermath for investors, especially individual investors, was grim. Interest rates had begun to rise as the economy strengthened; in the first five months of 1984, T-bond yields rose over two percentage points. The Dow slipped 20 percent from its mid-1983 level, while the previous year's new issues were decimated. The boom of hot deals had gone bust, as the results of these newly public companies disappointed their owners and the illiquidity of the shares left these holders with no easy way out.

By mid-1984, the gloom that pervaded Wall Street was reminiscent of a Russian film festival. The concerns of too weak an economy two years earlier had been replaced by those of excessive growth. Real economic growth in the first half of 1984 was an incredible 7.4 percent, which, in combination with a tightening monetary policy, had pushed long government rates near 14 percent.

The economy began to slow down under the weight of an unprecedented real interest rate: T-bond yields were ten percentage points above the inflation rate. As a result, rates began to fall in June, beginning another leg in the bond bull market. Stocks had an explosive one-week rally at the end of July and traded erratically higher with the bond market.

In the third quarter of 1985, the bond and stock markets had a brief correction. Two favorite names, Hospital Corp. and Burroughs, were hit hard after announcing disappointing earnings. Surprisingly, pessimism among investment newsletters reached the highest level since 1982, even though the Dow was 500 points higher by then.

Both markets resumed their rallies in September. Bonds turned sharply downward in early January 1986, but recovered to new highs due to the collapse in oil prices. The Saudis, angered by the lack of production discipline by its OPEC partners, engineered a price war. Spot prices fell from over $25 a barrel to under $10 by mid-1986. In April, stocks turned down sharply, even while bonds continued their blow-off on the upside. This move by the stock market, in advance of the bond market, was uncharacteristic. The bond market spiked on the upside soon afterward and then began to decline.

The market stepped onto a roller coaster for the next six months, rising through June, plummeting in July, climbing again in August, and then collapsing in September. Although the market had simply returned to its level in March, its participants were unsettled, and worse. Particularly hurt were a legion of trend followers, who had waited for the market to assert its "direction" before buying or selling. Each time a trend had seemed established, and they had climbed aboard, the market had turned sharply, whipsawing their positions. By late September 1986, pessimism had replaced the optimism of spring. The loss of the Senate by the Republican Party and the Boesky scandal in November didn't help the mood.

The wall of worry had been rebuilt, and stocks climbed it far into January, rising 400 points in two months. A violent one-hour (!) 100 point sell-off on January 23 raised another fear, that of volatility. The market kept climbing through the spring and summer but, for the first time in many years, without the bond market's lead. The existent and expected strength of the economy drove stocks on the hope for vastly improved corporate profits. Meanwhile, interest rates continued to rise. The significant overvaluation of stocks relative to bonds did not prevent the market from moving higher.

The success of the stock market in the face of the bond market's decline became almost a self-reinforcing mechanism. Optimism peaked in February, but momentum continued until March, and prices rose until August. Even the tightening of monetary policy engineered by the new Fed chairman did not create an attitude of fear. At least, not for a few months.

Investors had become conditioned to view sell-offs as buying opportunities, given the precedents of 1982, 1984, 1985, 1986, and early 1987. But when stocks declined in early October, it was not a buying opportunity. The magnitude of the sell-off that followed, fueled by portfolio insurance and program trading, was unlike anything most investors had ever seen—or, let's hope, will ever see again. The stock market lost $1 trillion in value in a matter of weeks.

After the Crash, investors—dazed by the collapse in prices and aware of the eerie similarities with 1929—waited for the next shoe to drop, the next disaster. Instead, since October 1987, stocks on average have advanced by over 50 percent, climbing to new highs. Meanwhile, bonds have performed handsomely since the afternoon of

Black Monday, with long-term Treasury yields falling by over two percentage points.

Brokerage firms have increasingly sought to encourage the return of retail investors, which had become the investment equivalent of black holes: we know they're out there; we just can't find them. *The Wall Street Journal* highlighted one interesting approach to lure back the individual investor: the euphemizing of the Crash. The word itself, with its ugly connotations of panic and poverty, has frequently been replaced in brokerage reports by less threatening terms, such as "correction" or "sell-off." Laszlo Birinyi had the final word on this out-of-sight, out-of-mind strategy, describing it as "Wall Street's version of 'I'm sorry, Mrs. Lincoln, but how did you like the play?'"

Two conclusions can be drawn from this review. First, the similar trading patterns of stocks and bonds highlighted the interrelationship between the two markets. Second, the ability of the market to confound the general consensus during these seven years argued the contrarian case; it demonstrated that the best values were created by pessimism and the worst by optimism. If you were a participant in this bull market, this summary might also remind you of how easy it was to believe the crowd, however wrong that belief now seems in retrospect.

CHAPTER 8

The Outlook for the 1990s: Conversations with Five Outstanding Investors

Let's take a look at the current decade, as seen in the minds of five highly regarded investment pros: John Templeton, Julian Robertson, Phil Fisher, Stan Salvigsen, and Mike Aronstein.

Their conclusions on the investment outlook vary, but they do share several attributes. They are men of unusual intelligence, with an underlying confidence in their own judgment. At the same time, they recognize and respect the obstacles that confine most investors to mediocrity. In the investment world, the best in the business know their strengths and their limits.

Fisher focuses on a few, superior companies, ignoring economic or market projections, while Salvigsen and Aronstein concentrate primarily on their overall economic forecast and its implications for U.S. investors. Templeton buys or sells stocks worldwide as the values in their markets warrant, while Robertson takes positions both long and short in each of the major equity markets.

The differences in their styles may seem great, but the similarities are greater still. In all cases, their investment approaches are driven by the classic themes of common sense, knowledge, patience, and flexibility.

The following interviews, which were conducted in September and October of 1989, are wide-ranging, and may touch on difficult topics at times. What's important is to learn a little of what these sophisticated investors expect, a little of why they expect it, and a little more of how they go about making money.

John Marks Templeton

John Templeton has been managing mutual fund money for almost half a century. He lives and works in Lyford Cay on New Providence Island, approximately one million miles southwest of Wall Street. His offices are located in a magnificent new building, the headquarters of Templeton, Galbraith, and Hansberger, Ltd.

Sir John is a man of strong faith and quiet charm. He is immensely likable, at all times, courteous and considerate—one of those rare people who seem genuinely content with life.

On the investment front, he remains optimistic about the potential for international achievement and advancement, but not without the expectation of substantial inflationary pressures. Both of these assumptions argue the long-term case for stocks.

DS: [Following your recent trip] I wanted to get your general thoughts on where Japan stands—the culture and the economy—at this time. It has been one of the great success stories of the 1980s.

TEMPLETON: I first went to Japan fifty-three years ago and it was quite different at that time, but even then, I could see that it was going to have a great future, because the people were very thrifty and well-organized and hard-working . . . reliable . . . clean.

So many good qualities there—even fifty-three years ago—that after the war, I began to study the stocks. But it was not permitted at that time to take your money out of Japan. You could buy stocks, but not take your money out. So I bought only for my personal investments until they changed the law and you could take your money out.

By that time, I had learned enough about the nation and the companies. And we were buying those shares at an average of only three times earnings for the finest rapid growth companies in Japan. The total stock market value of all stocks in Tokyo was about the same as the value of one stock in America—International Business Machines. There were just so many bargains twenty–twenty-five years ago that we kept buying and buying; at one point, about twenty years ago, our investors had 50 percent of their worldwide investments in these bargain stocks in Japan. And that proved to be very profitable

No one else was doing it, because at that time people said, "Oh, those Japanese—they can only make imitation goods. And what a small market." And it was not too long after the Second World War, so Americans just weren't interested. That's why the stocks sold on the bargain counter.

Now, we held those for a long time and made huge profits on them. A few years ago, we began to take those profits, because the share prices are so much higher now in Japan than they are in most of the world. Share prices for all stocks on the Tokyo Exchange got up to around seventy times earnings and are now about sixty times earnings, whereas American stocks today are only about twelve times what we think the companies will earn [in 1989]. So Japan, in terms of earnings, is five times as expensive. It's also expensive in terms of book value and dividends. You pay six times as much to buy a dollar of dividends in Japan as you would in America or England or other places. At present, share prices are just too high.

DS: Stepping back from the market for a moment, does it concern you that the image of the thrifty Japanese individual has now turned into an image of the heavy consumer? Did you see that when you were there?

TEMPLETON: Yes, but it's a slow process. They will still continue to save more than most of the world. It's true that they are learning to spend more—and even to borrow money, which is unusual—but, still, that's a long process. They are no further down that sad path than the United States was thirty years ago or England was thirty years ago.

DS: But do you see that they're in a process that will continue, or do you think this is just temporary?

TEMPLETON: Yes, it will continue but it's so long-range—twenty, thirty, forty years—that it's not a major factor in the question of whether you should invest there. Up until two years ago, we were worried that these very high prices in Japan might suddenly go down. But then we had the panic in America and worldwide, and the prices in Japan didn't go down as much as they did elsewhere, and they recovered more rapidly and reached new highs.

We now think that's because the people think differently, and the control that the brokers and the government have over the market is much greater than in other nations. So we no longer think there will be a sharp decline in prices in Japan.

However, we do think that in the very long run, values will have to come back into line with the rest of the world. It may be a slow process, but it means that—in that enormous area between twelve times earnings now in America and sixty times earnings in Japan, somewhere in that big middle ground—in the long run, the two will be selling on the same price-earnings ratio.

That doesn't necessarily mean that America will go way up or that Japan will go way down. It may be that, just over the years, the earnings will continue to rise in Japan until the price-earnings ratio is, therefore, lower on today's prices.

Now, to finish the answer to your question: From my many studies and visits to Japan, I believe that it will continue to be an industrial leader. It will continue to grow more rapidly than almost any major nation. The outlook—in terms of growing prosperity, available cash, and so forth—is still optimistic. The major problem there is not the prospects for the future, but the fact that the prices are already discounting it too greatly.

DS: You said that you no longer are afraid of a severe crack in the stock market—

TEMPLETON: Sudden crack.

DS: Are you concerned, though, [about] the real estate market? *The Economist* said that real estate prices went up by over 20 percent in '86, over 70 percent in '87, and over 40 percent in '88. With that kind of compound growth, with the kind of speculation we've seen, are you afraid of a severe crack in the real estate market, which could then feed into their stock market—to the borrowing that's been done off of real estate to finance investments?

TEMPLETON: That will not be sudden. The prices are high, but they may not go down on real estate. Real estate is so different from shares. Shares have a value from the standpoint of the dividends that you are going to get, and it is a world standard. Shares of a bank in Japan should sell about the same in relation to dividends as a bank in England, but real estate would be totally different, because you can't move the real estate from place to place. And real estate is in very short supply in Japan and will continue to be. So real estate prices can stay permanently out of line.

Now, that's not to say that real estate values won't go down. In every nation throughout investment history, there have been cycles in real estate prices. Not as quick as market cycles—the average market cycle is about once every five years, whereas the average real estate cycle is about once every twenty years. But still, there are cycles in every nation, and will be also in Japan.

There's much evidence—when I was there two weeks ago and when I was there in June—there's much evidence that real estate has already started to go down. The government, for example, has put a tax of 90 percent on the profits on real estate, provided you've held it only a short while. And that has stopped people from buying. There's no point in buying, if you have to give 90 percent of your profit to the government.

Also, there are changes occurring in the availability of land. Some of the crowding in the center of Tokyo is being alleviated by companies selling their downtown space and moving their headquarters ten, fifteen miles outside the city. So already there is, I believe, a beginning tendency toward lower prices but, again, I do not think it will be anything sudden—it will just be a gradual process.

DS: Do you see the other Asian countries—such as Hong Kong, Korea, Taiwan, and Singapore—in the same relationship to Japan as Japan was to the United States forty years ago, where they're just doing it better?

TEMPLETON: Yes, that's a very good analogy. Mainly on the basis of wage rates. Twenty or thirty years ago, the Japanese wage rates were a tiny fraction of American wage rates. Now, at the present exchange rate for the currencies, Japanese wages are a little higher than American wages. So they no longer have the advantage of low wages. On the other hand, wages are still very low in Korea— about one-fifth of what they are in Japan. Also, in Hong Kong, they are roughly one-quarter of what they are in Japan. In Thailand and other places, they are even lower.

Already, you can see that, whereas the low production costs for television sets in Japan have practically driven the American television companies out of business, the same thing is happening in Japan. When you travel and look in the stores there, the television sets are made in Hong Kong or even in Red China and other places. They are beginning to have the same situation as America had in competing with Japan twenty years ago.

But that applies mainly to wages. There's no other nation that has the other advantages that Japan has in terms of reliability, in terms of stable government, in terms of hard work and freedom from labor troubles. All of those things are better in Japan than they are in South Korea or Taiwan or Hong Kong or Mainland China or Thailand or Indonesia. None of those nations—called the Little Tigers—that are growing more rapidly than Japan, none of them have as many advantages as Japan had twenty years ago.

DS: Do you make much of the political turmoil that is going on in Japan, which threatens—at some point in the next five or ten years—to unseat the government that has been in power for the last thirty or forty years?

TEMPLETON: Yes. Yes, that is important. It's a very long-range factor, though. Every nation eventually gets a desire to have a different government. Surely, that will happen in Japan, eventually. And when it does, it is going to have a big effect.

You may remember when Churchill lost the elections [to the Labour Party] in England. When that happened forty-four years ago, it had a very depressing effect on the British nation and on share prices, and it led to more inflation. Now, I don't think that it will be quite that marked in Japan, but something like that is in the cards in the long run, because the people there are getting the same expensive habits and the same overexpectations that they did in England.

DS: Of course, in 1945, not only did Churchill lose, but, with the loss of [India the following year], the British Empire—as the world had known it—was in retrenchment. Do you think something that severe could happen in Japan?

TEMPLETON: They don't have an empire.

DS: I guess the analogy would be to their economic empire. That they've created expectations that can't be fulfilled.

TEMPLETON: Not particularly, no. It is true that some of the low-cost nations will grow more rapidly. But it's not a close analogy at all toward losing an empire. Already, the low costs in the Little Tigers are having an increasing effect on Japan, but it's a slow, steady process and has already been going on for several years. Nothing is likely to be startling or unexpected.

DS: Among the Little Tigers, do you see any that have—from an investment point of view—the same attractiveness that Japan had to you forty years ago?

TEMPLETON: No. No. Everybody keeps asking, "Where is the next Japan? I want to get in on the ground floor of the next Japan." And every investment counselor is always trying to find that. But that was a unique situation. There isn't any other nation that has the many, many advantages that Japan had thirty years ago.

There are some that come close. The one that comes closest now probably is South Korea because the people are somewhat the same—they also save money and they also work hard. South Korea is already beginning to grow twice as fast as Japan and will continue to do so.

For a different reason, Hong Kong is an excellent place to invest now because the prices are low. You don't buy shares because the outlook for the nation is good; you buy shares, because the price is low. And the price is low in Hong Kong now—[stocks] selling for no higher than they are in America, in relation to earnings, assets, and dividends. Whereas, in Japan, they are three, five, six times as high as America.

DS: You don't share the fear that many have that when the Chinese come in—as they've done with their own people—they will rewrite the rules as quickly as they want, and say to foreign investors, "Well, you no longer can take your money out"?

TEMPLETON: Oh yes. That's a very valid fear. Very valid. It is a major problem. But the only time you ever make money in the market is by buying when shares are very depressed in price, and shares do not ever get very depressed in price except facing a problem. So you have to expect that when you are going to buy shares on the bargain counter, you are going to have to buy at a time when other people are worried and selling. And that has happened in Hong Kong; in the month of June alone, the Hong Kong market went down 40 percent.

There were reasons for it; because of the problems in Mainland China. But if you don't buy it at a time like that, you just are never going to get shares at a bargain price. The thing to do is to buy despite those problems. You never know how, in the long run, it will turn out. But it won't become part of Mainland China for another eight years, and, in that time, all kinds of things can happen politically and economically. So that's far enough away that you can be sure that the problem will be largely forgotten within a year or two, and the attitudes toward Hong Kong stocks will be back to where they were last year or the year before.

Also, in the very long run, it's quite possible that becoming part of Mainland China will not be a problem. In fact, it may be a benefit, because the thing that Mainland China needs more than anything else is people who are good at running businesses. And they have so few, whereas Hong Kong is rich with thousands of experts at how to run a business efficiently.

So Mainland China needs Hong Kong. It needs the people of Hong Kong, and quite possibly after it becomes part of the mainland, it may turn out to be the commercial and economic center for a billion people in somewhat the way of New York. New York is not the political capital, but it is the commercial and economic capital of 250 million people. Hong Kong may become that type of capital for a billion people. If so, the entrepreneurs and the corporations in Hong Kong will benefit. So it is true there's a lot to fear, but on the other hand, there's even more to anticipate favorably.

DS: A former client of mine who was from Hong Kong made a similar point by saying that, actually, Hong Kong will be taking over China rather than China taking over Hong Kong. Looked at from your perspective, where do you see Hong Kong in ten years?

TEMPLETON: Ten years would only put us two years after it becomes part of Mainland China.

DS: You do expect that will go ahead as planned?

TEMPLETON: Oh, yes. That I think you can count on. Nine chances out of ten, easily, that it will become part of Mainland China in 1997.

DS: Even to go out fifteen years—

TEMPLETON: Yes, that would be an easier question. To go out fifteen years, they will have had time to adapt, to become a real part of the nation. And, on that basis, I would say that not all but most of the Hong Kong corporations will have become much bigger, because they will have expanded into such a huge market. The Hong Kong corporations will be bigger—probably more profitable—and share prices will be higher, because people will not have that worry to look forward to. Share prices are not harmed much by what has happened in the past; share prices are harmed by worries about the future.

And, once 1997 is past, that will no longer be a depressing effect, so Hong Kong share prices might go up greatly in the next fifteen years.

DS: As we look at Europe—the removal of trade barriers in 1992—what do you think the implications of the economic integration within Europe are to the American public, in general, and to the U.S. investor, in particular?

TEMPLETON: Splendid. Very favorable. When any part of the earth becomes more prosperous, it has an uplifting effect on almost all nations. And there's no doubt that free trade does speed up economic progress. The more free trade they have in Europe after 1992, the more the standard of living in Europe will rise. Our best estimates are that it will rise about 1 percent per year more quickly than it would have otherwise. Now that doesn't sound terribly fast, but it is. At 3.5 percent per year, your standard of living will double in twenty years, but at 2.5 percent per year, it will take thirty years to double your standard of living. So Europe is going to benefit greatly, and because Europe benefits, the whole world will benefit.

We, in our investment selection process, have been studying that carefully for more than two years, because when the trade barriers are removed, those companies that have the low costs and the most expert distribution will expand. So we have been identifying those companies in Europe that have low costs and excellent merchandizing—after 1992, they will have a field in which they can grow more rapidly than they ever did before. We do have, in our mutual funds, large holdings in European companies, carefully selected in anticipation of 1992.

DS: Do you ever fear that perhaps 1992 has not only been discounted, but overdiscounted? Well in advance of it happening, we are already starting to see signs of speculation. For example, recently, the Spain Fund has been running up wildly.

TEMPLETON: Yes, you're quite right on that. The time when a favorable development reaches the highest prices in the stock market is before it happens, not after it happens. It's too late now for people to go out and do what we did two years ago—that is, to identify those companies that are going to benefit from the freedom in Europe. But I do not think it's overdiscounted, no. European share prices are not especially high. In general, they are roughly the same as American or Canadian share prices. So there has not been any excess optimism yet.

DS: Where do you see the overlooked opportunities right now for the investor who is willing to look out five or ten years? Are there any particular countries that you have in mind as being unusually attractive?

TEMPLETON: Let me answer that in two parts. If you are writing this book for small investors, they are all going to expect my answer to be which nation has the most rapid growth future. On that score, the most rapid growth future is likely to be Mainland China, Thailand, Indonesia, Argentina, Brazil, Kuwait—those are the places [with] a brilliant future, with a rapidly expanding standard of living, sales volume, profits, and so forth.

But for your really experienced and sophisticated investors, the answer is not that at all. If you are going to make money in your investments, you have to buy when the prices are extremely depressed. And they're not depressed when everyone thinks the outlook is good. So you have to buy where there are big problems that are not necessarily permanent.

Now, on that score, it's well worth studying New Zealand. Because of a change to the Labour Party four years ago, they have been through at least two years of very severe depression, earnings are way down, and share prices are still 40 percent below where they were at the peak. So New Zealand is a nation that has a better than average long-range outlook with share prices that are temporarily depressed by major problems. And the same thing, as I already mentioned, in Hong Kong. Because of the terrible things going on in Mainland China and the big publicity that it got, it scared investors everywhere. So share prices are depressed. Therefore, that's a good place to buy. Share prices now are more than normally depressed in America and Canada, because there are big problems in those nations: unfavorable balance of trade, unbalanced budget, debts higher than ever before, and many other problems.

DS: Are there any particular themes that you feel are still attractive for the integration of Europe? Any themes that you feel have not already been picked over as we look out over the next ten years?

TEMPLETON: Throughout my forty-nine years of investment counsel, I have noticed that there are numerous themes—or as I call them, "fashions"—and they come and go just as they do in the women's clothing business. Every year, there are two or three new themes in America and two or three new themes in Japan, and so forth. The themes tend to be very popular for a few months, or a year or two, and then something else comes along. There's a danger in following themes for that reason. One of the wisest things you could put in your book is: Never follow themes. They're temporary.

DS: I guess if you take a broader [perspective]—for example, what you said about Japan earlier on: There was an underlying case to be made for the market, for the strength of character of the people, for the stability of the government—with all those factors, that was a theme that really lasted for forty years. Similarly, in Korea over the last ten years. So there are general themes that really evolve over a decade or two.

TEMPLETON: Then I wouldn't call them themes. I would call them underlying trends in economics and politics—long-range influences—and not themes, like shortage of oil, or whatever. It's obvious looking ahead, from the standpoint of many years, that those nations are going to increase in prosperity most rapidly that have the following characteristics: honesty, reliability, hard work, low taxes, and freedom from regulation. Nations that have those characteristics will grow much more rapidly than those that have the opposite.

Now which nations are those? One of those is Switzerland. And that has been the case for fifty years, and that's why Switzerland has been one of the best places to invest. People are so anxious to send their money to Switzerland that, a few years ago, the Swiss had to put on a negative interest rate of 35 percent to prevent flooding in of new money. So Switzerland is a good illustration that there are underlying forces—political and economic—that cause one nation, or one area or industry, to prosper and another one not to.

Switzerland still has them, but no more than it did before. Germany has those good characteristics. America, Canada, Japan—those are the ones that occur to me now. Those are the ones that, in the long run, will benefit from having attractive economic and political trends.

Between individual industries, obviously, the new industries will grow more rapidly than the old industries. For example, service industries, which were a small part of the national economy fifty years ago, are now two thirds or more of the total national economy. And those trends will continue.

But, in general, you do not make stock market profits by being in a new industry, because the highest prices come in anticipation. And to illustrate that more clearly, one of the industry trends that is most reliable is genetic engineering. But we don't own any shares in genetic engineering companies, because the prices went up so greatly as soon as the companies were formed. [The shares] have not behaved well recently and are not likely to, because the peak prices occurred long before those trends had any effect on earning power.

DS: What I've tried to emphasize throughout the book is for investors to understand the difference between a good company—and, by inference, a good country—and an attractive investment; often, it's not the most attractive company that's your most attractive investment.

TEMPLETON: Yes. I'd say in investing you have to give most of your attention to price. You're better off buying a very risky investment at an extremely low price than you are by buying a very safe investment at a high price.

DS: To follow up on Europe, do you think the takeover mania that we saw in the United States during the 1980s is going to carry into Europe in the 1990s?

TEMPLETON: Yes. Acquisitions and leveraged buy-outs and companies buying in their own stock are spreading rapidly into other nations, particularly Europe and Canada. They will eventually spread into Japan, but very little in Japan, because the stock market prices are so high that the acquisition people can't find any bargains.

DS: There are also hostile takeovers. We're in the midst now of Sir James Goldsmith's attempt to take over BAT [British-American Tobacco]. Do you think that is the first of what will be many hostile takeovers? Do you think the climate is changing now, where governments and the culture will allow hostile takeovers in Europe?

TEMPLETON: This popularity for hostile takeovers was very great in America, much greater than most people ever expected. It has already carried so far in America that you can't expect it to grow much more. But it has only recently begun in Europe. Therefore, the rate of increase of that type of activity will be greater in Europe than America. But it's not likely ever to become as large in Europe as it was in America, because the European governments and regulatory patterns are so different. For example, it's almost impossible to have a hostile takeover of any company in the Netherlands. Why? Because they won't allow you to vote. You can buy the majority of the shares of a Netherlands company, but that doesn't matter. You can't replace the board of directors—it's against the law.

DS: So we'll see a trend toward [takeovers] but nothing like we saw in the United States in the 1980s.

TEMPLETON: A trend, but it will not go anywhere near as far as it's already gone in America.

DS: Do you feel that it's a good trend or a bad trend?

TEMPLETON: It has gone far enough that the bad now outweighs the good. It's certainly desirable to have freedom . . . entrepreneurship . . . opportunities to replace less efficient management. All of those things are healthy, not only for the company and the investor but for the nation.

But, in America now, a high proportion of these acquisitions are based on government tax subsidy. Without the government tax subsidy, they wouldn't take place. They are based on the fact that the earning power of a corporation is taxed if it is paid out in dividends, but if the earning power of the corporation is paid out in interest, it's not taxed [dividend payments are not tax-deductible, whereas interest charges are].

That is likely to be changed. The disparity is so enormous that it has caused these acquisitors to be able to pay more than a company was worth and still have a good deal, because they no longer paid income taxes. Now, that's not good. That is a major factor in causing a bad deficit in the federal government's annual budget, and therefore, it is quite likely to be modified or stopped. So the acquisitions have gone to such extremes in terms of price that they are now a burden to the nation, rather than a benefit.

DS: Do you think the trend will be toward eliminating the double taxation of dividends? Do you think the trend will be toward tightening the deductions for interest? Or do you think it will be a combination of both?

TEMPLETON: Most likely a combination. America is very rare in the world, [in that it] allows total subtraction of all interest. For example, if you buy a home in Canada, you can't subtract the interest on your mortgage. America stands almost alone in the world in allowing total deduction of everybody's—corporate and individual—interest payments. On the other hand, America also stands almost alone in the world in not giving credit to the shareholder for the taxes paid by the corporation. So since America is so far out of line with the rest of the world, it is quite likely that, gradually over the next two or three years, there will be compromises made to come more in line in both directions—less benefits for interest deductions and more benefits for dividend payments.

DS: Arguably, each of the inconsistencies that you mentioned—full deduction of home mortgage on the one hand but not allowing [corporations to deduct dividend payments]—each of these seem to be a post-war phenomenon. After World War II, there was a national desire for home ownership, whereas there was generally a national aversion toward stocks.

Looking at the United States on a general basis—if we go back and compare 1950 with the beginning of the 1990s—there are some similarities and there are some differences. On the similar side, back then we were at peace; now we're at peace. In fact, we seem to be winning the cold war now. Technology was certainly an exciting factor as we entered the fifties; technology is an exciting factor now as we look at semiconductors, superconductors . . . biotechnology and health care, in general.

But there are also a certain number of differences. Back then, there was an aversion to debt; now there seems to be a love affair with debt. And, most important, since you've mentioned price, back then the dividend yield on stocks was almost three times what it was on bonds; now the dividend yield is roughly one third of what it is on bonds.

If we look at the United States in the 1990s, do you think that you can make anywhere near as powerful a case for common stocks as you could in the 1950s? Or, for that matter, do you think you could make a positive case for stocks in the 1990s?

TEMPLETON: There always have been numerous factors on both sides. In all of my forty-nine years of investment counsel, there have always been major factors toward higher prices and major factors toward lower prices—and always will be. But to try to be useful to your question, the new things that are coming along are more favorable than unfavorable.

Management has enormously increased its ability in the last thirty years. When I was born, there were only two places on earth to study business management in graduate school. Now there are 800, graduating over 80,000 Masters of Business Administration per year. And that is only one aspect of the improving management. That leads to lower costs, higher production, new products, greater variety, higher standard of living.

Another very powerful factor is scientific research. The world is now spending over a billion dollars a day on scientific research, whereas when I was born, they were spending 1 percent that much. Now, that has not stopped. It has not slowed down, even—it's still expanding. And it is not wasted, either. It leads to lower costs, new products, higher quality, greater variety, more richness of life.

So those are two powerful forces—and there are many more—that cause us to think that share prices are likely to go up as much in the future as they did in the past. It's true that the ratio of dividends to interest rates is not as favorable as it was thirty or fifty years ago, but it's still reasonably favorable.

And we are estimating that the standard of living worldwide—not just in America—may be able to quadruple in only forty years. Now that's extraordinary. It has never happened in history. In history, it often took a thousand years to double the standard of living. But the forces are so strong now that they probably will quadruple the standard of living of all the world in forty years.

In terms of prices, inflation is likely to continue. Almost every nation has inflation. The political condition is such that the people more or less force their governments to have inflation. So we think inflation will run at about the same rate in the future as it has in the past, which is the same as saying the cost of living will double about every ten years. Then, forty years out, that means it will cost you sixteen times as much to live, and you'll be living at four times the scale you are now, so the gross national product necessarily has to be sixty-four times as high as it is now. And if it's sixty-four times as high, that will be reflected in the sales volume of corporations and in their dividends and their earnings and, quite possibly, in their share

prices. In fact, it may be even more reflected in the share prices because there is developing a shortage of shares.

Because of this—and other similar factors—our best estimates
are, at present, that share prices will go up at least as much in the future as they did in the past. Now, how much is that? Well, it's
roughly a doubling every ten years. Share prices have been doubling
in America about every ten years and are likely to continue to double
about every ten years.

The volume of trading on the New York Stock Exchange is now
100 times as high as it was fifty years ago. The quantity of shares and
bonds available for trading is 100 times as great as it was when I became an investment counselor. The quantity of money in American
mutual funds is 1,000 times as great as it was just fifty-five years ago.
And those trends have not stopped. Those trends are still going on.
Maybe even speeding up.

So as you look forward to the future, there are offsetting factors.
I don't say there aren't problems. There are big problems that might
slow things down, and the bargains are not as great as they were in
1932, it's true. But these other factors are so enormous and so numerous that our best studies would indicate now that the probabilities
are that share prices can double about every ten years, not counting
the dividends. The dividends, of course, would mean an acceleration
to that.

DS: Do you feel that on a relative price basis you are better off
in the stock market, given your outlook, than you are in the bond
market?

TEMPLETON: Oh, very much so. Bonds are good now. They
pay well and the prices are likely to go up in the long run, so I
wouldn't want to discourage anybody from buying bonds at present.
But bonds give you no protection against inflation.

DS: What about the possibility of reduced inflation or even deflation, given the debt situation?

TEMPLETON: If you look back through the history of most
major nations and generations, you almost never find that debt led to
deflation. It led to inflation. The way that governments lighten the
burden is not to pay off the debt—that's practically unknown. They
lighten it by inflation, which reduces the burden. If the debt stays the
same and the cost of living doubles, then the burden of the debt is
half as great, you see

DS: In this country, though—100 years ago—we did have a deflation; sixty years ago, we did have a deflation. In both cases, it's been argued that the major factor was the debt that was built up, primarily during the two wars—the Civil War and World War I. So the precedent in this country has actually been that the buildup of debt has had a deflationary consequence.

TEMPLETON: Let's take some statistics on that. If you put one dollar into bonds sixty-two years ago and you reinvested your interest, you'd now have $5.00. If you put your money into stocks at that time and reinvested your dividends, you'd now have $1,400 instead of $5.00. And, as you say, that did include some years of deflation. It included wars and depressions and lots of big problems, but in the long run, you'd have been far better off in owning a share of something rather than owning a claim against it.

DS: And you feel that applies to the next five to ten years, as well?

TEMPLETON: If you give me ten years, I would say yes. Most themes, particularly investment themes, run in cycles. Not only do share prices go in cycles, but inflation goes in cycles, too. So who knows when those cycles will occur and, therefore, what will be the case a few years from now? It's possible that we might have a year with no inflation or 1 percent inflation but that would be very optimistic. If you're talking longer than that, then you're almost sure to have inflation. It's almost 100 percent certainty that cash will lose its value.

DS: We've discussed a lot on economics, as it applies to investing. How much do you let your economic scenario influence your investment decisions?

TEMPLETON: Very, very greatly but indirectly. Our investment decisions are based on this: Where in the world can we buy a share at the lowest possible price in relation to what that corporation is worth? Now the question is, what is that corporation worth? And what that corporation is worth depends on what its earnings are now. What is its growth rate? What's the competition? How good is the management? What's likely to happen to the nation where it operates? All these things enter into an appraisal of the value of the corporation. And once you have decided the value of, say, the telephone company of Mexico as compared with the telephone company of

Japan, you decide what each one is worth. Then your investment decision is, where is the lowest price, the price lowest in relation to what you previously decided it's worth? So all those factors do enter into appraising the values of corporations but only indirectly do they enter into the decision to buy this stock or that one.

Julian Robertson

A retail account executive before becoming a money manager, Robertson has headed Tiger Partners—a hedge fund—since May 1980. His performance in the '80s places him within the top 1 percent of equity portfolio managers anywhere; his investors have received a 32 percent annual return on their money.

The Tiger Partnership is managed out of a large office in midtown Manhattan, with a spectacular view that makes the city look, if not friendly, then at least pretty damn impressive. Robertson prefers to work in the middle of a mini-trading floor rather than in a private office. He retains the gracious style of his North Carolina roots, underscored by an intensity more typical of New York.

Looking forward, he is generally positive on stocks—particularly those in Europe and America—and negative on bonds, real estate, and gold.

DS: You had mentioned to me that you are a big fan of investing for the long term but not for investing in the market. Then, in looking at your literature, I see it says that you are not market-timers. It seems that there's a certain inconsistency there, because the first statement seems to say, "We go wherever the value is," and the second statement is, "We don't try to judge when the market is cheap or expensive."

ROBERTSON: But that's the whole point. We're looking for good companies and bad companies; we're looking for cheap companies and expensive companies. And because we're a hedge fund, we can buy the good companies and short* the bad companies. We find that easier, to operate in that kind of system, than picking markets.

When you pick a market, to be correct, you've got to be right when you get in and when you get out, and then get back in again. I don't know of anybody who has been successful doing that over the long term. That isn't Buffett's style, it certainly isn't Peter Lynch's style, it certainly isn't Templeton's style. Peter Lynch [states] flat out,

*As mentioned earlier, a short sale is the sale of a borrowed security, hoping for a price decline.

"Look, I've never seen foretold a downturn or an upturn. And I'm just as surprised when each one takes place."

We're not quite that doctrinaire, but we really feel that we are stock pickers, we are value judgers of what's overpriced and underpriced.

DS: In the United States, where do you think the individual investor should have his money as we go into the 1990s, in terms of stocks . . . bonds . . . real estate? If we look back ten years from now, where would the individual investor have done the best?

ROBERTSON: Looking ahead from this vantage point right now, one of the reasons why I'm reasonably bullish on equities is because we are the best game in town. I don't think there is any question that there's too much commercial real estate around; therefore, I don't think that's a good investment. That's not only true in New York, it's true all over the country. One of the . . . very viable alternatives during the last thirty years—or at least until about 1982 or 1983—was a second home or condominium.

DS: Not to mention a first home.

ROBERTSON: Well, of course, but you *have* to have a first home. So exactly right, first homes have been fabulous too—certainly here in this area—but I'm really talking about your disposable income, your savings. It seems to me that the bloom is off [the second home] rose. Young people have seen the success of that, and they have all piled into it. They're locked into apartments in Florida that they really don't want to go to every time they take a vacation, and they've seen those things begin to deteriorate in value. And they've seen the bother about owning them as [the homes] begin to get older and erode.

Gold—they're finding better ways to leach it out of the ground. There's more gold around. You've never been able to eat gold. It's been known as the storehouse of value for years. But why is that? I don't think it's really valid—

DS: It's the classic Greater Fool Theory. You hope somebody's willing to pay more for it. If they do, you will make money, and if they don't, you won't. There's no underlying value to it.

ROBERTSON: But, at the present time, supply comes in [to offset the demands of] the bigger fools. So I don't think that's a viable alternative.

Since I've been in the business, bonds have been a horrible long-term investment. It's very hard to make money when you see bond yields go from 4 percent to maybe 10 percent. Increasing yield and decreasing price of bonds—it's really hard to make money in that kind of environment.*

I see no indication, whatsoever, that there are any political things occurring which make bonds more attractive. I think, if anything, we're being more inflationary now than we were before, in terms of long-term policy. I don't think the politicians have the courage to be anti-inflationary; I certainly don't think the present administration does.

DS: Bonds have been a fabulous investment throughout the 1980s. One argument that has been made is that, even including the new politics since World War II which are inflationary policies, the bond market will preclude inflation with very high real yields.†

ROBERTSON: Well, if they have very high real yields, then you are not going to make any money in the bond market.

DS: If you buy with an exceptionally high real yield, and inflation comes down and the real yield narrows, then you win both ways, which has basically been the story of the 1980s.

ROBERTSON: Well, that's true to a certain extent . . . [rates] have done better off a huge spike up, but I still think it has been difficult to make money in [bonds].

DS: But, more important, you think it *will be* difficult to make money in that way.

ROBERTSON: So I think that the individual should have a mixture of cash and stocks. If he knows the [property], it's probably all right to get into real estate. But, generally speaking, that's a hard thing.

One of the enormous advantages of equities is the liquidity factor. You can get out in a minute. And [the individual investor], in my opinion, should be paying a huge premium for that liquidity. He's

---

*Bond prices move inversely with interest rates; when interest rates rise, bonds fall. The primary cause of a rise in rates is an increase in inflation—bondholders expect a return on their investment at least as high as the inflation rate.
†The "real" rate of interest is the current interest rate—the "nominal" rate—minus the inflation rate; it is the yield on a bond or a loan after adjusting for the loss of purchasing power because of inflation. A high real yield discourages borrowing, slows economic growth, and reduces inflation.

actually getting it at a discount. People who want to buy the whole ball of wax have to pay a premium. And that's, of course, what the takeover people do.

So I think [the investor] should have a backbone of cash and he should primarily be in equities. The long-term history would prove that good equities are better than bonds over a long period of time. Particularly if he runs his money properly, or goes with a good manager.

DS: What would you say to the individual investor in terms of managing money? That he's better off finding someone to manage it for him, or that individual investor can do very well on his own?

ROBERTSON: An individual investor with the same knowledge as an institutional investor should be able to beat the pants off the institutional investor, because he's dealing with less money. And that's a huge advantage for him. Obviously, [though, individual investors] don't have as much knowledge.

I haven't read the Peter Lynch book *(One Up on Wall Street)*, but what he talks about, I think, is very sound. Basically, he's saying that if, [for example,] you're a parent and you see that the Toys "R" Us stores have an enormous advantage over the competition, and if you know enough to check the growth rate against the P/E, and if the growth rate is much higher than the P/E—and that's likely to continue—it's pretty hard to lose money on [that investment] in the long run. It's a simplistic way of doing it, but I think it is possible for the investor to use just those kinds of simplistic tools and do quite well.

Of course, there are other things where he can't possibly make an evaluation. It would be impossible to grade an oil producer or refiner or anything of that nature, so I think that he is better off in most instances in getting a good manager.

DS: But that can be more difficult, in some ways, than finding a good stock.

ROBERTSON: That's true. But now there are people who will find you a good manager.

DS: But how good are *they*?

ROBERTSON: Well, you have that problem in everything. The fundamental [point] gets down to getting the best manager for your money, whether it be you or anybody else. And I don't think enough people pay enough attention to that. So it's a difficult problem.

I see so much opportunity in what we are doing here that it's just mind-boggling. For instance, one of our new people used to run the Japan Fund—a man named Tim Schildt. He goes to Japan about once a quarter, and he always takes one of our other people with him.

Why are we spending so much time in Japan? The reason is that we see an enormous dichotomy in their market; there's no rhyme or reason to where stocks sell. We can find really great companies selling at twenty-five and thirty times earnings; we can find awful companies selling at 200 times earnings.

An example of the former is a company called Ito-Yokado. It's sort of a WalMart of Japan. Now Japan has laws which protect the local retailer, much the way most countries have laws which protect the local farmer. And so Ito-Yokado has a more difficult time going into a smaller town than would WalMart.

Now, their cost of retailing has gone so high that the Japanese people are concerned about it. The government realizes it, and they will probably wipe out some of these laws that make it difficult for a company like Ito-Yokado to get into these towns. Ito-Yokado grows now at about 16 to 18 percent a year—that could jump up to 25 [percent]. It sells at twenty-five times earnings, which sounds high, but we are talking about a market that is averaging about sixty times earnings.

We can buy Ito-Yokado and short against that a chocolate company. Now, I don't know if you've eaten Japanese chocolates. I haven't, but my understanding is that they taste very much like cardboard. Meanwhile, the Japanese are importing Belgian, Swiss, and English chocolates. They adore them; they are wild over them. So they quit eating this cardboard. And we go in and see the cardboard manufacturer that's masquerading as a chocolate company, and say, "What are you going to do about it?" And they say, "Oh, no, we'll continue on." They have no plan to meet it.

The Japanese are not value-oriented at all, yet. It's just liquidity-driven; they do what Nomura [Japan's largest brokerage firm] says or what [others] say, and there are valuations all over the place. If you are willing to play for the long term, there's almost no way you can lose over there, if you do a hedging operation. And we are doing it.

There's a gradual movement toward the value approach, and it's just going to have to happen.

Just an example of how really naive they are, investment-wise: They have been buying the Spain Fund like crazy. They have gotten [the Fund up to] a 200 percent premium. You and I could go out and clone the same fund with ease, and there's no reason why that should sell at over a five or ten percent premium. It's not like the Korea Fund, where you don't have the right to go in and buy Korean stocks. Here, you have a perfect right to go ahead and do it.

DS: The excitement in the Spain Fund also suggests, not just the Japanese influence, but that the excitement over Europe 1992 is perhaps starting to sneak into speculation. Do you agree with that? Or, in a more general sense, how do you think Europe '92 shakes out? Where do you see the unconventional wisdom of the Europe play in the next decade?

ROBERTSON: I think there are enormous buys in Europe and anybody that doesn't look there is absolutely crazy. There is so much talk about '92 that there are a lot of people probably jumping in there just on the basis of 1992. I mean, you and I aren't the first people to talk about that; I get this all the time from partners and everybody else: "What are you doing in Europe in 1992?" Having said that, it is a huge development but even more important . . . it is an underresearched area, and we're more likely to find bargains [there] than we are elsewhere.

DS: But it has been a big theme for a couple of years now. Where do you see the values having disappeared, and where do you see the values still remaining in Europe? Taking a longer-term view— not just worrying about next year . . .

ROBERTSON: I think Europe is a very valid area to invest in. I don't believe in looking at the general area, though. I take more of a bottoms-up approach. I'd rather look for reasonable stocks within that area, and we are finding those.

DS: Taking it at the industry level . . . The industry tends to be a driving force very often in the success of a company.

ROBERTSON: I agree with that, but we are, again, more involved with individual companies. It's very hard to know how these things will evolve. You've got Telefonica, which is just dirt cheap. It's the Spanish telephone company. It has all the cellular [licenses]—

everything in Spain. It's a crappy company; the phone service over there is awful. What's going to be the situation? Is British Telephone going to come in there and take that over, or is it not? There's going to be politics involved, and I don't know what the ramifications are.

I do know, for instance, that the outlook for Cable and Wireless in England is fabulous. It's sort of the MCI of England with some cellular thrown in, and it has some business in Hong Kong. The outlook there is absolutely fantastic. I will buy that, and I think they'll do well, almost regardless.

And I think we will probably buy this company [Hoesch] that we talked to yesterday, which is at one-and-a-half times cash flow.

We are very excited about a company over there called Fisons, which is the leading allergy drug company in the world. We're excited over that because it's growing at about the rate of [good U.S. drug] companies. It's the size that it could be taken over by an international company, and it's selling probably at a 20 percent discount, valuation-wise, to American companies.

So we really take more of an individual approach [to companies] than a broad-brush approach as to what industries are going to do well because of 1992.

We do think [Europe] is a very fertile area of investment, and not only because of 1992. This flow of competent people from East Germany to West Germany is going to help alleviate one of their big problems, which is the lack of skilled labor and good young people.

There's also a move toward capitalism; we think there will be a move toward more markets. The percentage of German stocks, for instance, that are publicly held is just absolutely minute compared to [the percentage in] America, Britain, or Japan—it's literally 4 or 5 percent of those. There just is no liquid market over there. The wealth is very centralized and there will be an effort to decentralize it. I think you will have more listings [of stocks] and a better market. They've almost got to have a better market.

DS: Do you want to make a guess on where you think some of the biggest surprises will come over the next five or ten years?

ROBERTSON: I really don't know where they will come from. I think somewhere along the line the very driving force in the world [market] will be the coming together of the Japanese market and the world. We're in a one-world situation, and the Japanese market stands wildly above everything else. We think that it has to be insured against [and it can be] by the purchase of puts. We can buy two-year puts, which are unbelievably cheap [less than 2-percent annual cost]. We'd hedge our portfolio here if we could get anything like that.

You buy these puts and you hope that you never make any money off them, because if the Japanese market were to plunge remarkably, it would kill markets all over the world. So I think that there will be some meeting of valuations between the Japanese market and the rest of the world.

Why should Japan Airlines, which is a very high-cost producer— a very inefficient producer—why should it sell at seventeen times book when it doesn't even make any money, really, when an efficient producer like American Airlines—which if you add back in its Sabre [reservation] system—is selling at roughly book? Why should one sell at seventeen times the other? It just makes no sense—they both own the same [type of planes].

So there will be a coming together of these things. And, hopefully, they will come together with a gentle easing of the Japanese [market] and a gentle ascendancy of ours.

DS: So between the hedge strategy you have in Japan—some long, some short—and the puts, you're net negative [more short positions than long positions].

ROBERTSON: Yes, we are net negative on Japan. No question about that.

DS: And you sound very positive on Europe and reasonably positive on the United States.

ROBERTSON: That's fair to say. I would probably take it for a shorter span than you are asking the question for. I don't think anybody's been willing to bite some of the bullets that need to be bitten over here, and I think we're going to have to do that before we get completely out of the woods. And there are serious problems involving Japan. One of our biggest problems, to my way of thinking, is our dependence on Japan; I don't know whether they're willing to lend for the rest of [their] lives or not. They have all the money in the world but they also, generally speaking, have a very poor standard of living over there.

DS: And they're unstable politically.

ROBERTSON: Extremely It's now rapidly going socialist It's

probably gone from the most capitalistic political system in the world to one of the most socialistic.

DS: Right about now, we're patting ourselves on the back about victory in the cold war and the trend toward capitalism, and yet in Japan, we're seeing, as you say, a trend the other way. In the U.K., the government, which has been in power for ten years, is now behind in the polls—which may or may not mean anything, considering that the opposition has plenty of time to self-destruct. George Bush does not have the same philosophical beliefs about the free market that Ronald Reagan had.

Do you think that, in the 1990s, we'll start to see a shift back to the left, or do you think the momentum to the right is strong enough that the trend toward capitalism can be maintained worldwide? We're certainly seeing it in Eastern Europe, and we're seeing it in the Soviet Union, if not in capitalist countries.

ROBERTSON: I would again expect a coming together. I think that in the countries where capitalism is *not* now very vigorous, it will increase. Certainly in the Soviet Union and China and elsewhere, I expect that it will increase.

I think that in America, though, we're developing a serious problem between the haves and the have-nots. The haves have had it awfully good over the last nine or ten years, and I think there is too large a gap between rich and poor here. There are too many private jets clogging up the airways. And I think that these excesses of spending will have to be curbed, and it will either have to be by political action or something else.

I'm not sure that we're going to allow that law of uncontrolled capitalism to continue, and I'm not sure we should. So I suspect that there will be some controls here, but I think the trend in England is strong, and I suspect that it will continue. I think it'll continue in Europe. Even Mitterrand has become more capitalistic than people thought. The trend is strong but, here, we've almost taken it too far.

DS: Let's touch on [one] manifestation of that: takeovers. Do you think the takeover trend is going to slow down here, even as it picks up in Europe?

ROBERTSON: Very definitely, it will slow down here. On the other hand, our own takeover activity may be replaced by Japanese takeover activity, and actually we've seen great evidence of this in the last two weeks. Columbia Pictures was taken over by Sony. And then we have the Kyocera Corp. takeover of AVX [a U.S. manufacturer of electronic components]. It's the first all-stock takeover that's been done from Japan.

DS: The response to Sony's takeover of Columbia evidently has been very negative.

ROBERTSON: Very negative by whom?

DS: By the public. To some extent, that feeds its way into the regulators. Also, the Japanese are very sensitive about their image.

ROBERTSON: The Japanese are very sensitive about their image—there's no question about that.

DS: So are we seeing the beginning of a new major buyer coming in, or are we seeing almost the beginning of the end of the takeover trend when the new major buyer comes in and he's sufficiently rebuffed that he just stops?

ROBERTSON: I know that the polls show that [the public doesn't] like Japanese takeovers but if we were to stop that, the ramifications are enormous.

DS: But that's what I'm asking. Where do you think it will go?

ROBERTSON: I think it will continue. I don't think they can stop it. I think if they did, it would be a horrible mistake. And I think it's a way for [the Japanese] to get rid of their huge amount of cash. They're paying a million dollars a room for hotels now. They're buying horrible buildings, like the Exxon building, which is full of asbestos, and they're paying a lot for them. I think everybody makes out from that, and I think it's short-sighted of the public to be worried about Sony owning Columbia. I just think that if we were to say, "No more takeovers," it'd be crazy.

Now, the government really isn't acting the way it says. The government is making a big point of talking the dollar down. Not only talking it down, but selling dollars in the market to get the dollar down. If you want to stop [foreign] takeovers, you get the dollar up.*

DS: Two years ago, [Congressman] Rostenkowski tried to put a chill on takeovers, and that was one of the catalysts in the sell-off we had in October of '87. Doesn't [the Japanese buy-out threat] give the

---

*A rising dollar makes U.S. assets more expensive to potential acquirers from other countries.

more liberal side of Congress a strong excuse to try to stop take-overs—not by the free-market approach, but just to stop them by legislation?

ROBERTSON: I would think that would be a very, very difficult thing to do. And a foolish thing to do. I can see fighting over tariffs, but [the Japanese] are spreading the wealth, so to speak, by taking over our companies. I just don't see why we should say, "No, you can't take them over." It's the real world, and we can always na-tionalize them back if we desperately needed them—everybody's done that to us. They're paying too much, and it gets money into our system. I think it's an ideal setup. This is part of my theory of why the markets will come together.

DS: You wrote recently about an idea that you didn't want to touch because you thought [there] might be some inside knowledge. In your own mind, how do you define what is inside information and what is not, since the government has not done a very good job of being clear about it?

ROBERTSON: I couldn't agree with you more on that, and I think that it is a very difficult thing to do.

DS: Where do you draw the line between good insight, good analysis, and inside information?

ROBERTSON: I think the general rule would be: If it comes from the company, and the world does not have access to that infor-mation [and that information was substantive, we should not use it]. Now, I would not have any problem if in our own research, we dis-covered through various department stores around the country that Nintendo suddenly was not selling, and the rest of the world didn't know that. I wouldn't have any compunction about shorting Nin-tendo. But if the executive of Nintendo came in or called me on the phone and said, "Look, we're not selling any Nintendos," I don't think we should use it.

DS: What happens if you're the one that calls—if you pick up the phone and ask a question that maybe is a bit better than the other questions he's been asked?

ROBERTSON: That's where the problems are. You're exactly right. You have to [look at each situation] individually [to determine if the information is confidential and material]. It's a very difficult problem, and it's a very unfair problem. In the real estate business, if someone knew that a road was going through a particular area, they'd go right out and buy all the property they could properly get. And I don't think anybody would ever criticize them. In the securities business, you could be thrown in jail over that.

I really think that someone should bring that out to ameliorate the situation that Wigton, Freeman, and Tabor found themselves in.* Of course [in the case of] Wigton and Tabor, the charges have been dropped, but no apologies have been made, and their lives have been very, very disrupted and hurt. I happen to know Dick Wigton. He's a fine guy, and I think a lesser person, their life would have been ruined. He was strong enough to really handle that, but many people wouldn't be.

DS: You are a value investor. You mentioned about growth rates versus P/E, and you also seem to have a great deal of flexibility. What do you think were the driving factors in what has been one hell of a good decade for you?

ROBERTSON: I think the people that do well in this business are basically sound—there's no genius involved. I think we've taken a sound analytical approach to companies, and we have a big advantage over most of our competition in that we can buy good ones and sell bad ones.

DS: Actually, in the 1980s, your shorts† have probably not been the driving factor in your success.

ROBERTSON: What you've got to realize is that when we go short, that generally enables us to go long more. So if we can just break even on a short in a good market, we're thrilled, because that enables us to go long further.

The fact that we have been able to find these good shorts has enabled us to have a bigger long position. And that, of course, has helped us.

Certainly, the flexibility you talked about [is important]—a willingness to go into new things, which the young people bring to our attention. This year, one of our young people found a fixed-income instrument which yielded about 35 percent to maturity and on the basis of what we thought the maturity would be, was yielding

*Richard Wigton, Robert Freeman, and Timothy Tabor were Wall Street arbitrageurs who were arrested in 1987 on charges of trading on inside information.
†Short positions would have been hurt in a rising market.

over 50 percent. And this was in Hospital Corporation of America—
an essential [company].

Even though we're not experts in bankruptcies, we go into bankruptcies when there are opportunities that exist. [Another factor is the]
willingness not to say, "It's all over, we missed it."

We could have had that tendency in cellular, because these stocks
are up fifty and a hundred times. But the real fact of the matter is that
only about 1 percent of the potential market has been touched in
cellular. Is it over? We don't know. We're going to look at it now.

I think that [willingness to change] helps.

Philip A. Fisher

Phil Fisher has been a pioneer of the concept of long-term investments in exceptional companies. He is the author of one of the most influential books ever written on investing, Common Stocks and Uncommon Profits, *and is a successful portfolio manager himself. A thoughtful and unpretentious man, Fisher is still an active investor after almost sixty years, working out of a surprisingly modest office near Silicon Valley. His insights on the stock market—and his willingness to share them over the decades—have had considerable impact on the investment world.*

DS: You mentioned in *Developing an Investment Philosophy** that, going into the 1980s, you felt that this was potentially one of the three most attractive opportunities you had seen in your career—the 1930s and the late '40s being the other two. You said there were three factors that you felt, if resolved, would lead to a very successful market. One was the debt question, which actually has only gotten worse since. The other was high energy costs. And, in fact, energy costs did come down significantly. And the other was on the political side—the tendency toward the left—which in the 1980s became a strong tendency toward the right. So two of the three concerns that you had were resolved, and, in fact, the market did triple. In looking back on the 1980s, what do you feel were the dominant investment themes?

FISHER: I think some of the things that came out of the decade had good features and bad features. One of the most dominant, which I don't think people were really aware of as the decade started, was the importance and the significance of Japanese competition.

It might be a little bit like Pearl Harbor in its sequence. We suffered one defeat after another, but in due course, became totally victorious. And I think that the unawareness at the beginning of the decade of the very, very major strides the Japanese had made in increased manufacturing efficiency caused us to lose one industry after another—consumer electronics . . . motorcycles . . . you know what they all are.

---

*The Financial Analysts Research Foundation, (Charlottesville, Va. : University of Virginia, 1980). For a copy, send $10 to University of Virginia, P.O. Box 6550, Charlottesville, Virginia 22906.

But various companies began learning something from that and there have been—in the semiconductor industry, for example—sizable, sizable improvements in our manufacturing techniques by a few companies who were able to blend the best of what the Japanese were doing into the American culture: improve employee relations, vastly improve productivity, eliminate waste, and, above all, improve the quality of products. Enormous strides have been made. Some companies are becoming far, far stronger than they ever were, and many others are going to go by the wayside.

This is going to affect, in the 1990s, our whole economy. These are the kinds of things which are changing the face of manufacturing industry and, believe it or not, I see signs that some of these characteristics are going into the ever-growing service industry. I think that all this is forcing a stronger, better American economy.

DS: In line with this, takeovers of the 1980s also were a factor that forced discipline on American industry in the service area, as well as in manufacturing. Do you feel it has been a positive factor?

FISHER: I think it's been more of a negative factor than a positive factor, because so much of it has not been bringing greater efficiency into companies, but looting them. Those that have conducted their affairs prudently and have some surplus cash have been attractive—particularly if they are in lines of business that can be separated from each other so that some of the product lines can be sold to help pay off the debt of taking on and acquiring the company. And those companies which have followed what the Japanese do so successfully—ignore whether you're doing a little better or a little worse this quarter, and spend a lot of money on research that isn't going to pay off for five years, but can have an enormous payoff in the next five years after that—companies that do that have been vulnerable to these birds who come in, kill off long-term developments, and just parcel out the company, ending up with a nice piece of change.

DS: As an investor over the years in high-quality companies that spend a great deal on research and development without an immediate payoff . . . these companies which you invested in usually would sell at premiums to market. But you don't feel that the market has done, over time, a pretty good job of acknowledging those companies that have spent for the future and giving them a higher premium?

FISHER: No. I think that one of the worst effects of the developments of the past decade has been the steadily increasing thinking of the great majority of the investment community not of long-term investment, but ever-shorter range: "How can we buy something this quarter and sell it in a few months to make a profit?"

And I think that there can be a very great charge against those whose job it is to safeguard the American economy, because of presidents who just didn't understand it. There has been no attempt to use the influence of government to fight against the security markets being a Monte Carlo type of affair, instead of a place where people can take their savings—and want to take their savings—to grow over a long period of years, as has happened in Japan.

Now, I think the very success of the Japanese stock market is laying the seeds of its own destruction, because that sort of thing has been overappreciated. You're now getting a speculative froth which is quite dangerous.

But I think it was just appalling that the SEC, particularly, and the supervisory committees in Congress—who were supposed to watch over the affairs of investors—have let this thing go on. I think that this is one of the very ill effects of the 1980s which has not, *as yet,* affected the stock market, but will in time.

DS: At least during the 1980s, don't you feel that [the takeover boom] contributed to the success of the market?

FISHER: It contributed to a rise in prices in some companies short-term; I don't think it contributed to the success of the economy at all. I think the costs of this will come home to roost.

Fortunately, there are companies that in one way or another have been able to ignore this kind of trend, and those companies are developing maybe stronger than they would have otherwise, because they're not having as much competition from companies who can't ignore it. And that will show up in the years ahead.

I think that it has been a contributor to the rise in prices in the averages, but I think that if you go beyond the stock market, to fundamentals, it's been a very vicious development, which I know I didn't foresee at the end of the last decade—and I don't think that very many other people did either—that this sort of thing was coming, or if it did come, that the so-called guardian parts of the government would just ignore it.

DS: In the context of what we've discussed, how do you view the next decade? From the point of view of a common stock investor, are you excited . . . are you worried?

FISHER: When you ask if I'm worried, the answer is overwhelmingly yes. When you ask am I bullish or bearish, that's quite a different thing. I do not subscribe to the overwhelming current view—which would not have been the view fifty years ago at all—that hyperinflation, the kind of thing that we have seen in this last decade in most of the countries of Latin America, and which you saw in the 1920s in France and much more in Germany after World War I, is bearish on the market price of common stocks.

The evidence is overwhelming, in my opinion, that when you get a hyperinflation in the values of the currencies, the strongest stocks go up—not enough to completely equal the depreciation in the value of money, but to offset quite a bit of it.

I feel that the 1990s can be a decade when a lot of chickens will come home to roost.

DS: You're expecting inflation to come back in a big way?

FISHER: The roots of the average voter today are deeply imbedded in "What's in it for me?"—and the evidence of that is overwhelming. Look at the results in Fort Worth of the forced resignation of Speaker Wright. The voters of Fort Worth consider him a hero. Why? Because he brought a lot of bacon home to Fort Worth, and that same [attitude] is true all over the country.

In a situation of that sort, the forces that are going to create imbalance in the budget are bound to overcome the forces that will try and decrease it. The pressure to inflate the currency is just irresistable, and I don't think that's only true in the United States.

Now, I think that there is going to be much more political turmoil—gains by the left and so on—but with all that, I suspect that you are either better off or less worse off in outstandingly run companies than you are in most other forms of wealth.

I don't think you can forecast things precisely. There's an element of luck in it, but my own feeling is that it will be a decade of great turmoil—great mental worry regardless of progress technologically—and it's going to take real intelligence to steer your boat through highly troubled waters.

I think it is just fantastic to try and reach rigid conclusions. I'll give you a couple of examples of that. I attended one of these stock technological conferences, in about 1980. They showed a picture, done in 1940, of how cities would look in 1980. You had people landing on the roofs of big office buildings with helicopters and automobile driveways [spiraling up to the outside of] enormous storied buildings: Nothing of the way it happened.

That reminded me very vividly of a conversation I had had. I happened to meet two extremely intelligent investment men on a corner of Montgomery Street—the Wall Street of San Francisco—just a little bit before I got involved in World War II. The conversation was [about] how quickly this new hydroponic industry—the development of crops with types of water with chemical feeding—was starting to obsolete the business of the big agricultural implement companies—Deere and Harvester and whatnot, which were a much bigger factor in the economy than now. This [development], which a lot of wise people thought was going to be a major change in the face of the economy in the future—a complete change in agriculture—has not developed virtually at all.

I do not think that it is anything but an utter waste of time to be very precise in what the next decade is going to be. The factors are too complicated. I think—and I said this in one of my books—that it is possible, if you know your business and do enough homework, to judge an outstanding company from a run-of-the-mill company with 90 percent precision.

I don't think that any amount of work in judging what the general market is going to do about these broad influences is anything but futile, because there are too many variables, and the most brilliant guy in the world might have a 55 percent batting average against a 90 percent batting average otherwise. That's why it's a waste of time to spend too much time worrying about that. It's better to spend your time and energy on the thing you can do, not the thing that can't be done.

DS: You mentioned earlier the analogy of World War II. One of the big factors which helped us eventually beat the Japanese, oddly enough, was the fact that our technology was so superior. You have been identified with technology over the years, and it's been an interesting evolution—you've seen every stage of it, from the '30s, when there was very little research and development during the Depression, to the '40s, when there was tremendous research and development because of the war—

FISHER: I can go before that. There was a man by the name of Baker who was Secretary of War for Woodrow Wilson. At the beginning of our going into World War I, he received a letter from a man stating that he was a chemist and he would like to volunteer his services wherever they would be of the most use to this country. And he got a very polite letter back thanking him for his patriotism but that the War Department and the Army already had a chemist.

That shows you how things have changed. And I think this trend will continue. The people who feel that technological things are just too complicated for them to understand or invest in are ignoring the fact that more and more businesses are having technology—I hate that word because it's so imprecise—affect how they do things and the way they do things more and more. Whether it's a food manufacturer or a retailer or somebody in the magazine or newspaper business, technology is a bigger and bigger factor in what they're doing. And this is just going to continue.

DS: When we think about the concept of innovations in manufacturing, where do you see the greatest potential for the next decade?

FISHER: It's going to be through technology that we learn to do things better, no matter what industry you're in. And, by industry, I'm using that in the broadest sense. Regardless of what type of activity you or your company are endeavoring to serve the public, technology will play a bigger and bigger part, and it's coming in the service fields just as it came in the manufacturing field.

DS: You had said in an earlier piece that the 1980s would be the golden age for semiconductors. Looking back on the '80s and looking towards the '90s—being here in Silicon Valley—how does the outlook seem?

FISHER: I think the competitive pace will get faster. These are such obvious things: The demand for the product will go up, the price of the product will go down, and the companies that are very, very good will get better, and the companies that aren't will gradually fade from the picture. And that's no different from the course of that industry since it started.

DS: Back in the '50s, you were very excited about the potential for the introduction of semiconductors. Would you say, in retrospect, that the 1980s were as much a golden age as you had expected they would be?

FISHER: Look at the charts as to how [technology] has grown.

DS: Over time, you've introduced the idea that consumer franchises would be a worthwhile area for investment. Initially you were more focused on companies with a competitive edge across manufacturing and research and development. How did that evolve, your interest in the consumer franchise?

FISHER: It's the same thing. I don't think there's an enormous difference there than in manufacturing. Where you can do something that everybody and his brother can't, you've got something. Where you do something that everybody and his brother can do—such as running a chain of fried chicken shops—you've only got something if you can do it distinctly better, which means that everybody and his brother can't. And I don't think there's anything different in the franchise business than there is in running a factory.

My son, Ken, who writes a column for *Forbes,* phrases this pretty well when he says he likes to invest in the company that has an unfair edge. By unfair, he doesn't mean morally unfair; he means something that other people can't duplicate. Now, that may come from any one of a half-dozen different reasons. It may be because once you have built up a particular line of service, you're drawing on a data base—you're serving virtually the entire market, and it would just be too big a capital cost for somebody else to try and duplicate that after your business has grown for a number of years. That might be one way.

Another way is that, in the technological and manufacturing area, he who has, gets. If you're in the forefront and you're rapidly changing the technology and you keep the alertness of your research people, your competitor is shooting against a moving target. He has to rush to get into the campground that you used last night, whereas you're in the next night's campground. I think the significant part of the art of investment is finding the situation where a company has this kind of an edge, and a management which recognizes that edge won't be permanent unless they keep improving themselves, and therefore they keep that edge.

DS: Sometimes people will say they invest, then they investigate.

You have highlighted the importance of knowing what it is you're buying, first of all through the competitors, the suppliers, the customers, the people who are still there, the people who are no longer there—

FISHER: And I still make some mistakes.

DS: Yes, even having gone through all the thorough research—

FISHER: I'm proud of my batting average, but I've made a few investments that I've been ashamed of.

DS: When you look at the rest of the investment world—Wall Street in particular—do you feel that the analysis there is the kind that you would like to see on a company you were investing in?

FISHER: No, by and large. Now, there are some sharp exceptions to that. There are some people in Wall Street whose comments about a company or an industry I would pay great attention to. But, by and large, Wall Street has to please the customer, even though Wall Street has played a great part in giving the customer, let's say, taste for non-nutritious food that tickles the palate as it goes down and looks nice—rude analogy, but I think it's valid. And so much of Wall Street effort is focused on what, fundamentally, I feel doesn't matter—who's going to do better in the next three months?—than on the things that make a major difference in the change in the value of a person's holdings. I don't think that much of Wall Street's brain is focused on where the really big profits can be made.

DS: Would you say that the primary thing that Wall Street gives short shrift to is the importance of management?

FISHER: Not verbally but fundamentally. I don't think they spend as much time in regard to it. It is not a question that can be answered with accuracy, yes or no—it's a question of degree. Do I think enough people in Wall Street give enough attention to it? No. Do I think that most people in Wall Street ignore it? Also no. Now in between there's a gray area that varies with each individual.

DS: You've written that 80 percent of your best ideas come from a network of people that you have a very high respect for. The average investor out there hasn't the network, and they certainly don't have the time or the skills that you have to investigate companies. So for the average person out there who is interested in investing in common stocks, how do you recommend they go about it?

FISHER: I wish I knew the right answer to that. All that I can say is to get imbued with the right goals and then invest your money in things which you can know something about. Maybe things that are local. People who are in various lines of business have a good edge in knowing which are the people—among their suppliers, their competitors, the customers—who handle themselves right.

But it is not easy to make really big money out of investing, and with the kind of money that can be made, there's no reason it should be easy. It isn't a free lunch. You've got to put the effort into it.

DS: You pointed out ten years ago that you were concerned about the loss of investor confidence in the stock market, and the dangerous implications that had for the country, since the stock market is a method for raising capital. We're ten years later, and the market has gone up, but it has done it in the context of volatility. If we look towards the next decade, are you still as concerned . . . about the state of investor confidence?

FISHER: I would say that investor confidence is distinctly worse. It has gotten worse for reasons which to me are very understandable. I'm not so sure that that's any indication that it will continue to get worse or continue to get better. I think that will depend on things which are essentially unpredictable.

DS: You've said the SEC has shifted things from, [in the] 1920s, dishonest croupiers out there taking people's money, to honest croupiers—which is better, but implies that the small investor is still at a disadvantage in the market. Where do you see the disadvantage, and where do you think there should be a change in that?

FISHER: I think that our tax structure should develop into a way that encourages long-term investment rather than discourages it. I am a very, very strong believer in lower capital gains tax rates. I think the weakness is that, under the viciousness of politics, the capital gains tax was distorted to placate various interests in the financial business. For example, the idea that holding a stock for six months should make it a long-term capital gain is ridiculous.

Many years ago, we had here in California a capital gains tax where the tax rate was fairly low for those things that were held for ten years, somewhat higher for those things that were held for five, and I think only kicked in after two. That kind of approach makes real sense.

Another type of approach that might make real sense that nobody has talked about would be to [assess] a very much lower rate of tax on capital gains that are, within a very short period of time, reinvested in the same class of assets—common stocks to common stocks. A higher rate—but still a discount for capital gains that occur—for putting it into a form of savings bonds or bank account. But no capital gains reduction for what is spent for buying a car, or personal living and whatnot.

If we could build up a bank of personal savings in this country in the way that the Japanese have done, interest rates for productive activities might be at 3 or 4 percent as against the present 10 percent on up for industry. We would have a very much stronger economy.

I do not see much sense in the kind of capital gains tax that we had before, of holding a stock for six months and calling it a long-term gain. Nor do I see any possible reason—other than the purely political one of getting that many more supporters for what you want to do—to include, of all things, collectibles. Eliminating real estate from the capital gains tax would be productive because an overwhelming percentage of the illegitimate tax shelters . . . work through the real estate field.

I'm very much afraid that this whole matter of capital gains is going to be a political football for decades to come and there is nothing worse than having uncertainty on this sort of thing. And the fact that one Congress can't bind the next Congress makes it very difficult for the disadvantage to disappear.

DS: The government has been ambiguous about what exactly is inside information. Where does the individual investor draw the line between good, in-depth research and proprietary information?

FISHER: Everybody has to judge that for themselves. There is no sharp line. It's my own opinion that there should be a very short list of things which are inside information. Such things as receipt, or high probability of receipt, of a very big contract—big enough in relation to the company to affect the price of the stock; sales and earnings for the immediate accounting period before that is made public; and possibly two or three other things.

Beyond that, I think all that you're doing is both encouraging ignorance and encouraging managements that want to conceal things from their stockholders, by this vague idea of what is and what isn't inside information. I think this is just one of many areas where the regulatory authorities have been negligent.

The overwhelming number of people that get appointed to the SEC are lawyers. No attention is paid as to whether they really understand the investment process. I don't think anybody should be appointed to the SEC who hasn't made a definite record of success in handling his own investments. I think that there are plenty of people who can be found around the country who would have the knowledge to be good SEC commissioners.

Instead of which they appoint lawyers. And lawyers are people who live in an atmosphere where you make rules about a thing. Scientists are people who understand that you've got to understand how nature works, [that] just passing a fiat doesn't cause liquids to go uphill. I'm not accusing the people that have been SEC commissioners over the years of being anything but well-intentioned, but I think they're selected from a group that doesn't understand the problems.

I think that the failure to have a few clear-cut rules on what is inside information may be for the long-range good, because you get the job pretty well done with, say, five things, and you can bet your boots that—human nature being what it is—somebody will come along crusading for a sixth thing. And, in the course of five or eight years, instead of having five things, you've got fifty things, and now you're in a strait jacket. So maybe there's no solution to the problem.

DS: One generality: People tend to make what turns out to be their best investments, in retrospect, when they were the least confident. In reading your material over the years, I get a sense that when you're ready to step up, there is not a great crisis of confidence, that you're actually very positive.

FISHER: I have a tendency to go into stocks somewhat as I would go into a swimming pool on a cold day. Dip the toe in and go in slowly. It's not until a year after you've married a girl that you really know what she's like. And the same thing is true of investments.

Living with a management will show you over a period of years. Again, I'm talking about myself; I'm not sure that the average investor is in a position to do this, because he can't spend enough time with the management—either his own time or the management can't spend their time endlessly talking with investors. There is no business that doesn't run into trouble at times. That's how you tell the men from the boys—how they handle it.

I'll say that in the initial investment, usually the worst ones I have made have been after I've been highly successful for a few years. Unconsciously, the guard tends to go down and the speed of action tends to go up.

I think it is inevitable in my business to make some errors, and it's got to be allowed for in calculating the end results of net profit for me or my clients, just the same way that depreciation or the electric bill or something else has to be counted for as a business expense.

DS: You came into the business in 1928. You caught the end of that boom. You started your own business in 1932 at the bottom—

FISHER: No. March '31—pretty close.

DS: You've seen all the ups and downs over the last sixty years in the market as an active participant. What would you say is the best piece of advice that you've been given along the way?

FISHER: There are so many things I could quote. One of the wisest men I ever knew, who is no longer on this earth, said, "Nothing is black or white. It's various shades of gray."

Another one might be to never forget that nothing is permanent in the way of the world, and particularly in the economic world. Change is constant, and be constantly aware of managements as to how they're adjusting.

Another one might be to thoroughly understand the fundamentals so that you at least are setting yourself on the right course and not stubbing your toes by spending your time and energy on things that don't matter. That's not a fair statement—by things that matter less, rather than those that matter more.

Another one that comes to mind immediately is that the very bedrock of successful investment is complete honesty from people who are managing your funds. And, by honesty, I just don't mean that they won't steal, but a couple of other things. Second, that they are honest with you in talking about their situation; but, overwhelmingly first, that they're honest with themselves in sizing up the situation and don't see [only] what they want to see.

Stanley Salvigsen and Michael Aronstein

*Comstock Partners is not your typical money manager. Although lo-
cated in the heart of Wall Street, the firm has a relaxed atmosphere and
a very unusual point of view. Throughout the 1980s, Salvigsen and
Aronstein focused on the debilitating consequences of excessive debt
accumulation on our economy and its markets (see "The Dance of
Debt," p. 213). They believe that this thesis will be the dominant investment theme of the '90s, which would bode well for high-quality
bonds and poorly for almost everything else.*

DS: Your success has been driven very much by your economic
forecast, which, by and large, has been correct. You've highlighted
the negative implications for the country from the love affair that it
has had with debt over the last several decades, particularly during
the '80s. I thought two of the most interesting points you had made
were that the growth rate of debt has been running ahead of the
growth rate of the country and that the cost of debt has exceeded the
realistic return you could get on the money you were borrowing—
two conditions which are not sustainable. Now, for the 1990s, given
where we are right now, how does the U.S. economy look to you?

SALVIGSEN: In the 1980s, we reversed the sort of things that
were going on in the '70s. You had a lot of oil inflation, COLAs [cost
of living adjustments] were getting put into [labor] contracts, and you
were ramping up inflationary expectations. The 1980s were the reverse of that. In the '80s, while you were getting lower inflationary
expectations worked in, the big excess has been the acceleration in
the use of credit. The '90s will probably have some reversal of that.

In order to lighten up or lessen the debt burden, there has to be
a fairly sluggish growth period, almost by definition. The sluggishness
will lower inflationary expectations, and there will also be more of
the defaults and liquidations we have seen starting in the 1980s.
There's going to be some real growth, but if you look at inflation plus
real growth, our numbers look very light—very soft.

ARONSTEIN: We're still running abnormally high inflation
rates if you take a long-term prospective, but compared to what the
money is needed for—particularly in terms of debt service—it's too
low. So you may go through a whole decade during which your

growth rates return to more normal levels, which basically means no inflation. But with the debt burden still out there, it argues for pretty nasty times financially.

So the financial side of the economy may be sort of the albatross in here that prevents the physical side from moving as rapidly as it might move—you have all of these problems that are really clogging up the pipelines. The wheels of commerce have a little sand on them now, and the more the financial system gets bogged down in trying to reallocate assets and liabilities according to reality, the slower things will go, the harder it will be for the part of the system that really should be funded and should be advancing to get going.

DS: So basically what it comes down to is: You borrow too much and you have to pay it back. And paying it back is going to keep the economy from growing, and it may take us from the inflation of the '70s to the disinflation of the '80s to—

ARONSTEIN: Active deflation [declining prices]. You might have a lot of instances of active deflation in the '90s. We feel like the real estate problem is something that's going to be around for another decade or so.

DS: To touch on the real estate—you've highlighted in the last year or so concerns about real estate, particularly now in the Northeast. You've said that there has been [widespread] confidence from both borrowers and lenders and, accordingly, there has been too much borrowing and too much lending. [Also, you've noted] that implied in a great deal of building [projects] are capital gains, which in your mind won't happen.

ARONSTEIN: We think capital gains are generally an accidental occurrence that people very rarely anticipate. Ex post facto they are easy to explain. "Oh yes, we had a big demographics bulge. Yes, the city returned to favor and there was a big supply problem with housing in the city, so urban property got very expensive. Yes, we had a capital boom, so the capital-owning class of society got extremely wealthy, and we have a lot more people who could spend money on really lavish quarters."

DS: Even within real estate, it has never been monolithic. Now it's the Northeast in trouble; before, the area we read the most about was the Southwest. As we go into the 1990s, what would you tell the average investor? Would you say, "Well, if you live in this area, I would recommend this idea," or would you just say that real estate is not the place to be?

ARONSTEIN: We've never regarded [real estate]—at least for the past five years—as something somebody should consider as an investment. It's not an investment, it's a utility. It's part of the necessary capital goods of one's life; it's not in classical terms what you would call an investment. In hindsight, it turned out that it would have been an investment, but if you think of the people that really made a lot of money in ownership of single-family homes, most of [their profit] was purely accidental. They didn't go into it with the idea that was going to happen. It was kind of the classic value case: They were affordable, people bought them, and they became less affordable for a wide number of factors.

DS: You have to live in a house, so it really comes down to a question of whether you are going to own your house or rent your house. You have mentioned in the past that a pretty good rule of thumb is: three times your income is about as much as you should be paying, on average, for a mortgage. And by that standard, most people in the Northeast could not afford to buy their own homes.

ARONSTEIN: That's true on both coasts—all up and down.

DS: So there's nothing sacred about owning a house; if you can rent it at a better after-tax cost—

ARONSTEIN: Which you can anywhere within 200 miles of New York or Los Angeles, and it's not even close. There's nothing wrong with spending money to satisfy your personal needs, but what we're talking about is the ability to afford that sort of self-gratification. A lot of people own homes for that reason—because they want to own a home—which is fine. But we would say they can't afford to own the home that they're in unless the assumption is that it is going to go up 10 percent a year for the next twenty years.

DS: And, as long as everybody has that assumption, it won't happen.

ARONSTEIN: No, because it's hard to imagine that there are big segments of the population that haven't figured out that people have gotten wealthy owning homes. It's been going on for thirty years.

SALVIGSEN: I think the general answer to your question is, if we take real estate as an asset class that you could invest your money in—as opposed to, say, bonds or stocks—we'd say we would definitely underweight or have minimal amounts committed to that as an investment theme. If [you] push me and say, "You mean there's not going to be any place to make money?" I'd say, "Of course there will be." It's just that it will be much, much harder to make money; you won't get the big mark-up in value like you had been getting in Northeast real estate or in the stock market in the last six years. You just had to be in front of it. In stocks, you just had to be there. Selecting was almost secondary for most of that time.

ARONSTEIN: Just remaining invested was the whole game.

SALVIGSEN: So, in that sense, we would say that we would prefer to have little exposure to real estate over the next decade.

DS: How about other asset classes? Why don't we start with one of your favorites: bonds.

SALVIGSEN: Treasury bonds.

DS: [Concerning] high-yield bonds: In the 1980s, they have served you well as an owner and, so far, the companies that have sold them have done well. You don't expect that to continue, and I assume when you read of the recent problems with Campeau and Hooker and Integrated Resources, you think that we're starting to reach that inflection point where—

ARONSTEIN: Interest rates anywhere near double digits are not sustainable. Over time, compound interest is going to overwhelm.

People that have been successful were the people in first, who were able to dispose of aspects of their acquisitions by giving them to somebody who was able to releverage. The people who are in at the early stages of a chain letter make a lot of money.

But now what's happening is—as it has spread out—you have dozens of deals in the pipeline that depend upon somebody else being able to buy a division or two or three, in order to make the deals work.

DS: You mention a chain letter, which is a second cousin to a Ponzi scheme, essentially. Is that how you view what's going on in the LBO game and high-yield bonds?

ARONSTEIN: Sure. I don't believe any of these companies, if you stopped the music right now and things had to stay as they are— the capital structures and the operating structures—would be able to fulfill the terms of their long-term debt covenants over five or ten years. Half the deals out there admit as much in the prospectus.

DS: High-yield bonds are now selling about 600 basis points (six percentage points) above Treasuries. Do you still expect them to go to about 1,000 basis points?

ARONSTEIN: Yes, and part of it will be the [yield on] Treasuries coming down.

SALVIGSEN: It may take another cycle, but I think [the spread] will get larger and larger.

DS: Do you see that as a combination of Treasury yields coming down and high yields going up?

SALVIGSEN: More the Treasury [yields] coming down. We don't think you've got to drive [high-yield bond rates] up a whole lot higher.

DS: Well, if you eliminate inflation in the '90s, you will basically be driving up the real rate.

ARONSTEIN: Right.

SALVIGSEN: It's like the 1930s, where we saw [yields on] corporates—the lower-grade corporates—actually go up and the [rates on] T-bonds go down. In the beginning of the decade, you had maybe a one-point difference between the yield on the Treasuries and the corporates, and, by the end of the '30s, a difference of four or five or six hundred basis points in some issues.

ARONSTEIN: And those are the ones that survived.

SALVIGSEN: No record of the ones that didn't.

ARONSTEIN: So I think high-yield bonds are sort of like stocks with unrealistic dividend policies, where the people own them only for the dividend. [But] no enterprise on earth grows at 15 or 16 percent for a long period of time, and nothing ever has.

DS: Do you think that high-yield bonds have served a positive purpose—in terms of the takeovers of the 1980s—bringing a certain amount of discipline to managements that otherwise may not have been at risk?

ARONSTEIN: I don't think that it mattered one way or the other. It certainly has given management something to worry about, but good versus bad management is inconsequential. Price has not stopped anybody. A high stock price has not really stopped any of the deals. Some of these things are going out at three times, four times the price the stock was selling at two years ago.

DS: Can you argue that it's a good idea that has gone wrong? Originally, there were reasonable valuations paid in takeovers. It's only been in the last several years that it has fed on itself.

SALVIGSEN: The [deals] that have been done more recently are less well-off, largely because of the price tags. At the beginning of the decade, activity was so small but even by '82 or '83, the price you were paying for assets wasn't generally bad. The last two or three years they've paid huge prices.

Theoretically, it makes the management work harder, or whatever, but it seems like you put the companies in a very bad [position]. If you are in an oligopoly, competing with two or three others who have not leveraged up, the others can really put it to you in a competitive price war, because they don't have that burden.

ARONSTEIN: They don't have that constant ticking of the interest bill.

If you look at the last fifteen years—and particularly in the last ten—there has been a tremendous liberalization of access to credit. Fifteen or twenty years ago, you really had to be in a certain sort of loop in order to go into a lending institution and have capital raised for you. You had to play golf with the guys. You had to have the same tailor. You had to have gone to St. Paul's and Yale.

A guy running a medium-sized business who had big ideas just had no access to capital, whereas the treasurer of a Fortune 50 company would just come in and have lunch with his investment banker at the Union Club and the next day decide that he wanted one or two or three hundred million dollars in bonds sold.

I think the change—opening it up—is good, but what I really object to is the source of the money. It comes from places where people are not really forced to bear risk [savings and loans in particular] because it's somebody else's money. And that to me was the sort of distortion and perversion in this whole thing.

DS: I'd like to talk about the major asset class, from most people's point of view. What do you think about stocks in the next ten years, given your outlook on the world? Underweight them? Overweight them?

SALVIGSEN: There are going to be periods when they are good buys, but, point to point, I'd probably underweight them slightly. Not as badly as real estate. And I'd overweight Treasury bonds and underweight lower-grade corporate issues.

Everybody talks about how much stock has been bought back—the big shrinkage of shares outstanding. I would think that in the '90s you will see [equities] brought back out again.

ARONSTEIN: It's the answer to the overleverage. What does that make equity worth, if you are going to dilute the share base by that much over the next ten years? I don't care when you do it.

DS: So what you're saying is that over the next ten years, you're looking for a shortage of bonds—

SALVIGSEN: Of a higher quality.

ARONSTEIN: High quality non-callable bonds, and there are very few of them [primarily Treasury bonds.] And plenty of stock to go around. The oil shortage was amusing enough as a concept when you could look out the window and see the tankers sitting in the harbor in 1980 and '81, full. But shortage of paper, that's a real knee-slapper. Stock certificates are pretty easy to come by.

DS: Are there any industries that you think will be particularly interesting over the next decade? The airline group would be an interesting example of a real dog that, because of the structural change in the system, has taken off. Do you see that kind of thing happening anywhere else?

ARONSTEIN: The fundamental corollary to this financial condition we're talking about is lots of competition in a really free market, which very few companies are really exposed to now. The airlines got their feet wet—or up to their necks wet—with deregulation. Which was another way of saying they were going to have to operate in a free market. They went through nine years of that. And the remaining companies not only survived, but they turned out to be pretty well-run operations that had changed their way of doing business dramatically.

I think a lot of industries that have been apart from the free market for a variety of reasons, either due to labor constraints or government regulations—maybe things like the railroads, communications, utilities—when they go through that [competition] you will weed out an awful lot of the structural inefficiencies. While it's going on, it will be terribly painful. The airline industry was a pretty good reminder of that. It was a pretty doggy industry for a long time.

DS: Things worked out pretty well for the survivors, eventually, but there was this bloodbath in between.

ARONSTEIN: Sure. Efficiency sounds like a pleasant word [when] discussing economics, but not if you happen to be the target. If you are one of the elements of inefficiency, it's awful.

DS: It's the difference between a recession and a depression—a recession is when someone you know is fired, a depression is when you're fired.

ARONSTEIN: Yes. It's who it happens to.

DS: Going back to the debt [question]. Where in your thought process did you start to say that this really is the key economic and investment issue?

SALVIGSEN: It started in late '79, early '80, when rates hadn't gotten to their peak yet but were starting to get into the double-digit range. You really had to go back to the Civil War to see anything like that, so 10 percent looked incredible.

At 10 percent, you were starting to get into a range that was getting competitive with what stocks could do. Even though these were two completely different animals in the balance sheet, they started getting competitive.

That prompted more retrospective research, looking at how other inflations had come and gone in American history, and what were some of the early warning signals that inflation was, in fact, going to decelerate. I found out that the advent of very high real interest rates was one of the precursors to sustained low inflation, and liquidations of problem areas, and declining nominal rates.

Along the way our understanding of these problems has grown. We've lived with the concept almost a decade now, and it's amazing how few people still think we're right.

ARONSTEIN: Yeah. It still seems to people that this is a very fringe way of approaching things. We are both very convinced that when you want to analyze any investment opportunity or market economy, you really have to concentrate on price.

SALVIGSEN: It makes a great difference.

ARONSTEIN: It's the key determinant of trends . . . it is a big thing that has changed about credit, since we've never been through a sustained period in this country—or any industrialized country—where credit has come at this kind of cost for the broad sectors of the economy. There are always people that had to go to a dark alley and borrow money that way at two points a week, but we've sort of gotten into that on a national basis.

DS: One of the great mistakes of investors is when they start saying, "This time it's different." But when you looked at the economy in the post-war period, when the government started to take an active role in the economy—and the government can print money at cost—why didn't you two say, "This time it may be different. This time we may be on our way to a [serious] inflation?"

ARONSTEIN: The government did the same thing after the Civil War—the whole greenback era. That was a response to deflation, or the potential for serious deflation. People have tried all kinds of anti-deflationary fiscal and monetary tactics for centuries.

SALVIGSEN: We can find a lot of things that are different, but human nature doesn't change, really, over time.

ARONSTEIN: That's a constant.

SALVIGSEN: So the manifestation of these excesses or deeply ingrained beliefs show up in the same way as they did long ago. What's different is that, maybe, this problem is much worse than ever before, because you have exaggerated the excess by all the safety nets that were put in place during the last depression—those safety nets [such as deposit insurance at S&Ls] where the government stepped up and said, "We'll guarantee this, this, and this." That's coming home to roost here, and the cost of that is very high.

ARONSTEIN: In order to accomplish an inflation, you have to have somebody suffer from it. Otherwise, there would be no relative change in the burden or benefit. People who lent money to the government suffered for forty years. From 1941 to 1981, interest rates went from 2 percent to 15 [percent] at the long end.

SALVIGSEN: And inflation went up.

ARONSTEIN: You don't have a big class of people whose burden may be increased [by inflation] to smooth out the financial difficulties in the rest of society.

DS: What's the driving factor of hyperinflation in Brazil or Argentina?

ARONSTEIN: They have high real interest rates. I wouldn't call what's going on there "hyperinflation." Take a look at Mexico. The overnight deposit rate—even with the currency devaluation—has been sufficient to keep capital owners ahead of the cost of living.

DS: You say that the best single asset that the small investor can be in is a long-term Treasury bond. Yet, if we do get into a situation where inflation became a major factor, the person who is rolling over a Treasury bill might survive, but the person who owns a Treasury bond from January 1, 1990, would be murdered.

ARONSTEIN: Yes.

DS: And it's happened in other economies but you don't think it could happen in the United States?

ARONSTEIN: The reason it's happened in those other economies is through the currency mechanism. We still happen to be one of the reserve [currencies]—and maybe *the* reserve currency—in the world.

DS: You've suggested, though, that the yen was becoming the reserve currency.

ARONSTEIN: No. We said that there's a possibility that through the end of the cycle—maybe in a decade or more—the yen might emerge the same way the dollar did during the Second World War and replaced sterling, or stood alongside it. But you look at a history of the '30s, and the money fled right back to sterling when things got nasty in the United States.

We had the potential; this country was a good bet then. Japan has no land mass, no defense, and maybe in this day and age, that's not really germane. Maybe it is becoming more a world without the border problems, without the lack of access—with all the electronic transmission of capital and data, maybe Tokyo is just like Los Angeles, only a long swim. That might be true. But it takes a very long time.

DS: You have pointed out that the process of getting our house in order with debt is not going to be as quick and as painful as the '29 through '32 deflation. But the other side of the coin is that it will last longer. How long do you think the process will last before we're back into an accumulation phase again?

SALVIGSEN: We haven't stopped accumulating—so we haven't even gotten to that stage of it—but I think it will take a generation.

ARONSTEIN: Next generation.

DS: So if we sat down ten years from now . . .

ARONSTEIN: I think you'd be halfway through it. A whole attitude is going to arise with respect to debt very similar to the attitude that arose with respect to stocks after the '30s. It wasn't really until the late 1960s that people started with stocks again in a significant way. That was thirty-seven, thirty-eight years from the nadir of the last problem. And people don't like to hear that. They'd rather hear that it will be over in six months and back to their old way of living.

SALVIGSEN: You can't clean up something like this [quickly]—it's taken a whole generation and a half, two generations, to build up.

DS: It's the Kondratieff Theory of a fifty-year cycle—that's about two generations. It takes two generations to make the same mistakes.

ARONSTEIN: Yeah, it kind of fits that way. People tend not to make the same mistakes as their parents but the same as their grandparents. It makes some sense.

DS: Do you view [the market] as a level playing field for the individual investor? What would you want to change, from taxation to regulation?

SALVIGSEN: The tools available to individual investors are a lot greater than there have ever been before. There are a lot of shows on the subject where they're not only getting information from Wall Street directly—they're getting it from magazines . . . interviews with professionals on cable shows . . . on radio shows—so there is a lot of cross-filtering and cross-checking of ideas.

[Individual investors] seem to have also chosen to put their money into packaged products. They still have the element of risk in choosing the right asset class, and once they've made that choice, the right manager. But still there's a certain comfort in diversifying.

ARONSTEIN: Very few people can actually earn money simply by utilizing their own judgment. And what we're talking about in investing is earning monetary rewards from the use of judgment as opposed to hard physical labor.

It's much more common sense than anybody cares to admit. But Wall Street has turned into such a marketing mechanism, such a consumer products industry.

DS: So you don't feel there is any need for changing regulations or changing taxation?

ARONSTEIN: Taxation ought to be blind to the method by

which money is made [Tax rates should be the same on salary, dividends, and capital gains]. The marketplace does sort it out over time. And the worst abuses have come from distortions of tax policy that had no reason other than to promote a certain class of asset or certain method of behavior economically. But, immediately upon doing that, they became abused. There is no limit to the degree to which people will abuse things that were intended for benign purposes.

Disclosure, I think, is inadequate. As much as is required in a prospectus—and we've had to do a couple of them—the plain fact is that nobody reads them. The retail people don't. And there's a lot of stuff out there that seems intentionally deceptive.

DS: How would you change it?

ARONSTEIN: I'd probably make a short-form disclosure statement necessary with any kind of new product you issue—just the highlights.

DS: To wrap things up here, what's the best piece of advice either of you have ever been given?

SALVIGSEN: They used to say, "Check your answers over twice" when you took a test. I think this business is that way, too. I don't know how many times we've checked out answers on this theme that we're on with bonds. You should try to test your point of view against other things that you hold to be true to see if it holds up.

That's not a very profound answer, but being careful and thorough, in trying to think these things out, helps. It certainly gives you deeper conviction about how much of your resources you're willing to commit toward a certain thing. The more you've tested it and the more you've lived with it . . . your willingness to be more heavily entrenched in that investment increases.

Buyer beware is a good—

ARONSTEIN: Remember that life goes on, that nothing is ever as extreme as it may look. Because anything that seems contrary to the current tide of opinion at first glance seems quite extreme. But life does go on. The history of the world has been an oscillation between extremes. Don't get too excited about things going up a lot or down a lot. They do normally, and it doesn't mark the end or the beginning or a cataclysm—it's just part of the process.

That and patience, which is the hardest thing in this business, because every day someone wants some profound comment about what today's occurrences mean in the long run.

Also, I think you get into trouble when you assume the things that are clear to you—that you can just see for some reason, that may be a matter of your perspective or your emotional posture—are as accessible to other people. To us, the bond case for nine years has seemed as obvious as looking at the subway system and saying, "You know, if they don't fix this, it's going to fall down."

SALVIGSEN: But other people who look at it say, "I don't understand how they find any value in those bonds at these prices." That's because their perspective of what's turning this world is different from ours.

ARONSTEIN: It tends to make you discouraged when things don't happen as quickly as you would think they would happen. And that's why just sticking to things where you have not only some conviction, but some intellectual basis—and assuming that the market will gravitate toward the fundamentals at some point—is the only way to do it. But it makes for very boring viewing from the outside. To people who watch us, it looks like we don't do anything, other than keep writing about how this whole scenario works over a long period of time, and once in a while buying and selling bonds. But . . .

Conclusions

These five outstanding investors all have well-reasoned outlooks for the 1990's—but they don't agree on several important issues.

Stocks are the first choice of Templeton, Fisher, and Robertson, while Salvigsen and Aronstein prefer high-quality bonds. Their attitudes toward stocks are consistent with their expectations for inflation. The first three believe that inflation will rise, perhaps significantly, in coming years. Salvigsen and Aronstein, on the other hand, project that inflation may be replaced by deflation—accordingly, they recommend Treasury bonds (after all, deflation would reduce interest rates and increase bond prices, but only for those bonds that can maintain their interest payments in the dismal economic times they forecast).

Fisher's focus in on the shares of exceptional U.S. companies; Robertson's top choices are in the European and U.S. stock markets, while Templeton favors the markets of the United States, Canada, Hong Kong, and New Zealand. Both Robertson and Templeton are negative on the Japanese stock market, which is hardly surprising given that its P/E ratio is *five times* that of the U.S. market.

As for general advice, these professionals suggest that you avoid extremes, remain flexible, and make certain that you know what you're buying. Be right, then be patient.

There is little disagreement among the five on what it takes to be successful. In forecasting the future, however, differences of opinion are inevitable—historians have a much easier job than investors since they get to do their analysis looking backward. "Very few people can actually earn money simply by utilizing their own judgment," Mike Aronstein points out. As an investor, you have to decide whether you are willing to make the effort to be one of the few, or whether you are better off using what you know to find an exceptional money manager to make the decisions for you.

PART IV

Deeper Into the Market

"There's no cause for panic, Mrs. Munson, but, frankly, there are certain indicators that cannot be ignored."

Drawing by Chas. Addams © 1979
The New Yorker Magazine, Inc.

CHAPTER 9

Timing Your Investments: The Indicators

I bought stocks like they were going out of style.
And then they did.

—advertisement

The first two parts of this book focused on market realities and investment strategies. Part III then looked at the financial community and the investment outlook. In this chapter and in the next, we'll examine the market in greater detail before considering some general conclusions on investing.

The indicators provided here are designed to tell you when the stock market is an attractive investment and when it is not. They fall into three categories: monetary, sentiment, and trend. Some of them are easily quantified; others are downright esoteric.

If you choose to invest in mutual funds or low P/E stocks, you can use these indicators for timing your buy and sell decisions. Ignore any indicator that you find confusing.

Monetary Indicators

Monetary indicators are the most important of the three categories. They include various measures designed to value the market and to determine whether or not financial conditions in the economy are favorable for stocks.

Stocks Versus Bonds

This is the premier monetary indicator, measuring the attractiveness of the stock market relative to the bond market. You should compare the earnings yield of the S&P 400 (latest two years) to the yield of the long-term Treasury bond. (See Chapter 6.) If the earnings yield exceeds the bond yield, then stocks are an excellent choice, particularly if the yield is above 10 percent.

The Discount Rate Rule

Increases and decreases in the discount rate—the interest rate that the Federal Reserve charges its member banks to borrow money—tend to be a reliable indication of monetary tightness or ease. The Fed, once having signaled its preference by changing this largely symbolic rate, will arguably maintain its policy for some time. And faster growth in money is conducive to bull markets—the more money there is to buy goods and services and investments, the greater the benefit to the shares of the underlying companies.

This rule, popularized by stock market analyst Marty Zweig, works as follows:

1. A *cut* in the discount rate is a strongly *positive* signal for the next year; each subsequent cut extends that bullish time frame by an additional six months.
2. An *increase* in the rate is a *bearish* sign; the initial and subsequent increases are each negative for six months. If, for example, the Fed increases the discount rate twice, in December and February, this indicator would remain negative through the following December.

The Prime Rate Rule

This is similar in approach and intent to the Discount Rate Rule. In this case, the key variable is the prime rate—the interest rate that banks charge their most credit-worthy borrowers. These would include the likes of Unisys or GE, as opposed to the likes of you or me. When money is scarce, lenders will charge more for it; when the Fed is easy and money is plentiful, banks will charge less. Banks will vary the prime rate with the availability of money in the system. The

Prime Rate Rule, also popularized by Zweig, is a little more complicated than the Discount Rate Rule, but only a little:

1. If the prime rate exceeds 8 percent, as it does currently:

• an increase of at least ½ percent is a bearish signal.

• a decrease of at least 1 percent or two ½ percent declines is bullish.

2. If the prime rate is less than 8 percent:

• an increase of at least 1 percent or two ½ percent increments is necessary for a bearish signal.
• a decrease of at least ½ percent is bullish.

A high initial rate indicates a tight monetary policy at the time. In a tight-money environment, an investor would like a clearly positive signal—a sharp decline in the prime. The reverse holds true as well; when monetary policy is easy and the prime rate is low, the stock market already has a positive bias. Accordingly, even a small decline in the prime is a signal to buy. Zweig estimates that, by following the rules stated above, your return would have averaged 17.2 percent annually over the last thirty years, versus 6.2 percent a year for an investor who stayed fully invested at all times.

The T-Bill/Dividend Ratio

This indicator is similar to the first one—stocks versus bonds—in that we are comparing a fixed-income investment to an equity investment. In this case, the ratio is the three-month Treasury bill rate divided by the dividend yield on stocks. Since the T-bill rate is controlled by the Fed, its rise or fall gives an indication of a tightening or easing of policy, which usually precedes a decline or increase in stock prices.

In theory, this ratio compares a riskless short-term cash return from T-bills to a relatively riskless short-term cash return from stocks, since dividends are paid quarterly and are very rarely reduced or eliminated. When the ratio falls below 1.8, this has historically been positive for stocks; above 2.2, a negative outlook is indicated.

The Dividend Yield

Historically, a dividend yield on the S&P 400 above 6 percent is bullish for the stock market; below 3 percent, it is bearish. This is hardly the most impressive indicator in the list, which is one reason you have twenty of them to use. The thresholds for how high is positive and how low is negative should vary up or down as bond yields move up or down; in this indicator, however, competitive bond yields are ignored for no good reason, save simplicity. Someone once said that any idea that couldn't fit on a matchbook was too complicated to be useful. This one could fit on a match.

The Yield Curve

The yield curve is designed to show whether or not short-term interest rates are lower than long-term rates, which is generally the case (the longer the loan, the greater the risk, the higher the rate). It is a graph, with current interest rates as the vertical axis and debt maturity—the year when a loan must be repaid—on the horizontal axis.

An inverted yield curve—short rates higher than long rates—is considered bearish for the market, since it implies that monetary policy is tight, with the Fed pushing up short-term rates. A study by Raymond Dalio concluded that a $1,000 investment in the stock market in 1984 would have grown to $7,400 by early 1989. The same investment would have increased to $13,100 if you had avoided the market during periods when the yield curve was inverted.

Bond Quality

This indicator, developed by Salvigsen and Aronstein, is a bit esoteric, and you might prefer to skip it. However, it does make sense conceptually. When the risk-free bond yield is close to that of lesser quality bonds, this implies that investors are not particularly concerned about defaults. A tight spread between yields indicates a strong economy, in which companies can pay their debts easily (where corporate cash flows are substantially above debt service requirements).

In addition, the economy's strength will tend to create positive expectations for future growth—as usual, to excess. When the economic reality falls short of the expectations, the bond market will rally and interest rates will fall, since the demand for money will decline with the economy.

Within the bond market's rally, risk-free bonds will outperform their lesser-quality counterparts. Even though the riskier bonds benefit from falling interest rates, their performance *relative* to riskless bonds will suffer—investors will now begin to worry what a slowing economy might mean for corporations' ability to pay the interest on their bonds. They will demand a greater interest rate premium than before to compensate them for the greater perceived risk that lesser quality bonds won't pay them as promised.

On the other hand, when the spread between the risk-free bond yield and the lower-quality bond yield is exceptionally wide, this indicates that investors' concerns about the economy and its future outlook are too pessimistic. As economic performance begins to exceed expectations, interest rates will rise and bond prices will fall. In the decline, risk-free bonds will tend to do worse than the more economically sensitive corporate bonds—the decline in lesser quality bonds will be mitigated by the reduced likelihood that these bonds will default since the economy is strengthening.

Therefore, when yields on risk-free bonds are close to those on risky bonds, it is positive for the bond market in general and risk-free bonds in particular; a low ratio is a negative signal for bonds, especially for risk-free bonds. For this indicator, use the thirty-year Treasury bond yield as the risk-free rate and the ten-plus year medium quality corporate bond yield as the lesser quality rate; both are available daily on the Credit Markets page of *The Wall Street Journal*. Compute the ratio of the T-bond yield divided by the corporate bond yield. A ratio above .85 is positive for the bond market and, probably, for stocks as well. A ratio below .70 is negative for both.

Monetary Growth Versus Economic Growth

The money that is put into our economy can find its way to one of three areas: (1) real economic growth, which is nice; (2) prices of real assets (goods and services), which is inflation; and (3) prices of financial assets (stocks and bonds), which is a bull market. By definition, monetary growth in excess of nominal GNP growth—real growth plus inflation—implies good things for financial assets. The trick is to be able to project when this will happen in the future. Since most of us don't have a clue, we can look at what has happened in the recent past and hope that it will continue into the future.

On a practical level, compare the growth of M3 for the last three months against that of the nominal GNP* for the same period. (M3 is the broadest measure of the money supply and is reported monthly by the Fed.) Make certain that the figures are annualized so that you are comparing apples to apples. These figures are available in *The Wall Street Journal* and in *Barron's* (Market Laboratory/Economy). Also, *Grant's Interest Rate Observer* (212-608-7994) updates these numbers, in addition to giving excellent insights on the financial world in general.

Sentiment Indicators

Analyzing the market's fear and greed is not an exact science. The best approach is to observe sentiment from a number of different angles, without relying too heavily on any one indicator. Keep in mind that being a contrarian is most rewarding when the sentiment is at extremes. Much of the time the players will be half-hearted in their convictions, and the contrarian won't have a clear consensus to bet against. Also, remember that sentiment tends to be a leading indicator. The peaks and troughs of enthusiasm will tend to precede those of the market, since extreme greed and fear can feed on itself for a while.

Bearishness Among Advisers

The sentiment among advisers who publish investment newsletters has been tracked by Investors Intelligence for more than twenty

---

*Money manager Stan Druckenmiller makes a strong case for using the FRB Index of industrial production, which is a better measure of production, if a more difficult one to find. *Barron's* Market Laboratory/Economic Indicators publishes the year-to-year figures each week.

years. Over time, it has been a useful contrarian indicator and is available each week in *Barron's* on the Investor Sentiment page.

The problem with this measure highlights the problem with all sentiment indicators: Investor attitudes are difficult to measure and are not always reliable. A high level of bearishness is usually a good buying opportunity, whereas a low level justifies caution on your part. You should not depend on a set rule, however, since the buy and sell points may vary from one bull/bear market to the next.

In general, when the percentage of bears averages less than 20 percent, you should be negative on the market; when the percentage of bears remains above 35 percent for a few weeks, you should be positive.

Insider Transactions

"Insider transactions" refers to the on-going buying and selling of stock by corporate managers and directors.* In this situation, you *don't* want to bet against the consensus, since insiders have historically been accurate in judging the merits of their own companies. Insiders tend to be late in reporting their purchases or sales, but that's no problem, since they also tend to be one or two quarters early in being right.

The Insiders ($100/year; 1-800-327-6720) tracks the filings with the SEC and publishes an index of the percentage of buys as a percentage of total transactions—buys and sells. This index—a five-week average—is useful for market timing. Insiders tend to sell more often than they buy, since shares are often given to them through stock options. A level of 35 percent purchases to total transactions is considered neutral. Less than 20 percent is negative; more than 50 percent is positive. Pay particular attention to bearish or bullish readings that are sustained over several weeks or months.

Sentiment in the Futures Market

The *Bullish Consensus* tracks sentiment regarding the outlook for stock index futures. This weekly figure is also available in

---

*This is different from the illegal practice of trading on *inside information,* which is defined as material and nonpublic information.

Barron's. Here again, high levels of bullishness are dangerous, while low levels are encouraging. Specifically, readings above 60 percent should be viewed as a negative, whereas those below 30 percent should be considered a positive.

You might also keep an eye on the bullish percentage in the bond market, available each week on *Barron's* Capital Markets page. Due to the correlation between stocks and bonds, this indicator is most helpful when the readings for the stock market and the bond market are both positive or both negative.

Put/Call Ratios

The logic here is simple: If speculators are buying a lot of put options to bet on a market decline, you should bet on a market advance. And the opposite for call options. The stereotype of the option buyer is that of an individual hoping to parlay a small outlay into a large win, even though the odds are not good—theoretically, a good person to bet against. If you agree with the reasoning, then here are the rules:

- A ratio of six puts for every ten calls is neutral, since speculators are biased toward the upside, again due to human nature and a six-decade bull market.
- A reading above 70 percent is positive, while one below 50 percent is negative.
- Use the total open interest for the Chicago Board Options Exchange, which is published daily in the major newspapers, or the weekly numbers shown in the Options section of *Barron's*.
- Don't use the Index Options numbers; hedging by portfolio managers can severely distort these numbers.

Short Interest

This is another interesting, but not always reliable, indicator. Short Interest defines the number of shares that have been sold short; the higher the level, the more bullish the reading, since those shares will have to be bought back at some point. ("He who sells what isn't his'n/Must buy it back or go to prison.")

The complications arise when short positions are offset by ownership of options or convertible bonds. Phillip Erlanger of Advest computes a more useful ratio of short positions that are "at risk"—not hedged by options or converts—relative to average trading volume. The *Journal* mercifully includes his conclusions each month when they publish the short-interest figures.

Short-interest ratios are also published for individual stocks and are of value in stock selection. Look for high short-interest ratios, where a large number of days will be necessary to repurchase the shorted stock, based on its normal trading volume. But be aware of outstanding options or converts that might offset these readings.

Cash Levels

One indicator suggested by Richard Band, editor of *Personal Finance,* is the level of cash in investors' portfolios—the higher, the better. Since you need cash to buy stocks, this should be fairly obvious. What is less obvious is what those cash levels are at any given time. *Growth Fund Guide* (605-341-1971) publishes the monthly cash level among mutual funds that concentrate primarily on stocks. A cash level of 9 percent is the somewhat arbitrary neutral position; above that is bullish, below that is bearish. In the depths of two bear markets, October 1982 and September 1974, the readings were 12.2 percent and 11.8 percent, respectively.

Unfortunately, the trend of cash levels has risen over time, making historical comparisons less useful. Also, this approach is far from flawless—Merrill Lynch's survey of institutional cash positions was extremely encouraging at the end of September 1987, right before the Crash.

Stock Offerings/Repurchases

A large number of equity offerings indicates that investors are eager to buy, and managements are willing to sell, two conditions that imply that the market is overloved and overpriced. Unfortunately it is difficult to find reliable statistics and, therefore, this indicator should be used more for general insights than for specific conclusions. The *Journal* includes a list of expected offerings each

Monday on the Credit Markets page; *Barron's* offers a similar list on the Market Laboratory/Stocks page. Take a look each week at the number of stock offerings—ignore the bond offerings, which are listed as well. There are no hard-and-fast rules.

As for repurchases, which are a favorable sign for the underlying shares, there are even fewer statistics. However, it helps to keep an eye on the frequency of buy-back programs, which are usually discussed on *Barron's* The Trader page each week.

One study concluded that the performance of a stock subsequent to a share repurchase announcement was most directly influenced by the P/E ratio. It is hardly surprising that those shares bought at the lowest P/E's would tend to respond most positively. Certainly, the return on investment (ROI) for Company A buying its own shares at ten times earnings (a 10 percent earnings yield) is a great deal better than when its P/E is 20 (a 5 percent earnings yield).

In comparing different companies, the *initial* return on investment for Company A's buy-back at ten times earnings is clearly more attractive than Company B's ROI on its buy-back at twenty times earnings. That's why a share repurchase by a company like Ford (P/E of 5) will usually be more effective than one by a company like Merck (P/E of 22), even allowing for different growth rates.

To conclude, periods of heavy share repurchase announcements and completions, and positive price responses to that activity, are a favorable sign for the market.

Advertisements

Now we've really entered the world of the anecdotal. The number and tenor of ads related to the stock market is one contrarian indicator that Zweig has used. Although the approach of keeping an eye on investment-related advertising doesn't lend itself to formal buy or sell rules, it is helpful in maintaining a sense of the market. Logically, optimism will trigger a large number of positive ads, while pessimism will create a dearth of ads, with the few survivors suggesting caution or worse.

This applies to other markets, as well. For example, let's say, hypothetically, that *Barron's* contains quite a few ads extolling the virtues of gold, which we'll assume has been in a bull market. Perhaps there's a catchy headline or two: "Hyperinflation Is Just Around the Corner" or "How to Profit from the Mulching of the Financial System." Meanwhile, stocks have been in such a bear market that they have become something of a nonsubject among advertisers, with only an occasional subscription offer: "Free when you order *The Armageddon Letter* for a year, a new report from Dr. Guru Nehru, *The Hundred Years Bear Market*." This example is a bit extreme, but it does make a point, which is to hold your nose, buy some stocks, and sell the gold fillings in your teeth.

The Heavy Hitters

There are a number of people out there who understand the stock market better than most. As noted earlier, some of them are willing to manage your money; some are not. Regardless, most of them are proud of their points of view and are willing to share them. The weekly business publications and the daily newspapers often discuss the opinions of these great investors. Unfortunately, the media also highlights the thoughts of the many more not-so-great investors. To simplify things, here is an arbitrary Broker's Dozen:

Warren Buffett	Chairman, Berkshire Hathaway
I. W. Burnham	President, The Burnham Fund
Philip Fisher	President, Fisher and Co.
John Neff	Portfolio Manager, Vanguard Windsor Fund
Julian Robertson	General Partner, Tiger Fund
Jim Rogers	Professor, Columbia University
Stanley Salvigsen	Principals, Comstock Partners
Michael Aronstein	
George Soros	General Partner, Quantum Fund
John Templeton	Chairman, Templeton Funds
Robert Wilson	Private investor

You should also keep an eye out for comments by Peter Lynch of Fidelity's Magellan Fund, Michael Price of Mutual Shares, and Robert Menschel of Goldman Sachs.

These investors will rarely be in agreement, but if a consensus does develop among them, don't bet against it. This is the crowd to bet with.

Action and Reaction

The idea behind this indicator is to study the reaction of the "experts" to a very unusual, very major financial event. Discretion being the better part of valor, this one doesn't come into play too often, nor is it quantifiable. However, when it is of value, it is of great value. It really applies to two situations: an unexpected and dramatic rally in what has been a bear market or a similar collapse in what has been a bull market. If the reaction of the crowd to the event is one of apathy, watch out. Often, bull and bear markets begin with a bang that, at first, is explained away as a whimper. One example was the 90 point decline in the Dow Jones Industrial Average in early October 1987 that was heralded as a nonevent; two weeks later the Dow Jones Industrial Average bottomed out 800 points lower.

With all these indicators, especially with those that don't rely on set parameters, avoid any approach that you don't understand. Specific, but incorrect, answers are a good deal worse than no answers at all.

Trend Indicators

The underlying premise here is that a trend, once established, will continue for long enough to be profitable. After all, both the real world of the economy and the unreal world of fear and greed tend to move in cycles. In fact, as we have seen, the two worlds tend to reinforce each other.

An improvement in the economy encourages a shift from pessimism to optimism among investors. The shift reinforces the economy through increased consumer spending. This then encourages business to increase inventories and expand capacity, all of which feed the economic recovery. The further improvement in the economy and in the market, in turn, encourages further optimism.

In time, the once overly pessimistic market will come to reflect the improved fundamentals, and then to expect their continuation.

Unfortunately, economies are cyclical and are destined to disappoint expectations of endless improvement. The day of reckoning can be delayed for a while if the optimism of the players transforms itself into naked greed, which can become divorced from reality altogether.

This sequence is the trend-follower's dream, particularly at the end, when the market occasionally rises for no better reason than that it has been rising, and the players expect more of the same. Inevitably, the upcycle collapses and a downcycle begins, usually shorter and more violent. Unlike the deluded speculators who want to buy at the exact bottom and sell at the exact top, the trend-follower simply waits for a trend to establish itself, jumps aboard, and waits until it seems that a new trend has emerged.

The trick is to be able to ride a trend that will last long enough to do you some good, lest you get whipsawed into debtors' prison. As Peter Falk noted in *The In-Laws:* "Staying alive is the key to the benefits program."

The 2–1 Rule

For this indicator, compute the ten-day average of advancing stocks relative to declining stocks on the NYSE. When the ratio of up to down exceeds 2–1 over ten trading days, this is a positive signal.

According to Zweig, the average return from 1953 to 1985 in the six months following a 2–1 buy signal has been 16 percent (32 percent annualized).

Lopsided ratios of down-days to up-days are bearish, but, historically, are a less useful indicator. The figures for advancing stocks relative to declining ones are carried each week in *Barron's* on the first page of the Market Laboratory/Stocks.

The 9–1 Rule

A day when up-volume exceeds down-volume by a ratio of more than 9–1 is considered bullish for the market's subsequent performance, according to this indicator; two such days within a three-month period are a strongly positive signal. Zweig points out that the performance of the market in the year following two 9–1 days has averaged over 20 percent since 1960. Unfortunately, the advent of program trading with its concomitant volatility, he has noted, may have made such 9–1 days more common and, consequently, less valid.

Again, this is a more reliable indicator on the upside than on the downside. Again, *Barron's* is the best place to look, in this case on the second page of the Market Laboratory/Stocks.

What Now?

So what are you supposed to do with nearly twenty market indicators, some easily understood and followed, others not? Among those that are easy to quantify, my suggestion is to focus on the following three: stocks versus bonds, the discount rate rule, and the T-bill/dividend yield ratio. Check what they are suggesting on a monthly basis, and give primary emphasis to the stocks-versus-bonds indicator. In addition, keep an eye on the bearishness among advisory services for a reading on sentiment.

Among the indicators that are more qualitative, pay particular attention to what the heavy hitters are advising. As for the rest, use those indicators that you are comfortable with and forget about the others.

A Look Back

Now let's see what a few of these market indicators were suggesting at two significant points in the past, almost exactly five years apart. The first of these was early August 1982. The Dow Jones Industrial Average was trading below 800 and the S & P 400 Index was selling around 115. The earnings yield on stocks was over 13 percent, based on the latest two years earnings, versus 12.7 percent for the thirty-year Treasury bond. Therefore, stocks were more attractive than bonds, which, at double-digit levels, were a compelling value in their own right. At the same time, the T-bill/dividend yield ratio was below 1.5:1, and the discount rate was reduced on August 2 to 11 percent, the fourth cut from the December 1980 peak of 14 percent. (In addition, the three-week average of advisory bears was above 40 percent, another bullish signal.)

Therefore, all these indicators were positive in the weeks preceding the first leg of the 1982–1987 bull market.

And what was the state of the market in September 1987? By this time, the Dow had risen to 2500 and the S & P exceeded 350. However, the earnings yield had declined to less than 5 percent relative to the T-bond yield of approximately 9½ percent. This comparison shows that the stock market was significantly overvalued relative to bonds at that time; in the final analysis, that overvaluation was the dominant factor in the market's collapse.

Meanwhile, the T-bill/dividend yield ratio had climbed above 2.3:1. To make matters worse, the Fed raised the discount rate on September 11, the first change in almost a year and the first increase since April 1984. (As for the bearishness levels, the three-week average was around 25 percent, a neutral to negative reading.)

In this case, the indicators were quite negative on the market. Which was fortunate, since, during the subsequent five weeks, the average stock declined by over 40 percent.

When waiting for a buy signal, be patient—it's okay to join the party a bit late. When waiting for a sell signal, however, don't be afraid to get out early, since it may be impossible to get out otherwise. As Bernard Baruch replied when asked the secret of his success, "I always sold too soon."

CHAPTER 10

For the Serious Investor

By now, you know that you can become a successful investor with common sense, discipline, and some effort, but your chances will improve significantly if you also have a thorough understanding of what makes the market tick. This chapter provides an overview of such topics as stock valuation in theory, growth stock investing, economic and debt cycles, the impact of inflation, currency markets, the Japanese boom, short selling, convertible bonds, preferred stock, and leveraged buy-outs.

This is a difficult chapter, certainly—the toughest in the book. But it's worth the effort, if not now, then a month from now, or a year. I hope you give it a try. What the hell?

Micro

Valuation in Theory

You put up cash to buy a piece of a company and, over time, you receive cash in the form of dividends. As earnings grow, because of reinvestment by the company, the dividend grows.

The valuation issue is made a little more complicated by the concept of *present value*—namely, that $1 now is worth more than $1 a year from now. For example, if you could invest a dollar at 10 percent, you'd have $1.10 in a year. Therefore, the future value of $1 a year from now is $1.10; the present value of that $1.10 one year out is $1.

Similarly, in two years that $1 will be up to $1.21 (compounded at 10 percent for two years) and the present value of that $1.21 in year two is still $1. With the interest rate at 10 percent, there's no difference between $1 now and $1.10 a year from now and $1.21 two years from now. All three have a value at the present time of $1.

Now let's take that $1.10 a year from now and change the interest rate. If rates rise to 20 percent from 10 percent, the present value of that $1.10 is now $.92, not $1. That is to say, with rates at 20 percent, $.92 currently will grow to $1.10 in one year. If, instead, we reduce the interest rate to 5 percent, the present value of $1.10 a year hence rises to $1.05.

Don't panic—the concept of present value is not as difficult as it might seem on the first reading.

The value of a stock is the present value of all the future dividends—all the cash that you will receive from your investment discounted back to the present at the prevailing interest rate. If dividend expectations rise, the value of the stock rises. This is consistent with improved expectations for the earnings growth at the company. In addition, if the interest rate declines, the value of the stock rises.

A decrease in the interest rate helps the valuation in two ways. Most important, it reduces the attractiveness of an alternative use of your money. Bonds will be a less competitive investment when their yield is lower. A decline in the interest rate also helps indirectly by lowering the company's cost of doing business—debt expense—thus improving the dividend prospects. This helps to explain why stock prices are sensitive to movements in the bond market. (Interest rates vary indirectly with bond prices—if a bond pays a fixed $100/year, the current interest rate for a bond bought for $1,000 is 10 percent, while for one bought for $800, it is 12½ percent. Accordingly, bond prices decline as rates rise and rise as rates fall.)

Be aware that earnings and dividends are not very predictable. And interest rates are exceptionally volatile. It is little wonder, then, that stock prices move violently in reaction to changes in both interest rates and in the perception of future earnings and dividends.

Growth Stock Investing

Growth companies are those with exceptional prospects for growing their revenues and earnings at an unusually fast pace. Investing in them is particularly challenging, for the simple reason that the distant future is awfully difficult to predict.

Growth stocks generally sell at an above-average multiple of earnings to reflect the strong potential growth of those earnings. However, if the P/E is so high that the attractiveness of a stock is based on a forecast of extraordinary growth for many years, proceed with caution. The more vital it is to your decision that the company have an abnormally bright future, the more likely it is that you will be disappointed.

In addition to unpredictability, growth companies have another drawback: They also tend to be cash users. As they have grown, their expenditures to finance that growth have exceeded the cash generated from operating their businesses. The result is a negative free cash flow.

For a young company, there is nothing unusual about that. In fact, that is why we have stock exchanges in the first place, so that growth companies can raise money and keep growing. However, you should generally try to invest in companies that earn more than they need, not the reverse.

A case *can* be made for buying a cash-using company rather than a cash-generating company. If the negative free cash flow produces growth that will eventually generate enormous amounts of earnings in the future, the stock might be worth considerably more than the current price. This argument is similar to the justification for buying a company that currently pays little, if any, dividends and retains its earnings for growth—and for large future dividends.

Some investors believe a better measure of potential investment success than free cash flow is the *gross* cash flow (earnings plus depreciation). They feel that expenditures on plant and equipment which reflect attractive opportunities for growth are a positive for the shareholder.

This type of analysis obviously requires an extremely thorough knowledge of a company. An investor must be able to distinguish between expenditures that create exceptional growth and those that simply sustain an average or mediocre business. Some gifted investors, such as Philip Fisher and T. Rowe Price, were able to develop the conceptual framework for recognizing and valuing true growth companies. They were willing to pay a high multiple on current earnings for cash-using companies in those cases where certain criteria were met. And they prospered along with these companies. One example was Fisher's purchase of Texas Instruments in a 1956 stock offering, a position he sold for a 5,500 percent profit.

The potential losses, however, are enormous as well. In the wake of the few brilliant growth investors were strewn the remains of the many unsuccessful followers. Their reach of imagination was perhaps as broad, but their grasp of the risks was considerably less. They misunderstood what constituted an attractive growth stock, and were willing to pay extraordinary multiples of earnings for the shares of companies whose growth rates were unsustainable. In 1973, IBM, the niftiest of the Nifty Fifty, sold at a P/E of more than thirty-five times its trailing twelve months' earnings.

What were those investors expecting?

A Closer Look

Free Cash Flow: The previous section on growth stock investing alluded to a problem with free cash flow: Exactly how do you value it? Is the relevant figure gross cash flow minus all capital expenditures? Or is it gross cash flow minus just those expenditures necessary to maintain existing plant? Or is it something in between?

You might remember that the *average* company's capital spending allows it to grow in line with the economy. However, this average is comprised of thousands of companies that grow more slowly than nominal GNP and thousands that outgrow it.

When analyzing an individual company, the relevant free cash flow figure is the gross cash flow minus those capital expenditures that are necessary to generate average earnings growth—let's call this *normalized free cash flow*. If a company has excellent opportunities for expansion because there is a strong demand for its products, then its actual capital expenditures should be greater and its net income should grow faster than the economy. After all, more spending on plant and equipment allows for greater output and more efficient production.

An above-average rate of earnings growth for a company should be rewarded with an above-average P/E ratio for its stock. However, the greater the spending for future growth, the less the flexibility to repurchase shares or increase dividends. These are the tradeoffs that a management must decide on behalf of its shareholders.

Taking the issue from the theoretical to the practical naturally confuses matters. Specifically, what is the level of capital spending that will produce average growth? Should maintenance of existing plant and equipment be considered a capital expenditure to be deducted immediately as a cost of sales? Companies may vary in their treatment of capital spending; as an investor, you should prefer a management that takes the conservative approach of deducting maintenance entirely in the year it is incurred.

Normalized free cash flow is a difficult concept to understand and to value, but it is a vital one for a serious investor. It is the excess money that allows a company with a bright future to realize its potential or permits a company in a mature business to put cash in the hands of its shareholders through dividends and share buy-backs. A company that spends all its cash just to survive should be of little interest to an investor. On the other hand, a company that generates cash well beyond its realistic needs is a terrific investment at the right price. Not surprisingly, a company such as this is usually one with a strong franchise.

Growth Rates: There are several approaches to projecting a company's earnings growth rate, each of which is helpful, though not foolproof. In Chapter 5, it was assumed that the Washington Post would grow at a slower pace than its extraordinary rate of the previous five–ten years, to reflect a probable slowdown in the economy. Still, a 10–15 percent growth rate would almost certainly outpace that of the average company, which makes sense since the Post is an exceptional company.

A faster rate of gain appears indicated by the *implied growth rate,* which is determined by the amount of income retained by the company and the expected return on those retained earnings. WPOB pays out approximately 15 percent of its net income in dividends to its shareholders, and retains 85 percent for future earnings growth. The average return on equity over the past five years has exceeded 20 percent. A 20 percent return on 85 percent of the net income would result in an implied growth rate of 17 percent ($.20 \times .85 = .17$). However, this assumes that the company will be able to earn a 20 percent after-tax profit on its future retained earnings—difficult, at best.

Value Line's one-page summary of the Washington Post forecasts annual earnings growth of 16.5 percent on average. Unfortunately, that estimate is based on a time period from 1986–88 to 1992–94. (Value Line wisely averages three years together in each case to mitigate the effects of recession in recovery years.) Therefore, the projection includes the rapid growth—almost 20 percent a year—of the 1988–90 period, while our estimate is concerned with 1990–95.

Let's look at this issue from another angle: A 10–15 percent growth rate will be easily reached if economic growth is 7 percent (including inflation). Assuming that both revenues and costs grow in line with the economy, the earnings growth from current operations will be 7 percent, as well. The remaining 5+ percentage points of earnings gains could be achieved from the reinvestment of the free cash flow—all that is needed is about a 10 percent pretax return on that money.

Of course, if inflation rebounds to the levels of the late 1970s, earnings growth at the Post will be higher than estimated. On the other hand, if economic growth (again including inflation) is less than expected, earnings growth at the company might not even reach 10 percent a year. The fact is, we just don't know.

Assuming for a minute that growth at WPOB will be at the high end of the 10–15 percent range, earnings would double between 1990 and 1995. This would imply an increase of $3/share from our previous estimate, to $34/share. Again using a multiple of 6× the 1995 estimate, our buy point for the company would rise by less than $20/share and would still be some 20 percent below its current price.

All things considered, it's better to err on the side of caution, with this company or with any other. Bear in mind that even 10 percent growth—the low end of our estimated range—is not in the bag, given the sensitivity of advertising revenues to the economy. An earnings decline at the Washington Post is not out of the question: It's unlikely, but it did happen in 1975 and 1980.

If a down year did occur, it probably would be necessary to reduce your 1995 estimate and your buy point. On the positive side, however, the market might overreact to the temporarily bad news and give you a buying opportunity sooner.

The Income Statement: The Washington Post defines operating profit differently from Value Line and S&P. The Post defines it as sales minus cost of goods sold minus selling, general, and administrative expenses *minus depreciation/amortization.* According to both *Cost Accounting* by Horngren and *Fundamentals of Financial Accounting* by Welsh and Anthony, this is the correct approach. However, Value Line and S&P *do not* subtract out depreciation/amortization in determining operating profit. To be consistent with Value Line and S&P—both of which you'll probably rely upon in the future when analyzing stocks—this book uses their definition. This is a variation of the Golden Rule: He who has the gold makes the rules.

Book Value: A company's book value—its assets minus its liabilities—is a useful figure if the recorded value of these assets and liabilities is close to their market value. If so, book value is a reasonable estimate of the company's *break-up value:* what it would be worth if it were sold off piecemeal.

Value investors pay close attention to four assets in which the balance sheet figures, determined by accounting rules, can significantly differ from fair market value:

- inventories, which may be comprised of obsolete products worth less than their cost of production.
- accounts receivable, which may have a substantial volume of delinquent accounts.
- plant and equipment, which are recorded at historical cost minus depreciation, and may be worth substantially more or less than their recorded value. For example, a steel foundry might be recorded at zero value after ten years although it could last three times as long. On the other hand, a computer department may need to be replaced every three years.
- Land, which is carried on the books at cost and is normally worth significantly more.

Turnarounds: A careful reading of Chapter 2 will raise what might seem to be a contradiction. The favorable investment viewpoint on Geico and American Express in the discussion of margin appears to violate the advice in "Don't Play Turnarounds" a few pages later.

The distinction here is subtle, but important. Geico and American Express suffered *temporary* setbacks. Their underlying competitive advantage was not lost; in this sense, they were not strategic turnarounds. In fact, temporary problems at great companies many times offer the opportunity to invest at an unusually low cost.

The strategy of buying low P/E stocks will at times result in the purchase of what are clearly turnaround situations. In this case, you can either weed out the turnarounds or you can opt to ignore this general rule in favor of an investment approach that has proven itself over time.

Let's hope that the turnarounds you buy will be the extremely profitable exceptions to the rule. Some sophisticated investors focus on turnarounds, particularly those with low margins, but with production costs below that of the competition. Such companies have a great deal of leverage in profits and in stock price if operations change for the better.

Lawsuits: Wall Street hates a courtroom. The financial community is uncomfortable with legal issues and is generally unwilling to make the effort to become knowledgeable. From a Wall Streeter's point of view, the most compelling feature of the legal profession is its ability to give everyone else a warm feeling of moral superiority.

There is an old saying that you should never buy a lawsuit: If a company may be significantly affected by a pending case, avoid it. However, the exceptions can be quite lucrative. In Chapter 2, it was noted that investors, faced with the issue of tobacco litigation, severely overreacted to the financial implications of a legal defeat. A similar reaction followed Monsanto's loss in a Copper-7 IUD trial. On the other hand, product liability cases bankrupted Johns Manville and wiped out its shareholders.

What separated the first two situations from the third? The difference between these cases was that only the third one involved a class action, in which all of the plaintiffs consolidate their claims into one lawsuit. For the courts to certify a class action, according to liability expert Victor Schwartz, there must be reasonable evidence that the defendant both caused specific harm with its product and failed to warn its customers of the risk. In the tobacco and IUD litigation, the courts determined that these requirements were not met, forcing plaintiffs to try their cases individually, an extremely time-consuming and expensive process. The Manville asbestos case, however, was very different, involving both a specific injury—asbestosis—and a failure to warn the public of a recognized danger.

The bottom line is that lawsuits offer an opportunity to the serious investor precisely because legal issues are so unfamiliar to Wall Street. If you are willing to put in the hours studying legal documents and talking with lawyers, you may find an occasional market inefficiency that makes all the effort worthwhile. But tread carefully where class actions are threatened; if you cannot rule them out or easily quantify the risk, look elsewhere.

Future Shock· Companies set aside reserves for anticipated pension expenses, which are deductible from the income statement and recorded on the balance sheet. In Chapter 5, it was suggested that you should be wary of a company with a large unfunded pension liability, whereby the money set aside is substantially less than the expected cost.

What was not mentioned is that in the next several years, companies may be required to set aside funds—in this case, *non-deductible* funds—for another retirement cost: medical coverage. The effect of this proposal will vary from company to company, depending upon the number of employees and the amounts already set aside voluntarily. In general, this rule, as currently proposed, will have an enormous impact on the financial statements of corporate America. Stay tuned.

Macro

Economics for Non-Economists

The economy and its business cycles of expansions and recessions are not easily understood. Economic growth, interest rates, government policy, trade, inflation—almost everything seems to affect everything else.

Let's think about the value of stocks again, this time for all companies together. The economy determines the level of earnings from which dividends are paid. The income distribution in our economy is made up of wages, investment income, and corporate profits. The output of the economy—the other side of the same coin—is represented by the Gross National Product (GNP), which is the sum of Consumption, Investment, Government Spending, and Net Exports (Exports minus Imports). In recent years, C was 66 percent of the total, I was 15 percent, G was 20 percent, and X was −1 percent, a deficit of some $80 billion. Over time, corporate earnings and dividend growth are closely correlated with economic growth.

The rate at which future dividends are discounted back to the present is determined by the interest rate on bonds. An interest rate is simply the price of money and, like other prices, is determined by supply and demand. In the short term, the demand for money is relatively fixed, while the supply is controlled by the Federal Reserve. Therefore, the Fed controls short-term rates.

We are interested in the long-term rate, however, since our dividends are paid over a long period. The interest rate that we use in valuing these dividends can be viewed as an *opportunity cost*—namely, the return we could have received if we had invested in a long-term bond rather than in a stock (which, after all, is a long-term equity investment in a company).

The demand for long-term credit is determined by the economy. Growth and the expectations for future growth will influence production and expansion decisions, both of which require financing. These capital expenditure decisions are heavily influenced by the real cost of money—the interest rate minus the expected inflation rate. The higher the real cost of money, the less attractive these decisions to expand and borrow.

As for the supply of long-term money, the Federal Reserve must be considered a factor, since it does have a printing press. More important than the generosity of the Fed, however, is the influence of investors: These are the people who lend their money to long-term borrowers by buying bonds. These investors want to receive a return on their money that more than compensates them for the loss of purchasing power—each dollar buying less—because of inflation. Therefore, the interest rate that investors require is based on their expectations of inflation.

Unfortunately for the Fed, the more generous its policy of supplying money, the more likely investors will raise their expectations of inflation. Since inflation is a general rise in the price level, it is easy to see how investors might get nervous at the inflationary prospect of more money chasing a relatively fixed amount of goods.

To summarize: economic growth produces earnings and dividends, and long-term interest rates determine the present value of that income, which is reflected in stock prices. The Fed may influence the level of interest rates in the short run through its control of the money supply, but inflation is the determining factor over time.

And now let's look at the business cycle, starting at a point late in the process, when the economy has been rising strongly for some time. Shortages of labor and materials are beginning to appear. Accordingly, wages and costs are beginning to rise sharply. Businesses gear up to expand, since consumer demand is strong; however, there is a time lag before new capacity will be ready to relieve the shortages.

Expansion costs add to the need for money that an overheated economy is already demanding to finance the various stages of current production. Interest rates are bid up. Meanwhile, the Fed, fearing further rises in inflation, begins to tighten the money supply, putting further upward pressure on rates, particularly short-term rates. Compounding the inflation problem is the hoarding of finished goods and raw materials by consumers and businesses who buy now in the expectation that prices will only go higher.

As consumer purchases and then industrial production begin to level off under the weight of rising interest rates, net business investment drops off. This is due to the Acceleration Principle, which economist Helen Hotchkiss describes as a "self-feeding downward spiral" of net investment (check out Paul Samuelson's *Economics* if you are interested in more information). It will cause GNP growth to slow, and then turn negative, as the decline in investment more than offsets the ongoing increase in consumption. At this point, production will begin to decline as well, to adjust to the reduction in the overall demand. The growth of net investment will turn even more negative in response.

The capacity additions that were begun when the economy was

booming now come on line, creating further excess production. All of these factors cause inflation to moderate, which encourages the hoarders of the previous up-cycle to dump their speculative purchases of finished goods and raw materials on the currently declining economy. This is a further depressant on both economic growth and inflation.

The Fed, now believing that it's tightened not too wisely but too well, eases up and drives short rates lower. Long rates also begin to fall as new money enters the system, demand continues to weaken with the economy, and inflationary expectations follow actual inflation downward. As the decline in production begins to slow, the Acceleration Principle works in reverse, net investment turns up, and the next up-cycle begins. This, in a nutshell, is the business cycle, from the expansion peak to the recession trough.

The stock market contributes to the process through the *wealth effect*—by declining as interest rates rise and the corporate profit outlook clouds, the value of people's wealth declines, and they become more cautious about their purchases.

In general, the bond market and the stock market will move together. However, at economic turning points, the bond market will tend to precede the stock market by one or two quarters, on average. For example, late in an economic recovery, stocks will rise in the face of rising interest rates as people focus on the corporate profit outlook, with a perspective narrowed by greed. Many will argue that the two markets will go their separate ways indefinitely, that "this time it's different." Usually, however, it's not different at all.

But let's not take all of this too seriously. One economist defined his peers as people who, if you forget your phone number, will try to forecast it for you.

The Dance of Debt: The Credit Cycle

Nikolai Kondratieff was a Russian economist who observed that capitalist societies went through long secular waves of economic growth and decline lasting approximately fifty years. Within these waves occurred the much discussed and overanalyzed cyclical expansions and recessions (as outlined in the previous section). Kondratieff's observations of the secular cycles did not please Stalin, who wasn't fond of economists who believed that free market economies could recover from declines; he preferred those who predicted the inevitable collapse of capitalism, period. Given the marshal's characteristic sense of justice, Kondratieff was sent to Siberia, from which he never returned.

The secular wave argument has validity when one considers the credit cycle. The expansion of debt in the economy is a drawn-out process that transcends the typical three-to-five year cyclical expansion. It is influenced by a factor that may take more than a full generation to shift: the attitude of individuals toward risk and borrowing.

Among the experts who have highlighted the credit cycle are George Soros and Al Sommers, but none have done so more thoroughly than Stan Salvigsen and Mike Aronstein. They have been accurate forecasters of the financial markets in the 1980s, and their underlying theme has been the peaking, and eventual crash, of the credit wave. Their basic argument is that credit growth, not monetary growth, is the driving factor in inflation, a force that applies to the inflation of real assets (land, oil, or other commodities) as well as financial assets (bonds and stocks).

In this century, the rise in the prices of real assets and financial assets has been driven by a phenomenal expansion of credit. Since the 1950s, domestic nonfinancial debt* has grown from less than 130 percent of GNP at its low to 180 percent by 1988. In fact, total debt as a percentage of GNP is now considerably higher than it was in 1929, right before the Great Depression. Since 1973, credit outstanding has risen by 340 percent, while GNP had grown by only 69 percent. Total debt rose 17 percent in 1985, 10 percent in 1986, 9 percent in 1987, and 9 percent in 1988, ending that year at 9.05 trillion!

Yet, if people were still borrowing or, more importantly, if banks were still lending, the debt expansion party could continue. Jam yesterday, jam today, and to hell with tomorrow—why sweat the hangover if it's off in the future? However, it looks as if the future is now. As Salvigsen and Aronstein have pointed out, the banking system is running out of markets where it hasn't already been burned. The Third World, energy, agriculture—the great lending opportunities of

---

*American debt owed by individuals, government, and corporations (except banks and S&Ls).

the past—are the ruins of the present. In time, even the once and future LBOs will probably suffer, as well.

Meanwhile, the baby boomers, who have borrowed to finance a life-style that they considered a birthright, are starting to reach an age where saving predominates over spending. In the next decade, people may become more interested in paying back debt than in borrowing more. Certainly, Eastern Europe and the Soviet Union may become eager borrowers, and the Pacific Rim—Japan, South Korea, Taiwan, Hong Kong, and Singapore—may become a willing lender, though this would arguably only defer and magnify the eventual credit problem.

The end of the credit-expansion cycle has very serious implications, if and when it happens. As the major sectors of the world economy are viewed as unattractive lending risks by the banks, the likelihood of a credit contraction increases.

When credit is expanding, the new loans provide the money to finance economic growth. The increase in prices—of exports, land, oil, companies, housing, whatever—stimulates further lending. For example, the run-up in oil prices in the 1970s encouraged banks to lend more to energy companies for further exploration.

The boom, however, sows the seeds of its own self-destruction, as loans are used to increase supply, eventually overwhelming demand. Prices, which were expected to rise indefinitely, begin to head lower. New loans dry up and existing loans become less secure. Projects in various stages of development are abandoned as economic growth stagnates, or slips into decline.

As loans are called in, assets are sold to pay the loans, causing prices to plummet. As the value of the assets on which other loans are based decline, other banks will worry about the safety of their loans. And as these banks try to get their money back, more asset sales become necessary, further depressing their prices and continuing the downward spiral. Since fear is more basic than greed, the downward process of credit contraction is usually quicker and less orderly than the upward process of credit expansion.

I hope this analysis is wrong. If not, then let's hope that the Fed offsets the deflationary impact of credit contraction with a generous monetary policy. Unfortunately, however, we tend to fight the last war, which in our economy was the inflation of the 1970s; few are left to remember the deflation of the 1930s.

The Fed is accustomed to a world in which the economy has grown faster than the money supply. In the postwar period, a given percentage of increase in money has resulted in a greater increase in nominal economic growth—an easy monetary policy, as in the 1970s, led to rising inflation. However, in the 1930s, nominal economic growth was significantly less than money growth. If the next decade has more in common with the credit collapse of the 1930s than with the credit expansion of the 1970s, we are going to need a generous monetary policy. And a great deal more.

An expansion of credit is, in effect, an expansion of money, due to an increase in the *velocity* of the money supply. A dollar that is spent ten times in a year—as each recipient buys something from someone else who in turn spends it, and so on—will have as much impact on the economy as ten dollars that are turned over only once a year. Increases in credit create increases in velocity and in buying power. This raises the price of goods and services, which is inflation. Inflation, in turn, encourages a further increase in velocity: As real assets rise in value and are worth more dollars, each dollar is worth correspondingly less; therefore, people tend to spend their money more quickly to buy real assets rather than save it in dollars of declining value.

While credit expansion is positive for real assets, debt contraction is positive for financial assets. In this case, the value of each dollar increases relative to real assets (deflation). If you knew that the economy was in a credit contraction, you would want to own long-term government bonds, which will pay you in dollars for many years without risk of default. On the other hand, a credit expansion would be a reason to invest in real estate.

Stocks are really a hybrid between financial assets and real assets. They are usually considered financial assets, since they are a claim on the income of a corporation; however, that income is derived from the company's real assets—the products it makes, the services it provides, and the assets it owns.

The question of where we are in the debt cycle is an important one and, as with most important questions, a tough one to answer.

One way to approach it is to examine the long-term trend of velocity. Charles Eaton of Nikko Securities has estimated that velocity declined from 1920 to 1946, then rose over the next thirty-five years, and has declined since the beginning of the 1980s. A logical inference is that we are in the early stages of a long-term decline in velocity, a conclusion that is consistent with the anecdotal evidence presented by Salvigsen and Aronstein.

This discussion, already confusing, can become a good deal more complicated without much effort. An optimist would argue that the members of the Fed, although rookies, are pragmatists, not card-carrying monetarists, and will provide whatever amount of money is necessary. Maybe, replies the pessimist, but what if investors in their inflationary paranoia react to monetary ease by tanking the bond market, driving up long-term interest rates to levels that might preclude economic recovery? Will businesses be able to adjust with inexpensive short-term financing instead, as economist Richard Hoey has argued, or will investment be crippled, triggering a depression? These are difficult questions to answer. For that matter, they are difficult questions to read.

The Impact of Inflation

Inflation has been criticized as a method for government to give itself purchasing power without direct taxation. By printing money, the government receives something for nothing, while everyone else is left with a smaller share of the pie.

Regardless, common wisdom has held that stocks were a good hedge against inflation since revenues and profits should increase with prices. However, Warren Buffett offered a different point of view in a 1977 *Fortune* article entitled "Why Inflation Swindles the Equity Investor."

Buffett argued that, even through decades of rising prices, companies have tended to maintain a steady 12 percent return on equity—net profits as a percentage of the shareholders' investment. Since this important measure of profitability had not risen with prices, then the logical conclusion was that equities were not a hedge against inflation.

His analysis broke down the ROE measure into five components:

asset turnover, cost of debt, amount of debt, tax rate, and operating profit margin. Although asset turnover—sales divided by assets—had increased somewhat, operating profit margin had decreased, offsetting it. Buffett argued that the debt burden of corporations had already increased to more than comfortable levels, and that tax rates would more likely rise than fall. Therefore, the return on equity, which had been stable, would probably remain stable. Profitability would not rise to reflect higher prices, and the real value of stocks—after allowing for that inflation—would decline.

Actually, in the subsequent twelve years, ROE has risen. Certainly, the increase in corporate debt to even more dangerous levels has been a factor, as has the reduction in tax rates, since a cut in taxes raises profitability. Perhaps asset turnover has also increased, which is a logical response to higher sales.

More important is the original question of whether ROE should increase with inflation. The answer, I believe, is yes. Simply put, in a world of 5 percent inflation, all components of revenues and costs should rise by 5 percent, and the resulting profits should rise, as well. Thus, the "return" portion of the return on equity would be higher, raising the ROE. The reason that ROE had not risen for decades may be due to the fact that the profit margin—profits as a percentage of sales—has been declining as the economy has aged in the postwar period. Therefore, without inflation, the ROE would have declined over time. In essence, the growth in profitability due to inflation was offset by the decline in profitability due to the economy.

The conclusion that one can draw is that stocks, in theory, are a hedge against inflation, so long as the inflation rate is steady (prices increase by the same percentage each year). In the event of *rising* inflation (prices rising at an *accelerating* rate), stocks offer a partial hedge. Company profits will increase with rising prices; however, interest rates will rise as well, somewhat offsetting the present value of this higher stream of income. Still, a partial hedge is better than no hedge at all, which is the unfortunate situation with bonds in an environment of rising inflation.

Currency Markets

Considering the importance of the dollar in world trade, its extreme volatility may seem a bit surprising. Various governments do intervene, alone or in combination, by buying or selling currencies; their goal is usually to smooth out fluctuations in the foreign exchange market, and sometimes to give it a specific direction. Still, the best-laid plans of central banks are often submerged under the flood of money from private investors and speculators.

The value of assets in this country is stated in terms of dollars, obviously. If, for example, a stock doubles from $10/share, the stock is now worth twice as many dollars. At the same time, the dollar—in terms of that stock—is worth less. In this case, the dollar has fallen from 1/10 of a share to 1/20. The foreign exchange market is similar, as dollars are valued in terms of Japanese yen, British pounds, West German marks, etc.

The finest discussion that I'm aware of regarding the currency market was written by George Soros. In his book, *The Alchemy of Finance,* he attributes the strength of the dollar in the first half of the 1980s to what he calls Reagan's Imperial Circle, a self-reinforcing but precarious combination of high real interest rates, a strong economy, a massive trade deficit, and a large budget deficit.

Our trade deficit—the result of imports significantly in excess of exports—would normally have been expected to drive the dollar lower, as the demand for foreign currencies to pay for imports from these countries exceeded their demand for dollars to buy our exports. However, as Soros pointed out, the high real interest rates, caused by our economic strength and budget deficit, attracted investment inflows of dollars that offset the trade-related outflows.

By early 1985, however, the economy was well into a slowdown and interest rates into a decline; speculative inflows by trend followers into the dollar were exhausting themselves as well. The dollar peaked and began a three-year decline.

In theory, the value of a currency responds to the Interest Rate Parity Theory (IRPT) and the Purchasing Power Parity Hypothesis (PPP). The IRPT states that money will flow into the currency that offers the highest return on that money, after adjusting for the gain or loss of translating that return back into your currency (through foreign exchange futures).

For example, let's say that you can earn 10 percent on your money in the United States for a year and 6 percent in Germany, but the Deutschmark—the German unit of currency—is selling at a 5 percent premium one year out. Your total return of 11 percent in marks would be higher than the 10 percent in the United States, encouraging you to invest in Germany: Buy marks, invest them at 5 percent, and sell mark futures so that you can convert your marks back to dollars in one year.

Similar to this theory is the argument that you should invest in countries with the highest real interest rates—the stated rate minus inflation—with a subjective adjustment for political risk, without worrying about buying or selling currency futures.

On the other front, the PPP argues that currencies should sell at levels that equalize the cost of purchasing the same products in different countries. Unfortunately, this parity is difficult to determine, since even similar products can vary widely in quality between countries.

In the real world, the value of a currency should tend toward these parities over time, as a stock will tend toward its intrinsic value. Soros disagrees with this conclusion, however, and further argues that the speculative flows in the foreign exchange markets are even more dominant than those in the stock market. The influence of trend-followers is a destabilizing and growing force, he points out. A recognition of this should help the average investor understand the often confusing movements in the currency markets.

Fluctuations in the dollar's value will impact both the economy and corporations. A weaker dollar makes exports cheaper and imports more expensive, which is inflationary. On the positive side, a depreciating currency will improve the competitive position of businesses; this, in turn, should benefit our balance of trade with other countries.

The Japanese Market Mania

The Japanese market has risen by over 3,000 percent in the past twenty-five years. During the 1985–1987 period, the strong yen and the weak Japanese economy fueled its stock market boom, as George Soros has pointed out. The currency's strength attracted speculative funds, some of which found their way into the market. The Ministry of Finance meanwhile tried to limit the yen's appreciation through an easy monetary policy (an increase in the supply of money will reduce its price, all things being equal). With weak domestic growth, this government-supplied liquidity benefited the market, as well.

These factors have reversed since 1988, however. The Japanese currently have a stable-to-declining currency, which encourages an outflow of speculative money. In addition, if the yen becomes too weak for the comfort of the central banks, the monetary authorities may be forced to reduce the growth of the money supply significantly, in order to raise interest rates and support the currency. Moreover, Japan's strong domestic economy must compete with the financial markets for whatever money is available. Meanwhile, their Pacific neighbors—Taiwan, Korea, and Hong Kong—have become more formidable competitors in the export market.

Another factor to consider is that Japan's emergent status as an economic superpower may bring with it a responsibility to pay for its own defense. Currently, Japan spends 1 percent of its GNP on the military, compared to 5 percent for the United States. To put this in a strange kind of perspective: Ford pays more for the defense of Japan than Toyota does. At some point, Japan's most important military ally—the American public—may start hoping that the Russian armies hop over the Sea of Japan and botch up its economy for a decade or two.

In the face of all these current and potential concerns, the Japanese market still rises. Is it worth what it's selling for? The long-term government bond yield is above 5 percent, while the earnings yield on stocks is less than 2 percent. Or, looked at another way, the free market is valuing Japan at more than the United States. Which would you rather own, from sea to shining sea?

The success of the Japanese market in recent years seems to be following the classic late-cycle pattern of a bull market. There are explanations to justify the overvaluation—in this case, the Japanese cultural preference for consensus and the activism of its government. A consensus to buy-and-hold is easily maintained in a bull market, but, as Mark Twain observed, "A virtue that has not been tested in the fire is no virtue at all." As for government intervention, it might mitigate a bear market but, even if the government is willing to buy stocks as it did in 1965, it had better wait until they are cheap enough or it just may end up losing a great deal of money.

Meanwhile, Japan's corporations boost their profits by playing the stock market, and brokers sell shares door-to-door. The market keeps rising and common sense is increasingly discredited as a peculiarly Western approach to valuation.

The Japanese people, justifiably proud of their accomplishments since World War II, have perhaps allowed that pride to slide into arrogance regarding their culture, their economy, and their market. As one American visitor observed, the only thing that the Japanese can't figure out is how they could have lost the war.

All of which *does* matter to us thousands of miles away. A substantial decline in Japan's stock market—the world's largest—would likely have serious ramifications for the United States, much as our 1930–1932 debacle had a significant effect on the rest of the world.

Miscellaneous:

Technically Speaking

Investors often discard their out-of-favor stocks at the end of the year, in spite of underlying value. Individuals are motivated to sell in order to lock in their losses for tax purposes in the current year, while institutions are eager to remove the ogres from their portfolios in advance of the year-end reviews by their clients. This year-end selling pressure, driven by noninvestment consideration, helps to explain the so-called January effect, whereby the dogs of December tend to outperform in the following month.

Individuals who tried to buy or sell during Black Monday in October 1987 faced a difficult situation, at best. Quoted prices were out of sync with the actual reality on the trading floor, the automated order system was overloaded, and some of the pros decided to let the phones just ring. This chaos was hardly unique to 1987; in 1929, baskets full of orders were left unexecuted on the trading floor of the Exchange.

How then does a value investor take advantage of Mr. Market's panics—assuming that real values are created—if trading is haphazard? Once you have determined a price you would be thrilled to pay, put in a *buy-limit order,* which tells the specialist to execute your order only at your stated price or better. Place your order in advance

of a panic, when investors are pessimistic but calm, and specify that
the order is *good till canceled (GTC)*.

On a related issue, one school of thought argues that traders
should bravely and blindly buy stocks during a Crash. The relevant
analogy is that of a cat which falls off a skyscraper; when its plummet
is over, healthy or not, it will bounce. The problem is that it's very
difficult to know when the fall will end. In 1929, this approach might
have had you buying when the market was hit hard on October 24,
25, or 28, in advance of what is now known as Black Tuesday. In
1987, the sell-offs on Friday, October 16, or on the morning of Monday, October 19, may have mistakenly seemed like excellent short-
term opportunities.

Short Selling

As noted earlier, a short sale is the sale of a stock that you don't
own. Your hope is that it will decline and you can repurchase it—
cover your short—at a lower price. The difference is your profit. This
approach is just "buy low, sell high," but in reverse order. After all,
why shouldn't an astute investor have the opportunity to profit from
temporarily inflated prices?

Short selling even provides a beneficial function to an overvalued
stock or market that is riding a wave of hope. By shorting into the
rise, the seller moderates the rise; by covering the short in the subsequent decline, the buyer moderates the intensity of the fall.

The short seller does not have a reputation as a moderating influence, however. Historically, this person has been viewed as a heart-
less, unpatriotic speculator who profits from the misery of those who
have bet on a bright future. Indeed, it may be argued that this individual contributes to economic misery by beating down the wealth of
the country. Thriving in an environment of panic, this speculator con-
tentedly watches as consumers (their investments damaged) purchase
less, while corporations (their opportunities diminished and their access to cheap equity financing reduced) expand less.

Prior to the Crash—the 1929 one—the short sellers' lousy reputation was probably justified. They would occasionally attack a stock,
selling aggressively and driving down the price. Eventually, margin
calls would force out speculators who had borrowed heavily to buy

the stock. (In the 1920s, individuals could borrow up to 80–90 percent of the stock purchase price; as a result, a 10–20 percent decline could wipe them out.)

Even more insidious were those unethical speculators who were given access to the order books of the stock exchange specialists, whose job it was to maintain "orderly markets" for stocks to trade. These supposedly confidential books recorded the stop-loss orders of investors, specifying at what price to sell their shares and cut their losses. Knowing these orders in advance allowed the short sellers of the '20s and early '30s to determine how far down the stock needed to be sold before investors would automatically sell, forcing down the stock further.

Such "bear raids" were effective for three reasons. First, it was legal in those days to short stocks as they declined, creating a downward spiral that appealed to investors' natural sense of panic. Second, margin calls and stop-loss orders created additional selling pressure on the way down. Third, the lack of full disclosure by companies made it difficult for average investors to have any idea what their investments were really worth, leaving them at the mercy of the market.

Given the mystery and the manipulation of some short sellers, it is little wonder that they became the favorite scapegoats of the Crash. Few people wanted to acknowledge that maybe the market was just too high to begin with. In reality, however, a study done after the 1929 debacle showed that short selling had very little to do with the decline. But in the much-loved pattern of ignoring the facts when they don't fit the theory, restrictions were placed on short selling. A stock may now be shorted only on an *up-tick*—a higher price than the previous trade—thereby preventing continuous and overwhelming selling pressure. (But imagine the reaction if someone proposed allowing the purchase of a stock only on a *down-tick*.)

Short sellers currently maintain a poor reputation, although it is undeserved. The up-tick rule, the strict confidentiality of stop-loss orders, the more reasonable levels of margin, and the full disclosure rules for public companies preclude most unfair trading in stocks. Equally important, free markets need the rationality of people who are willing to sell overvalued stocks and buy undervalued ones, regardless of the order in which they buy or sell.

As a practical matter, short selling is generally a poor idea for individual investors. Stocks tend to rise in price over time, since the underlying companies tend to rise in value. And, although you are selling shares, your broker holds onto the proceeds, and requires you to put up margin, as well. For the professional investor, however, shorting stocks can be a smart strategy, particularly when the short positions are hedged by long positions, as Julian Robertson described in Chapter 8.

Modern Portfolio Theory

The volatility of a diversified portfolio of many stocks is less than that of the individual stocks that make up that portfolio.

Modern Portfolio Theory asserts that a well-diversified portfolio—approximately thirty stocks—will eliminate essentially all the stock price impact of company-related surprises. The negative surprises from some companies in the portfolio will be offset by the positive surprises of others. Therefore, the portfolio's total value won't be affected by these unexpected developments. This *nonmarket risk* has been eliminated through diversification; the portfolio is now less volatile than any of its individual stocks. All that remains is the *market risk*—some stocks will react more than proportionally to moves in the general market and others less.

The relative performance of a stock in response to a market move is called the *beta*. A beta greater than 1 indicates that, for a 10 percent move in the market, the stock will move more than 10 percent; betas less than 1 indicate less than a 10 percent move. For example, AT&T has a beta of .85—if the market declines by 10 percent, it will fall by 8.5 percent, on average. Apollo Computer has a beta of 1.90—if the market rises by 10 percent, its expected rise is 19 percent.

Convertible Bonds

Convertible bonds pay a fixed interest rate and can be exchanged for stock in the company. For example, let's say that ABC Inc. is selling at $20/share and issues a "convert" with an 8 percent yield, convertible at a 25 percent premium, or $25/share—this would be

referred to as "8's up 25." As a buyer of this security, you receive
$80/year for each $1,000 bond; if the underlying stock rises, you will
also share in its appreciation beyond $25/share. You benefit from re-
ceiving a fixed income like a bondholder and participating in the potential growth of the company like a stockholder. In addition, your
claim on the company's assets in the event of bankruptcy is ahead of
those of shareholders.

But every coin has two sides. The convertible bond's yield will
be higher than the dividend yield, but it will be lower than non-con-
vertible (straight) bonds of equal quality. And you will not participate in some of the stock's appreciation; in this example, you miss
the initial 25 percent move from 20 to 25. Also, the convert market is
a great deal less liquid than the equity market. This may seem unimportant until you try to sell your bonds at a reasonable price, at
which point it may become very important indeed.

The question is when to buy a convert. For the beginner, my
suggestion is to steer clear. For those who want to understand and
perhaps purchase converts, the determining factor, as always, is valuation. First and foremost, you need to be certain that you would like
to own the underlying stock, since a convert should be viewed as
another way to buy the stock. If you don't like the stock, forget it.

Second, determine the "payback" period on the convertible
bond. This is the amount of time it will take for the *incremental* income from the convert to offset the *additional* cost of buying the
stock by way of the convert, rather than directly.

The incremental income from ABC's convert is the interest income minus the dividend income. Since we will assume that ABC
doesn't pay a dividend, the incremental income is $80 (8 percent of
the $1,000 face value of the bond). Next is the cost of the premium,
which is the difference between the $1,000 cost and the value of the
common shares that you could buy immediately. Since the conversion
price is $25, you could convert the bond into forty shares ($1,000
divided by $25). At the current price of $20 and a conversion ratio of
40, the immediate value of the convert is $800. Therefore, the cost of
the premium is $200 ($1,000 − $800).

The payback period is the incremental cost divided by the incremental income—the number of years it will take for the additional
income to pay for the additional cost. In this example, the payback

period is two and one half years ($200 divided by $80). Less than three years is considered acceptable, and less than two and one half years is considered attractive. Paybacks of less than two years have become rare, and are often associated with companies that won't pass the first question: Do you want to own the stock?

For companies with dividends and for converts not selling at par, the calculations are more complicated. Here's the general formula, but you probably shouldn't waste much time memorizing it:

$$\frac{I - (B \div S \times D)}{B - (C \times S)}$$

I = interest income on the convert
B = current price of the convert
S = current price of the stock
D = annual dividend per share of stock
C = conversion ratio
E = mc^2

In recent years, new features have been added to converts to make them more attractive, if more difficult to value. The most interesting of these is a reset feature. In this case, the yield or conversion price is reset after a certain amount of time, such that the bond will trade at par ($1,000) at that time. This feature is designed to reduce the downside risk on the convert. However, you probably should leave it to the professionals to determine how much these bells and whistles are worth.

Preferred Stock

Preferred stocks have many of the disadvantages of bonds and stocks. For investors, the dividend is fixed and does not increase over time like a bond. Unlike a bond—even a convert—the dividend is not required to be paid, although preferred dividends must be paid in full before common stock dividends are declared. (Cumulative preferreds require that all dividends, past and present, must be paid before common shareholders receive anything; noncumulative preferreds require only that the current year's dividends be distributed ahead of common dividends.) In the event of bankruptcy, preferred shareholders are senior to common shareholders. However, they are junior to all bondholders and shouldn't expect much, if anything, once all the fixed-income investors have been paid.

From the company's point of view, preferred stock is usually the most expensive form of financing. The dividend is higher than that paid to the common stockholders to compensate for the absence of growth potential. And it is not deductible for tax purposes, which is allowed for the interest expense on bonds.

So why do we have preferred stock? It allows companies to raise money when their debt level is already unacceptably high and/or when the stock price is unacceptably low. From the buyer's standpoint, there is a huge tax advantage if the purchaser is a corporation. The income from dividends is 80 percent excludable—only 20 percent need be recognized for tax purposes. In time, however, this tax exclusion may be phased out by Congress, reducing the attractiveness of preferreds as an investment for corporations. It is already unattractive for individuals.

Market Efficiency

A favorite debate among academics is whether or not investors can consistently outperform the market. The vast majority would probably still argue that the market cannot be beaten by relying only on past price movements. In their lingo, the market is efficient in the *weak form*. However, the success of Value Line, the 9–1 Rule, and the 2–1 Rule offer a strong opposing case.

Efficiency in the *semistrong form* implies that an investor could not expect to outperform the market in the long term, even with access to all publicly available information. If this were the case, almost everything that you have read in this book would be useless. Fortunately for both of us, several of the investors mentioned earlier have track records that easily dispute this point of view.

As for *strong form* efficiency—that you can't beat the market even with inside information—well, that's not true. However, truth and justice are on two different sides of this issue.

LBO's (Leveraged Buy-Outs)

You might wonder why a management or a raider might be willing and eager to pay enormous premiums to acquire a company. Often, the eventual takeover price is more than twice what a conservative investor was comfortable paying for shares of the stock when the company was trading publicly.

One reason for these premiums is the leverage involved, which can dramatically change the investment equation. Since the buyers' contribution is only a sliver of equity under a mountain of debt, their potential losses are small relative to that of the lenders. At the same time, their potential profits are enormous; after all, the bondholders do not share in the appreciation of the company's value.

If you can borrow almost all of the purchase price, your initial concern is the interest expense. As long as you can earn enough to pay the cost of the debt, you are still in business. Assisting your cause is the government, which permits interest costs to be deducted for tax purposes; therefore, the taxpayer picks up approximately one third of the interest costs.

In time, improvements in productivity and normal growth in operating earnings will allow you to repay debt, and your investment will grow dramatically in percentage terms. Also working in your favor is the potential to sell off various assets of the company to strategic buyers for top dollar. Your hope is that the private market values of the assets will rise as well, as they have during the bull market of the 1980s.

Let's consider an example. Company XYZ has revenues of $60 million, operating profit* of $10 million, depreciation of $4 million, no interest costs (debt-free), and a tax rate of 33 percent. Therefore, net earnings are $4 million; earnings per share are $4, based on 1 million shares outstanding. If a buyer could borrow money at 12½ percent, he/she could afford to pay eight times operating profit, or $80 million.

On the other hand, if you or I wanted to buy shares in this same

---

*Operating profit, as defined earlier, is the same as EBDIT: The Earnings Before Depreciation (a *noncash* cost), Interest, and Taxes. EBDIT must be high enough to pay interest costs and, therefore, to avoid bankruptcy.

public company, we must focus on net earnings (*after* depreciation, interest, and taxes). If we are willing to pay ten times these earnings, then the total value of the company from our point of view is $40 million—only half of what a leveraged buyer might pay.

Let's assume that this leveraged buyer puts up one tenth of the cost and improves operating margins to 20 percent from the initial 10 percent due to cost-cutting, etc. If the top line grows by 7 percent annually for six years, revenues would reach $90 million. Operating profit would be approximately $22 million net of depreciation of $4 million. After deducting interest charges of $9 million and taxes of $3 million, net earnings would be $6 million. If the company went public again and investors were willing to pay eight times net earnings, the original buyer would receive $48 million six years after investing $8 million, or a 500 percent profit.*

Leverage works nicely if you can find someone to lend you the money, and the economy continues to grow. Should the economy falter, however, companies with significant debt on top of modest equity may find themselves in very bad shape. Campeau Corp., for example, has found itself in a financial mess less than two years after its $6.6 billion LBO of Federated Department Stores.

Another factor to consider is that leveraged buyers should not ignore depreciation charges, unless they don't plan on replacing plant and equipment as it ages. And, if they don't, what will they use to build their products in five or ten years?†

The point of this overview is to show why leveraged buyers of companies are willing to pay significantly more than what you should consider good value. The LBO boom is usually a bull market phenomenon and, as such, is rarely sustainable.

---

*The total value of the company would be $120 million since there is debt of $72 million from the LBO that must be assumed by the new buyers.

†For this reason, operating profit net of depreciation may be a more relevant starting point for an LBO analysis. In the case of The Washington Post, examined in Chapter 5, net operating profit would be approximately $70 million less and the LBO value would be reduced by $630 million, or $50/share.

PART V

The Bottom Line

CHAPTER 11

How to Invest in the Market

Americans look much too much at the short term, because they think it's so simple to make a right decision, that all you need to know is which company is going to have good earnings next year. But it's not as easy as that. . . .

The best discipline for an investor is common sense. And common sense tells you that if you buy something for a small fraction of its true value and are patient, in the long run you're more likely to make a large profit than if you had paid full value in the first place.

—John Templeton
in an ad for Shearson Lehman

• As the above quotation suggests, success in the market is both easier and more difficult than most investors realize. While others are overwhelmed by the complexity and the sheer volume of information, you should rely on the simple strategies discussed earlier and on your own discipline and common sense. At the same time, while other investors focus on the apparent and the irrelevant, you should remember that "if it's obvious, it's obviously wrong."

• Respect the market's ability to respond to information quickly and to reward value eventually. If you play "Beat the Clock," trying to react immediately to new information—an earnings surprise or an unexpected event, for example—you will probably lose. The market quickly reacts, and often overreacts, to news; speculators who chase the headlines, hoping for short-term gains, do more for their brokers than for themselves.

At the other extreme, those who think that stocks will remain overpriced or underpriced forever are ignoring the long-term intelligence and rationality of the free market. Which is to say, you should find stocks that you have strong reasons to believe are significantly undervalued, and hold them until they are not.

- The market occasionally offers an opportunity for your money to grow considerably faster than it otherwise would. When an unusually attractive investment presents itself, grab it; otherwise don't bother. There are several basic needs in life, but owning stocks is not one of them. You can live fully—and, in some cases, longer—without being a shareholder.

- Remember that when you buy stock, you are buying a stake in a company's future. Make certain that you are buying reality, not hype. There is an old story of a sardine trader who opened a can and found sand inside. "Don't worry," he was assured. "That can is only for trading."

- Try to find a few attractive investments in simple companies with strong, sustainable market positions that generate substantial free cash flow.

- Look for talented and trustworthy managers, those who recognize that the shareholders are the owners. In addition, invest with people who treat their employees with fairness, but still believe in a work ethic according to Vince Lombardi: "If you are not fired with enthusiasm, you will be fired with enthusiasm."

- An awareness of sentiment is a useful complement to an understanding of valuation. Pay particular attention to a consensus that is overwhelmingly negative or positive. Look for situations in which the general viewpoint of investors is that the market is either "cheap but will get cheaper" or "expensive but going higher."

- To the extent you are uncomfortable with the various sentiment indicators, you should rely upon valuation alone. Simply put, value wins out over time.

- A decline in a stock's price—even a substantial one—only means that the shares cost less. It does not necessarily mean that the price is a "bargain"; rather, the decline may only be highlighting just how overvalued the stock was to begin with.

- Don't buy a stock because it has been rising and you hope it will keep rising. Stocks rarely follow a defined sequence from significant undervaluation to significant overvaluation, and back again. A trend will last only as long as it lasts, and you probably won't know how long that will be.

  The stock market as a whole is more likely to demonstrate trends since the psychology of a large crowd takes time to swing from long-term bearishness to bullishness. However, playing the trend is easier in theory than practice; your time is better served focusing on valuation rather than on trend-following.

- Don't try to buy at the exact bottom or sell at the top—you can't expect to make a rational prediction of what is usually an irrational event.

- Get rich slow. A small amount of money will become a small fortune over time if invested wisely. (Baron Rothschild referred to compound growth as "the ninth wonder of the world.")

- Be skeptical. Don't take what the "experts" say at face value, particularly in regard to their track records. It's difficult to know whether they are reciting or rewriting history.

- Be flexible within your disciplines. Focus on those industries and companies that pass your screens. And don't harbor prejudices against a stock that meets these standards ("I lost money in that dog once, and I'll never buy it again").

- Be patient. Recognize that it may be a long wait between such opportunities. If you are averaging more than one or two decisions a year using the Buffett Approach, ask yourself why.

  In addition, don't let the market wear you down. Look for cheap stocks, and don't concern yourself about when they will move higher. Try to view price declines as good news, since, as a value investor, you can pick up bargains at a better price. If you are right, the market will eventually get around to balancing the scales, occasionally with a violence that you would not have thought possible.

- Be thorough. Do your homework. Your purchases of stocks and bonds probably dwarf your purchases of cars and clothes; the amount of time and thought that goes into these decisions should reflect their importance.

  (When I was just starting out on Wall Street, I met with a young investment banker regarding the projections for a company in need of financing. He assured me that he had reviewed the numbers twenty times—he was obviously not willing to make a stupid mistake. He went on to become fantastically successful. Ironically, however, the company went bankrupt, which brings us to the next point. . .)

- Don't be seduced by numbers. Projections are educated guesses, at best—necessary information but not gospel. Leave yourself a generous margin for error.

- Remember that no matter how smart and motivated and deserving you are, sometimes you are going to lose, sometimes badly. Perhaps you weren't as smart, motivated, or deserving as you thought; perhaps you were just unlucky. It's all part of the challenge.

  To your advantage, you probably know a great deal more about the stock market than most investors, and you certainly have made more effort than most. That's a pretty fair achievement, in my book at least. Now it's time for those efforts to pay off.

Appendix

Reading: What's Worth Your Time

The financial press provides an overwhelming amount of information about what is happening or, more precisely, about what has just happened. Unfortunately, investors too often race about, hoping to profit from new developments more quickly than the competition. They would be better served by using the information as a foundation for long-term investment decisions.

Most investors put themselves at a disadvantage by not reading enough. Part of the problem is laziness. Part of the problem is the mistaken belief that you can't draw lessons for the future from the past.

There is also the problem of locating the few really excellent sources of financial information among the many choices available. Any well-stocked investment book section offers a bewildering array of interesting titles and intriguing approaches. At the same time, newspapers and magazines offer seemingly unlimited advice. The investor is a victim of information overkill, most of which appears to be helpful and most of which isn't. The following summaries should keep you going in the right direction.

Periodicals

The Wall Street Journal is the finest daily paper on the subject of American business, as you probably know. You should at least glance at the index on page B2 each day to see if there are any important developments at your companies of interest.

Among the weeklies, *Barron's* is quite useful to an investor—its writers, both in-house and contributing, are generally excellent, and occasionally controversial. In addition to the feature articles, look at the weekly summaries of the various financial markets on a regular basis.

You should also try to find the time for *Fortune, Forbes,* and *Business Week.* These are of value in keeping you up to date on general economic and investment thinking, as well as on specific events at companies.

Warren Buffett, *Berkshire Hathaway Annual Reports.*

As the chairman of Berkshire Hathaway, an Omaha-based holding company, Buffett publishes an annual letter to shareholders, in which he discusses his activities and his investment approach. This approach was directly influenced by the insights of Benjamin Graham and Philip Fisher, with considerable help from his own talents. He is also fortunate to have a partner and friend in Charles Munger, one of the most underrated investors in this country. (Munger managed an investment partnership from 1962 to 1975, averaging 19.8 percent annual returns versus 5 percent for the market.)

Many of the recent annual reports are available free of charge (402-346-1400). They offer a good look at how a management should treat its stockholders.

Buffett's approach is deceptively simple, a combination of unusual insight and discipline. "We never learned how to jump over seven-foot bars," he once said. "But occasionally we find two-foot bars." As you know, his focus is on extremely well-managed companies with distinct franchises that generate a great deal of cash. Over the years, he has taken sizable positions in American Express, Disney, Geico, the advertising industry, the newspaper industry, and the broadcasting industry. And throughout an investment career spanning four decades, he has remained remarkably true to his Two Rules:

Rule No. 1: Never lose money.
Rule No. 2: Never forget Rule No. 1.

Books

Benjamin Graham, *Security Analysis* and *The Intelligent Investor*

In 1934, following the worst bear market in this century, *Security Analysis* was published. Benjamin Graham and his coauthor, David Dodd, emphasized conservative, quantitative measures of performance and offered a rigorous approach to stock and bond analysis that, for the first time, made investing more science than art. It is an acknowledged classic of this industry, but it is a very long and difficult read.

Graham perhaps recognized this himself since, in 1947, he published the first edition of *The Intelligent Investor,* a common-sense, insightful approach to investing designed for any interested reader. The central arguments of the book—highlighted in Chapters 8 and 20—are familiar to you by now: (1) view a stock position as a minority ownership of an ongoing business; (2) be willing to buy when your manic-depressive partner, Mr. Market, is desperate to sell; and (3) leave yourself a margin of safety since even the best analysis is hardly flawless.

The overall approach is disciplined, contrarian, and conservative—hardly surprising for a brilliant investor who lived through the 1929–1932 massacre and the subsequent seventeen-year roller coaster. Graham directs his discussion both to defensive and to active investors, and includes several rules for each. He also includes his one sure-fire investment approach: Buy companies at two thirds or less of current assets minus *all* liabilities. Unfortunately, these days you're as likely to find a unicorn as a stock selling at a one-third discount to "net-net."

The Intelligent Investor also contains interesting material on the history of the stock market, and even a mention of Graham's unsuccessful attempt to get his employer to buy shares of National Tabulating and Recording in 1914; the company subsequently changed its name to International Business Machines.

In addition, there are discussions of accounting red flags, private market value, and Wall Street's penchant for recommending good companies regardless of price. Two pages under the title "To Sum

Up" can be read in a few minutes and will probably persuade you to read the rest.

Philip Fisher, *Common Stocks and Uncommon Profits*

Phil Fisher's philosophy is apparent from his first comments: "This book is dedicated to all investors, large and small, who do NOT adhere to the philosophy: I have already made up my mind, don't confuse me with facts." Three decades ago, Fisher argued what was an unusual case for stocks: Buy innovative, well-managed companies as long-term investments.

He outlines fifteen rules for selecting the rare exceptional company from a host of pretenders:

1. Excellent market potential for its products
2. Management commitment to the development of new products
3. Superior research and development relative to the company's size
4. Strong sales organization
5. Acceptable profit margins
6. Commitment to the maintenance or improvement of margins
7. Excellent labor relations
8. Excellent morale among managers
9. Management depth
10. Tight cost and accounting controls
11. Competitive advantages in quality and/or cost
12. Long-range approach to profits
13. Ability to grow with minimal equity financing
14. Respect for the shareholders
15. Management integrity

When you have found such a company—and you won't find many— Fisher recommends that you ignore economic or market forecasts in determining a buy point for the stock. Focus instead on an opportune time in the company's new product cycle, most prominently when profits are hurt due to expansion costs. The likely delays in getting the new product into production and the costs of promoting it may cause disappointment among investors. That, Fisher asserts, is the time to buy.

And when to sell? Not because of economic or market reasons, he advises. Not even when the stock seems overpriced on current results—if it is still attractive relative to future expectations. And certainly not just because the stock has risen. If you've found the right company and have bought it wisely, Fisher argues, you need not sell at all. Your profit potential should be measured in thousands of percent, and the temporary fluctuations of the economy, the market, and the stock itself are just so much distracting background noise.

As an investor, Fisher relied on a network of industry sources providing him with information and insights on current and prospective investments. Unfortunately, access to such scuttlebutt is only a distant dream for the average investor.

Fisher also offers some observations on diversification (focus on a few great ideas rather than a bunch of above-average ones), dividends (managements should be consistent in their payouts, and those payouts should depend on the opportunities for reinvestment of earnings), comic opera insights (don't be obsessed with meaningless statistics), and crowds (avoid them).

Peter Lynch with John Rothchild, *One Up on Wall Street*

As a mutual fund manager, Peter Lynch's career has been a succession of hard-earned achievements. In this book, the investment strategies that contributed to his phenomenal results are described, and in a manner that is accessible to the average investor.

Lynch prefers small companies that have found a successful niche for themselves and have been able to duplicate that success outside of their original locations. He also likes companies in mundane industries that, through price increases, cost cuts, and market share gains, can consistently produce exceptional earnings growth. A believer in diversification, Lynch analyzes how to tackle each of six investment categories: fast and slow growers, turnarounds, asset plays, cyclicals, and "stalwarts."

He recommends that investors look for companies, in which they have an edge over the pros—for example, firms that they deal with in the course of their jobs. He describes how to develop an investment case for a stock, and advises on when to buy and when to sell.

The suggestions that Peter Lynch offers are pure gold for the investor who is willing to do the necessary legwork.

George Soros, *The Alchemy of Finance*

This is a marvelous book to give to people who have an exaggerated perception of their own investment talents. By page 10, they will probably feel overwhelmed. It is unquestionably a difficult book, written by a man who views himself more as a philosopher than a money manager. However, if you are willing to make the effort, it will be time well spent. Soros is that rare commodity, a truly original and brilliant thinker, and one who is self-critical without being falsely humble.

While most great investors are able to simplify a complex world, Soros is able to make the world *more* complex and still understand it. His is an approach to be admired, but not one to be easily followed. The value of Soros's book is not in his day-to-day investment approach, but in his economic and market insights.

Soros's basic premise is *reflexivity:* Events create expectations which influence the financial markets; the markets, in turn, then influence these events. For example, a strong stock market based on the perception of a strong economy will boost the confidence of investors and consumers. This confidence will result in greater purchases by individuals, which, in turn, will help to boost the economy.

Soros believes that reflexivity applies to the credit, currency, and stock markets. He also contends that regulation is subject to the process of reflexivity, and that its relative popularity tends to run in tandem with the bust-and-boom cycles of the financial markets—the greater the bust, the greater the regulation, and vice versa. In addition, he believes that free markets, left to their own devices, will not tend toward equilibrium.

The second half of the book focuses on the decisions made in Soros's own Quantum Fund between August 1985 and November 1986. His results were extraordinary—an advance of 113.7 percent. Unfortunately, his fund is registered outside this country and is not available to United States citizens.

The most interesting conclusion Soros draws from his "real-time experiment" is that the market is an excellent early warning system for potential economic catastrophes. By reflecting the fears of investors, the market encourages the powers-that-be to correct the underlying problems before they become unmanageable. In this regard, the market appears to worry constantly about possibilities that never seem to happen, when, in fact, the market's concerns help to forestall these potential catastrophes.

Soros also professes to be an *anti*contrarian, preferring to bet *with* the crowd rather than against it. Since "events tend to reinforce prevailing expectations most of the time," he argues, the contrarian only wins at the elusive turning points.

(Certainly, at the end of a bull or bear market, expectations do become temporarily self-fulfilling, as described earlier. However, playing the trend is not an approach that the individual investor should rely upon. Even as brilliant a trader as Soros was unable to avoid the October 1987 massacre; his fund lost 30 percent of its assets, some $800 million! All things considered, you should try to be a long-term investor focusing on the less popular, since these are the investments that are most likely to be undervalued.)

Soros is also wary of what he perceives to be the popularity of the contrarian approach. However, contrarian thinking cannot become the consensus viewpoint, by definition. Its apparent popularity among investors is usually not reflected in their actions, recalling the old saying: Do as I say, not as I do.

John Train, *The Money Masters*

The focus of this book is on the investment approaches of nine exceptional investors: Warren Buffett, Paul Cabot, Philip Fisher, Benjamin Graham, Stanley Kroll, T. Rowe Price, John Templeton, Larry Tisch, and Robert Wilson. The strategies of these men vary widely, but the similarities in their underlying approaches to the market are also apparent: They each focus on a logical and disciplined investment philosophy developed over years of experience. And they like to win.

As Train shows, these investors are also blessed with unusual degrees of intelligence and common sense, which unfortunately are not as transferable as their strategies. Regardless, this book offers a great deal of insight to the beginning investor and should be read early on in the process. Even the veterans of the investment business could benefit from another look at the excellent discussions about and with these money managers. John Train also offers a number of worthwhile comparisons and conclusions of his own at the end of the book.

Adam Smith, *The Money Game* and *Supermoney*

The chief strength of these two highly readable books, published in 1968 and 1972, is the sense they give of the personality of the Street in its bull-market glory and in its subsequent fall from grace. Throughout, Adam Smith's insights are funny and cynical and fair.

For example, during the buying panic of April 1, 1968, the author found himself with a major portfolio manager who was desperate to throw $42 million at the market:

> "I never bought any Carbide," Poor Grenville said. "I would never buy a tired old mother like Carbide."
> "Well, I didn't buy it either," I said. We stared at each other, and then at a smudged, penciled slip.
> "It followed us home," Poor Grenville said. "What the hell. Just go out and get it some warm milk and a blanket."
> The next day a *New York Times* reporter called Poor Grenville to check on the block. Poor Grenville learns fast, and he was ready. "Our fund," he said, "did not follow the mass panic into such highfliers as Burroughs and Control Data. In these times of turmoil, we are seeking value. Union Carbide, for example, whose additions to net plant make it attractive. We believe, after exhaustive research, that the chemicals are ready to turn." Next thing you know, *Newsweek* was about to quote Poor Grenville on value in these troubled times. Four more funds bought Carbide. Grenville the Statesman.

Adam Smith's personal investment preference is for a limited portfolio of small companies with unique characteristics that will permit them above-average compounded earnings growth. Not surprisingly, his approach is based on the suggestions of Phil Fisher (and on those of Winthrop Knowlton, author of *Growth Opportunities in Common Stocks*).

David Dreman, *The New Contrarian Investment Strategy*

The investment approach recommended by this book is to focus on the out-of-favor in general and the low P/E in particular. David

Dreman is also a regular contributor to *Forbes*, which should keep you up to date on his thinking. To give credit where credit is due, Dreman made a magnificent call on the market by turning bearish in September 1987, after many rewarding years in the bullish camp.

Edward Lefevre, *Reminiscences of a Stock Operator*

This is the story of the legendary speculator, Jesse Livermore; almost seventy years after its original publication, his observations on the market and its players are still amazingly relevant.

Some things have changed in the stock market, certainly, since the first two decades of the century. In that era, the abundance of insider trading and the absence of reliable company data made speculation the name of the game. Directors and officers were free to trade their company's stock in advance of the public release of significant news and, accordingly, the best indicator of what was happening with a company was the price movement of its stock.

However, many aspects of the financial markets are still very much the same as they were in Livermore's day. As he pointed out, human nature is a constant—an observation that is as true today as it was then. Among the many other insights in this book, here is a brief collection of a few of the best:

> One of the most helpful things that anybody can learn is to give up trying to catch the last eighth—or the first. These two are the most expensive eighths in the world. They have cost stock traders, in the aggregate, enough millions of dollars to build a concrete highway across the continent.

> I am so accustomed to losing money that I never think first of that phase of my mistakes. It is always the play itself, the reason why. In the first place I wish to know my own limitations and habits of thought. Another reason is that I do not wish to make the same mistake a second time. A man can excuse his mistakes only by capitalizing them to his subsequent profit.

> In every boom companies are formed primarily, if not exclusively, to take advantage of the public's appetite for all kinds of stocks. Also there are belated promotions. The reason why promoters make that mistake is that being human they are unwilling to see the end of the boom. Moreover, it is good business

to take chances when the possible profit is big enough. The top is never in sight when the vision is vitiated by hope. The average man sees a stock that nobody wanted at twelve dollars or four-teen dollars a share suddenly advance to thirty—which surely is the top—until it rises to fifty. That is absolutely the end of the rise. Then it goes to sixty; to seventy; to seventy-five. It then becomes a certainty that this stock, which a few weeks ago was selling for less than fifteen, can't go any higher. But it goes to eighty; and to eighty-five. Whereupon the average man, who never thinks of values but of prices, and is not governed in his actions by conditions but by fears, takes the easiest way—he stops thinking that there must be a limit to the advances. That is why those outsiders who are wise enough not to buy at the top make up for it by not taking profits. The big money in booms is always made first by the public—on paper. And it remains on paper.

This book was published seven years before the 1929 Crash. Al-though Livermore avoided the first mistake of speculators (getting out too late), he made the second: getting back in too early. The market declines of late 1931 and 1932 drove him to bankruptcy and, eventually, to suicide.

Fred Schwed, *Where Are the Customers' Yachts?*

The title of this 1955 book is based on the question asked by a visitor to Wall Street upon seeing the yachts owned by the various titans of the brokerage industry. Throughout, the author does an effective job of both educating and entertaining; the following ex-cerpts should give you an idea of his excellent sense of insight and humor:

> Your average Wall Streeter, faced with nothing profitable to do, does nothing for only a brief time. Then, suddenly and hys-terically, he does something which turns out to be extremely un-profitable. He is not a lazy man.

> For one thing, customers have an unfortunate habit of ask-ing about the financial future. Now if you do someone the signal honor of asking him a difficult question, you may be assured that you will get a detailed answer. Rarely will it be the most difficult of all answers—"I don't know."

There was always a scattering of bears, "aginners" by temperament, who spent their business days having their ears knocked off. Many of them, bowing to a force which finally seemed cosmic, switched to being bulls at a sadly late period in the era. The remainder who were still short at the time of the crash covered too soon (as who wouldn't?). Then, after prices had gone inconceivably lower, they took their profits and bought stocks (as who wouldn't?). In due course of time, if they bought on margin, they went to "the Cleaners," that mythical establishment to which their brother speculators had repaired some time earlier. "The Cleaners" was not one of those exclusive clubs; by 1932 everybody who had ever tried speculation had been admitted to membership.

When there is a stock-market boom, and everyone is scrambling for common stocks, take all your common stocks and sell them. Take the proceeds and buy conservative bonds. No doubt the stocks you sold will go higher. Pay no attention to this—just wait for the depression which will come sooner or later. When this depression—or panic—becomes a national catastrophe, sell out the bonds (perhaps at a loss) and buy back the stocks. No doubt the stocks will go still lower. Again pay no attention. Wait for the next boom. Continue to repeat this operation as long as you live, and you'll have the pleasure of dying rich.

Andrew Tobias, *The Only Investment Guide You'll Ever Need; Getting by on $100,000 a Year;* and *Money Angles*

These three books, written over a six-year period, offer an excellent and enjoyable introduction to personal investing. Tobias is fun to read—an accusation that can't be leveled at many investment writers—and I doubt that you can finish these books without gaining a much better sense of how to make money and how to keep it.

One example is a six-page chapter, written in January 1979, that is included in *Getting by on $100,000 a Year.* Titled "The Case for Stocks," it is clear, concise and correct: "I am not suggesting that we have in today's stock market the chance of a lifetime. . . . Nor am I predicting that stock prices next month won't be lower than they are today. They well could be. . . . What I am telling you is that stocks are a bargain." The DJIA was near 800 at the time versus its current price above 2700.

Tobias's investment preference is for low multiple/high dividend stocks, with a few high quality Fisher-types thrown in for good measure.

John Brooks, *Once in Golconda*

This book focuses on Wall Street in the 1920s and 1930s, and describes the rise and subsequent disgrace of the NYSE's president, Richard Whitney. The main character became the hero of the 1929 Crash, resolute and reassuring—the quintessential business statesman. And yet, in Jekyll and Hyde fashion, he was personally bankrupt at the time, a victim of his speculations in the Florida land debacle. He eventually resorted to embezzlement and ended up in prison. This story of arrogance, greed, and misplaced idolatry is more than a bit relevant to this decade, and not only to this country.

Glossary

AMEX—The American Stock Exchange; the second largest stock exchange after the NYSE, where 1,067 companies, mostly medium-sized, are listed and traded.

"And the market don't ring no bells."—The end of a bull or bear market is clear only in retrospect.

broker—The firm which executes your trades; the person whom you speak with is an account executive, formerly known as a customers' man.

capital—Money.

capitalization—Debt plus equity, the money available to a corporation to fund its operations.

closed-end fund—An investment fund with a fixed number of shares that trade publicly; since these shares are not redeemable at net asset value, they tend to sell at discounts of 10–15 percent to reflect this illiquidity; in the 1920s, these funds were called investment companies; in the 1930s, they were called other things not generally printable.

correction—A price decline to a "proper" level, whatever that might be; a mitigated disaster for shareholders.

discount rate—The interest rate that banks pay to borrow directly from the Federal Reserve.

DJIA—The Dow Jones Industrial Average is an index of thirty major industrial stocks; although it is less representative than the Standard & Poor's 400, most investors are referring to this when they talk about "the market."

earnings per share (EPS)—The net earnings of a company divided by the number of shares outstanding.

equity—The ownership position in an asset, such as a corporation's stock.

fed funds rate—the interest rate that banks pay on overnight loans to each other.

fixed income security—A bond; the borrower is obligated to pay you a fixed amount of interest—no more, no less—usually semiannually.

fear—The only thing to fear; that is, if you're less than five years old.

golden parachute—A generous severance payment to a manager, usually offered by a management-approved acquirer, easily confused with a payoff.

good till canceled (GTC)—A limit order that is not canceled until you request it; if, instead, you want your order to be effective only for that day, place a *day order*.

greenmail—When the management of a company repurchases the stock of one shareholder at an unfairly high price to protect itself from a possible acquirer.

inverted yield curve—When the yield on short-term interest rates exceeds that on long-term rates; the result of a tightening of Fed policy, often leading to a recession.

investment—Ownership of an asset that's selling for less than it's worth.

"Know Thyself . . . Nothing in Excess"—Advice inscribed on the Temple of Apollo at Delphi a few thousand years before the Crash.

leverage—The use of debt.

limit order—A set price at which an order is placed for execution; if a better price is available, fine.

liquidity—The ease of exchanging a stock or another asset into cash.

margin call—Occurs when your investment in a margined security declines below 33 percent of its total value due to a price decline; you are required to put up additional funds to avoid a forced sale of security by your broker.

margin debt—Funds lent by a brokerage firm so that a customer can put up less than 100 percent of the cost; currently, maximum margin debt is 50 percent on a stock purchase and an astounding 90+ percent on a stock index future.

market order—An order to execute at the current level; this usually means the offer/ask price for a buy order and the bid price for a sell order

NASDAQ—The National Association of Security Dealers Quotations; provides current quotes and transaction prices on stocks that are traded over the counter.

NAV—Net asset value; in closed-end and open-end funds, the NAV is the market value of the securities that the fund owns.

NYSE—The New York Stock Exchange, where 1,600 of the largest companies are listed; minimum capital requirements determine which companies are traded here rather than on the smaller exchanges or over the counter (OTC).

OTC—The over-the-counter market where stocks which are not listed on any stock exchange are traded by phone; most OTC stocks will have at least two registered dealers who will buy or sell for their own account to make markets in the stocks.

open-end fund—Mutual fund; investors can buy or redeem shares at the current NAV.

option contract—The right to buy (call option) or sell (put option) 100 shares of a specific stock for a specific price within a specific period of time.

poison pill—An attempt to prevent a hostile takeover by creating artificial barriers designed to make a company financially unpleasant or fatal to swallow.

Rule of 72—A rule-of-thumb approach for determining how long it will take for a certain sum to double if you know its compound annual growth rate. If the growth is 12 percent, it will take six years (72 divided 12); at 4 percent it will take eighteen years. Alternately, if you know how long something took to double, you can determine its growth rate.

S&P 400—Standard & Poor's Index of 400 of the largest stocks; a more representative though less frequently used measure of market performance than the DJIA.

security—A stock or a bond.

specialists—The people who are responsible for maintaining an orderly, liquid market for securities listed on the exchanges; their primary goal is to match buyers and sellers, but in the event of an imbalance, they are expected to buy or sell for their own accounts.

speculation—An attempt to make money by betting on the irrationality of the other players; a highly leveraged or time-constrained investment would qualify as well.

stock—A piece of the action, a designation of partial ownership in the equity of a corporation.

stockholder—A shareholder, an owner.

stock exchange—A place where buyers and sellers of specific stocks can trade their shares.

stop-loss order—A price below the current one, designated by the investor, at which he wishes his stock to be sold at the market—the next available price.

The Market—The stock market, as defined by the S&P 400, S&P 500, DJIA, Wilshire 5000, whatever.

"This too shall pass"—Let's hope so.

white knight—The acquirer of a company at the request of its management to preclude an unfriendly takeover.

white squire—The acquirer of a significant, but not controlling, stake in a company at management's request to discourage an unwanted suitor.

Wilshire 5000—Index of 5,000 stocks, which offer an approximation of total market value; recent price of 3,300 equates to a value of $3.3 billion.

Index